Changing Society Through Drama

MORAL RE-ARMAMENT AT THE WESTMINSTER THEATRE, LONDON

PAMELA JENNER

Pinocchio Press

ISBN: 9781720182641

Published by Pinocchio Press, Culver House, Exeter Road, Crediton EX17 3BH

Cover illustration: The Westminster Theatre, by William Cameron-Johnson

Set in Goudy Old Style a serif typeface originally created by
Frederic W. Goudy in 1915

DEDICATION

This book is dedicated to my cousin Frank Gent who has been a constant
source of inspiration and encouragement throughout my research

CONTENTS

ILLUSTRATIONS

APPENDICES

Note: short emails and brief conversations are listed in the bibliography rather than appendices.

ACKNOWLEDGEMENTS

I am grateful to Anglia Ruskin University (ARU) for awarding me a three-year bursary in order to research this PhD. My thanks also go to my supervisory team: first supervisor Dr Susan Wilson, second supervisor Dr Nigel Ward, third supervisor Dr Jonathan Davis, fourth supervisor Dr Aldo Zammit Borda and also to IT advisor at ARU, Peter Carlton. I am indebted to Initiatives of Change for permission to access and publish material from its archives and in particular to contributions from IofC supporters including Hilary Belden, Dr Philip Boobbyer, Christine Channer, Fiona Daukes, Anne Evans, Chris Evans, David Hassell, Kay Hassell, Michael Henderson, David Locke, Elizabeth Locke, John Locke; also to the late Stanley Kiaer, Louis Fleming and Hugh Steadman Williams. Without their enthusiasm and unfailing support this book could not have been written. I would also like to thank my family, Daniel, Moses and Richard Brett and Sanjukta Ghosh for their ongoing support.

PREFACE

This book is the result of a PhD thesis. It investigates the rise and fall of the propagandist theatre of Moral Re-Armament (MRA), which owned the Westminster Theatre in London, from 1946 to 1997. MRA operated a unique theatre movement which was initially extremely successful in taking a stand against the avant-garde drama of the twentieth century. Its own controversial plays promoted an ideology of living by four absolute moral standards: honesty, purity, unselfishness and love.

My research explores the way in which MRA sought to change society through drama and investigates the reasons for the eventual demise of the Westminster Theatre operation. Because MRA theatre has not featured in secondary criticism on twentieth-century British drama, my information has been gathered from MRA archives, interviews with key figures associated with the movement and a performance in London of one of its political plays. This book fills a gap in the history of twentieth century British theatre, which so far has not acknowledged MRA's contribution.

Initially the Westminster Theatre, which was administered entirely by volunteers, was a huge success, attracting a working-class audience and even helping to resolve industrial disputes. However, the movement was unable to adapt to the cultural revolution of the 1960s. Its plays became less relevant and therefore less effective and the costs of maintaining a London theatre began to soar. The final production at the Westminster in 1990 of Václav Havel's *Temptation* was boycotted by many MRA members and proved to be a moral and financial disaster that led to the closure of the theatre.

Although MRA theatre was ultimately not sustainable, it achieved much during its fifty-year existence. It delivered plays that not only promoted its ideology and dealt with controversial issues but also provided a valid and valuable alternative to the left-wing and experimental theatre of the twentieth century.

Introduction

Could theatre speak to Russia and China with an idea more revolutionary, more effective and more satisfying than communism? Could theatre speak to the Free World with a programme more revolutionary, more satisfying and more compelling than affluence? ... That is what we would like to do at the Westminster Theatre. That is our policy. It may not appeal to everyone in modern theatre, but it will appeal to the overwhelming majority of the British public.
–Belden, 1963, p.2

This book provides the first in-depth critical analysis of a movement which aimed to revolutionise British theatre. Theatre has always been a useful tool to promote ideologies and in the twentieth century left-wing propagandist groups such as the Workers' Theatre Movement, founded in 1926, Unity Theatre formed in 1936, Joan Littlewood's Theatre Workshop, the Royal Court Theatre and the English Stage Company dominated political drama in Britain. These groups have all been researched and documented.[1] However, there was another theatre movement operating in Britain during

---

[1] Publications include: *Joan Littlewood's Theatre* by Nadine Holdsworth; *Joan's Book: The Autobiography of Joan Littlewood* by Joan Littlewood; *The Royal Court Theatre and the Modern Stage* by Philip Roberts; *The Royal Court Theatre Inside Out* by Ruth Little and Emily McLaughlin; *Theatre of the Left 1880–1935: Workers' Theatre Movement in Britain and America* by Raphael Samuel

the latter half of the twentieth century that initially had a major influence on the working class in British industry. Moral Re-Armament (MRA), which owned the Westminster Theatre, London, from 1946 to 1997, was idealistic, anti-communist and backed by many leading figures in the establishment. Its plays were highly controversial – described by some as right-wing and out of touch but by others as providing a solution to the world's problems – yet its work has never been objectively researched and documented. Richard Palmer states: 'The success of MRA theatre eclipsed any comparable producing organisation in the left-wing theatre but, unlike its ideological opposite, MRA drama has been ignored by theatre historians' (Palmer, 1979, pp.172-173). This book seeks to address such an omission and to provide the first comprehensive, critical analysis of the movement's work at the Westminster.

My research has been based on answering the following questions: what was the message MRA was attempting to convey, what strategies did it use within theatre to promote that message, how successful was it as a propagandist theatre movement and why did it eventually fail in its mission to change society. Cultural materialism has been a useful basis for my investigations and the works of literary theorists Raymond Williams and Alan Sinfield have been key to analysing the way in which MRA attempted to use theatre as a means of changing society. Williams posits that it is not possible to separate literature from society and its attachment and relevance to history. He argues that, whilst 'the art of writing and creating performance is central to articulating the dominant culture', a great deal of literature is 're-sidual' in its ideology, reflecting the values belonging to cultural achievements of past societies (Williams, 1980, p.44-45). Although MRA aimed to transform the dominant culture, its critics maintained it was merely reflecting the values of a bygone age. The theories developed by Sinfield, on the difficulties that certain cultural groups encounter when attempting to ensure their work is relevant within the wider community, are particularly pertinent to MRA. Sinfield argues that literary culture is 'developed by certain groups in ways that enable them to identify themselves through it; to others it is a matter of indifference and, to some, an object of detestation' (Sinfield, 1983, p.6). He adds: 'The diversity of codes is probably healthy. What is not, I should say, is the tendency of each group to insist upon the exclusive validity of its particular mode' (Sinfield, 1983, p.7). MRA dismissed the theatrical forms that were emerging in the post-war era, insisting that its own theatre would 'appeal to the overwhelming majority of the British public' (Belden, 1963, p.2). Initially it seemed the movement's predictions were correct, but its ideology conflicted with the changing culture of the twentieth century and eventually led to the closure of the Westminster.

MRA was initially known as the Oxford Group because in the 1920s its founder, the American Lutheran pastor Frank Buchman, used Oxford University as the base for his recruitment campaigns. In 1938 the Oxford Group launched a new initiative, Moral Re-Armament (MRA), to emphasise the need for moral and spiritual re-armament at a time when European nations were literally re-arming for war. The movement was also conscious of the need to attract the working class as well as those in academia and hoped that the launch of MRA would widen its appeal. In 2001 the name was changed to Initiatives of Change (IofC) in the belief that in the twenty-first century the words 'moral re-armament' no longer had the same resonance. However the Oxford Group remains the overall management body in Britain[2]. The movement's ideology has a religious basis: listen daily in silence for guidance from God and live by four absolute standards; honesty, purity, unselfishness and love. The word 'absolute' is significant because MRA brooked no compromise. The standards had to be completely adhered to and, as Rex Dilly says, 'You can't join it and you can't resign. You are in or out according to the quality of life you are living at the moment' (Dilly, 1995, p.95).

In order to analyse MRA theatre, I needed to understand the belief system of the movement and how it originated. MRA itself has been the subject of many investigations, some written by those unconnected with the movement and some of which consist of reports and others of published works.[3] MRA's own archives contain copious books, pamphlets and magazines, written by supporters of the movement, which give an in-depth insight into its origins, aims and objectives. This publication, however, is not an investigation into the movement as a whole but into its work at the Westminster Theatre. My research uncovered two articles in academic journals about aspects of the movement's contribution to theatre. These articles are by historian Dr Philip Boobbyer and American Professor Richard Palmer; Boobbyer also has a chapter containing references to MRA theatre in the book *Missions Nations and the End of Empire* (2003). There are brief references to the movement's theatre work in Tom Driberg's book *The Mystery of Moral*

<hr>

[2] In Britain the Oxford Group is the legal body of the movement. The UK annual report is entitled *The Oxford Group operating as Initiatives of Change*.

[3] Publications relating to MRA include: *The Spiritual Vision of Frank Buchman* by P. Boobbyer; *The Oxford Group its History and Significance* by W.H. Clark; *Discovering Moral Re-Armament*, by R. Dilly; *Is it True What They Say About MRA? – A Trade Unionist's look at MRA*, by J. Hodgson and *Moral Re-Armament: The Reinventions of an American Religious Movement* by D. Sack.

Re-Armament: A Study of Frank Buchman and His Movement (1964). None of these publications[4] provide an in-depth analysis of the work of MRA at the Westminster Theatre.

The absence of any substantial secondary criticism meant I had to investigate alternative ways of obtaining material. MRA has produced many pamphlets and articles about the aims of the Westminster Theatre and its archives proved to be an invaluable resource. Minutes of meetings and letters relating to activities at the Westminster – not only from supporters but also from members of the public – conference reports, evaluations from schools, articles in the national and local press, together with minutes of trade union meetings provided an insight into the way in which MRA used theatre to promote its message. The most valuable aspect of my research has been the information gathered from interviews with those who worked at the Westminster Theatre on behalf of MRA, several from as far back as 1946. They include actors, writers, stage managers, producers and administrators. All worked on a voluntary basis whilst living in large houses leased by the movement in the vicinity of the theatre. Twenty were interviewed in depth; most of them in face-to-face interviews, two by telephone and four by email. The majority were recruited following an article I wrote for the IofC newsletter appealing for interviewees with memories of the Westminster Theatre. Several leading figures were interviewed more than once. Their memories have been essential in painting a picture of the way in which the

---

[4] Publications referencing MRA theatre are: 'The Cold War in the Plays of Peter Howard' by P. Boobbyer in *Contemporary British Theatre (2005)*, Vol. 19. No. 2; 'Moral Re-Armament in Africa in the Era of Decolonization' by P. Boobbyer in *Missions, Nations and the End of Empire* (2003) edited by Brian Stanley; *Mystery of Moral Re-Armament: A Study of Frank Buchman and His Movement* (1964) by T. Driberg and 'Moral Re-Armament Drama: Right Wing Theatre in America' by R. Palmer in *Theatre Journal* (1979) Vol. 31. No. 2.

theatre operated. One of those interviewed provided previously un-published photographs of the official opening ceremony at the Westminster Theatre and of a tour of British industry undertaken in 1947 by the cast of MRA's inaugural play *The Forgotten Factor*.

It was also essential to investigate not only what was happening at the Westminster but what was taking place elsewhere. Publications by John Bull, Peter Hennessy, Steve Nicholson, Dominic Shellard and Alan Sin-field,[5] are among the works I consulted to gain an overview not only of the-atre but of the changes in British culture. My own experience of theatre in Britain from the early 1960s onwards, as a theatre reviewer and member of the Royal Court's English Stage Company, helped me to contextualise MRA theatre. I have also used material from my own archive of theatre programmes and newspaper cuttings spanning the last forty years of the twentieth century.

I wanted to discover not only how MRA compared with other theatri-cal movements in the twentieth century but how its propaganda plays would be regarded in the present day. To that end, I staged a production, in 2013, of *The Diplomats*, by Peter Howard, a leading figure in the movement in the 1950s and 1960s. The event, at the London headquarters of IofC, marked the fiftieth anniversary of the play's first performance at the Westminster Theatre in 1963 and is described in greater detail in chapter two. The audi-ence in 2013, ranging in age from twenty-one to ninety years, included life-

---

[5] Publications relating to twentieth century British theatre history include: *Stage Right* by J. Bull; *Having it So Good* by Peter Hennessy; *Modern British Playwriting: the 1960s* by Steve Ni-cholson; *The Royal Court Theatre* by P. Roberts; *British Theatre Since the War* by D. Shellard and *Literature, Politics and Culture in Post-War Britain* by A. Sinfield.

long MRA supporters and those with no previous knowledge of the movement. Verbal and written feedback from the audience revealed that, while the themes were still relevant fifty years later, many regarded it not as a propagandist play but as an entertaining, even farcical, historical piece. The changes in culture and society resulted in very different interpretations of the play. This supports the view held by literary theorist Terry Eagleton that 'No work, and no current evaluation of it can simply be extended to new groups of people without being changed, perhaps almost unrecognisably in the process' (Eagleton, 1983, p.12).

MRA believed passionately that conflicts could be resolved and peace restored on all levels – personal, national and international – through adherence to the absolute standards. This unshakeable belief created many enemies, in particular Tom Driberg, the journalist, MP and former chairman of the Labour Party, who wrote a highly critical book *The Mystery of Moral Re-Armament: A Study of Frank Buchman and His Movement*. When I interviewed those who had been associated with the Westminster since its early days, I encountered a real fear that I would, as had others before me, paint a picture of an arrogant, cultish and possibly naïve organisation. And in a sense their concern is valid. Although MRA did not exercise excessive control over its followers and therefore could not be considered a 'cult', it clearly believed that it had a solution to the world's problems and as a result may well have appeared to some to be both arrogant and naïve. However I discovered, through my interviews, that its supporters are genuine in their desire to improve the lives of others and remain deeply concerned about the plight of the world. Their ideology has developed and the twenty-first century Initiatives of Change places less emphasis on specific religious beliefs and more on having regular Quiet Times and respecting all religions.

7

This book, which seeks to explain the reasons for both the success and ultimate failure of MRA theatre, is structured both chronologically and by themes. The first chapter provides an explanation of the ideology of the movement and the reasons for its use of theatre as a vehicle for promoting its message and gaining converts. Palmer describes MRA as a right-wing organisation but that is not how those within the movement viewed themselves. Whilst attracting many members of the British establishment, it has always described itself as politically neutral and has called not for change in political regimes but for a moral and ethical change in the individual. It considered both capitalism and communism to be corrupt and sought to align itself not only with influential members of British society but with the trade unions and the working class. MRA purchased the Westminster in 1946, when Britain was still reeling from the aftermath of the Second World War, in order to stage plays promoting its ideology of living by the four absolute moral standards. It fought against the emerging kitchen sink drama of the 1950s and managed, in its early years, to attract both the working class, not usually associated with the theatre, and members of the establishment. The leading West End impresario Bill Kenwright directed and performed for MRA at the Westminster Theatre; Elaine Page, the musical theatre actress, made her debut there and other well-known performers of stage and screen, Dame Sybil Thorndike, Hannah Gordon, and Cliff Richard are among the many famous names to be associated with MRA theatre.

The second chapter investigates the effectiveness of MRA's propaganda theatre through an analysis of two plays, each written by a leading playwright within the movement and presented at the Westminster, Rev Alan Thornhill's *The Forgotten Factor* and Peter Howard's *The Diplomats*. When it was first performed in Britain in 1946, *The Forgotten Factor* received an extremely positive reaction from both management and unions in a variety of industries. *The Diplomats*, presented nearly twenty years later in 1963, had very mixed reviews as did *The Forgotten Factor* when it was restaged in 1970. Thomas Postlewait argues, 'Our interpretation of "political drama" does not necessarily require our understanding of the initial – and often initiating – context' (Postlewait, 2002, p.11). However, 'political drama' has to be relevant to the audience for it to have the desired effect. MRA's choice of theatre as its main propaganda tool proved to be hugely problematic for a movement at loggerheads with the emerging culture of the 1960s and beyond. Although MRA was aware that it needed to be both entertaining and relevant to get across its message, this was always going to be difficult without, to some degree, acquiescing to cultural norms that were in opposition to its own values. When Howard, a former *Daily Express* political journalist, began to take on a leading role in MRA, in the late 1950s and early 1960s he introduced a new professionalism at the Westminster in terms of performance and production. Well-known actors such as Bryan Coleman, Richard Warner and Phyllis Konstam took the place of MRA volunteer performers, but the structure and content of the plays remained the same.

Chapter three investigates the life and work of Howard, who went on to lead the movement for a brief period following Buchman's death in 1961. Howard was very clear about his role in MRA's battle to revolutionise society through theatre but an examination of his writing, in the context of the rapidly changing culture of the 1960s, indicates that this was a fight he was not going to win. He had hoped his plays would attract the working class but his lack of understanding of that section of society meant he was unable to achieve his aim. His approach to theatre is compared in this chapter with that of another propagandist playwright, Bertolt Brecht. Both men aimed to use theatre to bring about fundamental changes in society and their historical context is important. Their plays can be re-interpreted within the political landscape of the twenty-first century but both failed in their attempts to convert audiences to their own ideologies. Howard, today, is virtually unknown as a playwright and Brecht is renowned more for his skills as a writer and for the way in which he transformed the theory and practice of theatre than for his political message.

In the preface to his play *Mr Brown Comes Down the Hill*, Howard states the reasons for his writing:

> I write to preach. I write for the sake of propaganda. I write with a message and for no other reason ... My plays are propaganda plays. I write them to give people a purpose. The purpose is clear. The aim is simple. It is to encourage men to accept the growth in character that is essential if civilisation is to survive ... It is to end the censorship of virtue which creates [a] vicious society [sic]. It is to enlist everybody, everywhere in a revolution to remake the world (Howard, 1964a, pp 15-16).

Howard may have been confident in declaring himself to be a propagandist but many in the movement today are uncomfortable with this concept. The word 'propaganda' has had very negative connotations in the past, especially during and just after the Second World War, when it was associated, in particular, with the Nazi regime. David Welch, in his book *Propaganda, Power and Persuasion*, quotes a leading figure from that time: 'Propaganda is a much maligned and often misunderstood word. The layman uses it to mean something inferior or even despicable. The word propaganda always has a bitter after-taste'. These are wise words; however, they come from the mouth of Joseph Goebbels immediately following his appointment in 1933 as Minister for Popular Enlightenment and Propaganda in Adolf

Hitler's first government (Goebbels cited in Welch, 2013, p.2). It is not surprising therefore that those in IofC, who were previously involved with MRA from the launch of its work at the Westminster in 1946, remain uncomfortable with the use of such a word. And, as MRA discovered, propaganda has its disadvantages. Welch writes:

> A great deal of recent research on the subject has forced us to reappraise previous simplistic assumptions by looking at 'resistance' or 'immunity' to propaganda. In the short term propaganda may carry its audience on a wave of fervour, like the patriotic surges that can accompany the outbreak of war. In the longer term, however, it becomes less effective, because the audience has got the time and opportunity to question its underlying assumptions (Welch, 2013, p.30).

This is what happened to MRA. In 1946 *The Forgotten Factor* was greeted with immense 'fervour' by audiences at the Westminster but, as culture and society changed, the message in its plays was considered to be too emotional and too obvious. Welch writes: 'If propaganda is too rational, it can become boring; if it is too emotional, too strident, it can become transparent and laughable. As in other forms of human interaction, propaganda has to strike the right balance' (Welch, 2013, p.30). As will be demonstrated throughout this book, the MRA message presented in plays at the Westminster was mocked and vilified because it was delivered with an undisguised passion which many, particularly newspaper theatre critics, could not treat seriously. Welch maintains that propaganda can be defined as not only a 'deliberate attempt to influence the public opinions of an audience' but as a way in which to 'serve the self-interest of the propagandist, either directly or indirectly' (Welch, 2013, p.2). MRA, whilst wanting to influence public opinion, was not concerned with self-promotion but rather with encouraging people to exercise personal responsibility and promote its ideology on an individual basis. When using the word propaganda in relation to MRA I use it in its broadest sense; it was a movement with a message and a belief that theatre was one of the most effective means of delivering that message. It hoped people would come to the theatre, be introduced to its ideology and then go back to their homes and institutions prepared to put the four 'absolutes' into practice. Kenneth Belden, chairman of the trustees of the Westminster Theatre throughout the 1960s and 1970s, states, 'Men and women in a key British industry, whose actions affect the lives and livelihoods of at least a hundred thousand people, have come to the theatre and have since been finding ways of replacing conflict by constructive action' (Belden, 1970b, p.1).

The fourth chapter in this book concentrates on the development of the Westminster Theatre following Howard's death in 1965 and the movement's opposition to contemporary drama. During this period, MRA extended the theatre; it built an arts centre and became the first theatre in the country to introduce simultaneous translation, but the genre of its plays, and the manner in which the message was delivered, did not change. The movement believed theatre was key to changing society and as such offered an alternative to the experimental and avant-garde drama of the 1960s and 1970s. According to MRA, 'modern theatre' portrayed a world of pessimism and did not inspire people to want to change it. Belden claimed that the Theatre of the Absurd was doing nothing to enable people to 'deal with the world in which we have to live ... It is a theatre which goes on probing endlessly, in ever greater detail and so-called frankness, the problems that everyone knows already but offers no glimmer of hope of how to deal with them ... It makes the world appear so impossible, so frustrating, so lost in its own selfishness, that nothing can be done about it' (Belden, 1965a, p.6).

By the late 1960s, MRA theatre was clearly no longer representing the dominant culture as it had done in the 1940s and 1950s. It was unable to counteract the experimental theatre of the Royal Court and Joan Littlewood's Theatre Royal, Stratford, which appeared to represent a rapidly growing new society. Sinfield highlights the rebellious mood of the 1960s and the desire of those working within the arts to experiment with new forms and subject-matter, adding 'not surprisingly, this led to headlong assaults upon established forms and values' (Sinfield, 1983, p.43). However, as the left-wing theatre practitioner John McGrath points out, the Royal Court was not as ground-breaking as it initially appeared. Like the Westminster Theatre, it appealed chiefly to the middle and upper classes, even though it was aiming its productions at the working class. McGrath says of the work of John Osborne and others at the Royal Court in the 1950s and 60s:

> Its greatest claim to social significance is that it produced a new 'working-class' art, that it somehow stormed the Winter Palace of bourgeois culture and threw out the old regime and turned the place into a temple of workers' art. Of course it did nothing of the kind. What Osborne and his clever director Tony Richardson had achieved was a method of translating some areas of non-middle-class life in Britain into a form of entertainment that could be sold to the middle classes (McGrath, 1984, p. 9/10).

Chapter five examines the most innovative of all the projects at the Westminster — The Day of London Theatre, which introduced schoolchildren to life behind the scenes and to the mechanics of staging a play. Launched in 1967, at a time when Theatre in Education was in its infancy, The Day of London Theatre ran for twenty-two years, attracting thousands of children from London and the Home Counties and receiving praise from the Inner London Education Authority as well as individual schools. MRA also staged a number of plays especially for children and the most successful of these was the pantomime *Give a Dog a Bone* written by Peter Howard. It opened at Christmas 1964 and ran for eleven seasons, helping to launch the career of West End musical star Elaine Page. The show was also filmed and broadcast on British television as well as screens around the world. This chapter also includes an analysis of two plays, written by MRA supporters in the 1980s, which aimed to confront current concerns; one dealing with illegal drug use and the other with the plight of young ethnic minorities in Britain's cities.

The final chapter in this book, chapter six, highlights a project created by a new generation of MRA supporters who, in the late 1980s, made a concerted effort to become more relevant to the changing culture. They developed First Floor Theatre, inspired by Theatre Upstairs at the Royal Court, to stage plays tackling controversial issues. Unfortunately First Floor Theatre, whilst a great success, lasted for only one year. A decision to stage *Temptation* by the Czechoslovakian political dissident Václav Havel, in the main theatre, proved to have catastrophic consequences which are also investigated in this chapter. The director, James Roose-Evans, included scenes that simulated sex, which proved too much for many of the older members of MRA to tolerate. The result was a financial disaster. A growing faction within MRA, that wanted to sell the theatre and replace it with a conference centre, seized their opportunity. The theatre was closed and put on the market. Those who recognised that MRA theatre needed to adapt to a changing society in order to become relevant again were over-powered by others who believed that theatre was no longer an effective way of promoting the message.

Despite attempts to appeal to all races and creeds, MRA appeared, during the latter half of the twentieth century, to be unable to reconcile itself with the prevailing culture. A female supporter, who lived in one of the MRA houses near the Westminster Theatre in the 1960s, told me she was advised to dress 'modestly' in clothes with sleeves and to avoid being alone in the company of men. Another said her experience, on becoming involved with the movement in the 1970s, was that women were not encouraged or expected to take on management roles. MRA talked of 'revolution', of 'changing the world' through the theatre, but because they lived and worked together in a tight-knit community, its supporters may not have been fully aware of the cultural shifts that were taking place around them. The movement did, however, provide an alternative to the new theatrical forms that were emerging in the twentieth century and for many people this was a comfort. William Cook, writing in *City Limits*, says First Floor Theatre involved 'conservative audiences in a debate from which less cuddly drama excludes them' (Cook, 1990). The Westminster Theatre stood as a bastion against what MRA regarded as the evils of an emerging culture. Ultimately, it failed in its aims and the reasons for that failure are examined in my conclusion to this book. But regardless of the end result, the unique way in which the Westminster operated makes it worthy of a place in British theatre history.

1

The Origins of Moral Re-Armament

and its Theatre Movement

I do not think that there is any one single message for the world today that has so much significance as MRA. You are embarked on a most essential if difficult mission and if you fail, the world fails
(Devadas Gandhi cited in New World News, 1956a, p.47)

Devadas Gandhi, editor of the *Hindustan Times* and son of Mahatma Gandhi, epitomised the belief of all MRA supporters when he announced 'If you fail, the world fails'. The movement was convinced that the most effective way to save civilisation from what it regarded as impending moral and spiritual doom, was through its own ideology. To appreciate the principles of MRA and to understand the aims and objectives of the Westminster Theatre, it is necessary to examine the roots of the movement in America and the vision of its founder, Frank Buchman. This chapter researches the origins of MRA and explores the way in which it began to develop its use of theatre to promote its ideology.

Philip Boobbyer, an academic who is also chairman of the trustees of IofC UK, analyses Buchman's life and work in *The Spiritual Vision of Frank Buchman*. Boobbyer states that since his youth Buchman had been interested in the theatre and regarded plays as 'weapons' in MRA's spiritual battle (Boobbyer, 2013, p.114-115). Born in 1878 in Pennsylvania, Buchman was the son of an enterprising merchant who owned first a store and then a hotel profiting from the Philadelphia and Reading railroad. In 1902 Buchman was ordained a Lutheran minister and in 1906 he established a project for the poor in downtown Philadelphia, where he was housefather at a hostel for young men. Disagreements with the board over its decision to cut back on some of the amenities, in the belief that the hostel should make a profit, soon led to him leaving the post. Buchman's health suffered from the stress of this dispute and, following advice to go on a long holiday, his father gave him one thousand US dollars to enable him to visit Europe in January 1908. During his time in England, Buchman underwent a spiritual experience at a church in Keswick which eventually led to the birth of Moral Re-Armament. He attended a church service of just seventeen people and heard evangelist Jessie Penn-Lewis, a descendant of the family of William Penn, speak about Christ on the Cross. For Buchman that sermon was life changing:

> I began to see myself as God saw me, which was a very different picture than the one I had of myself. I don't know how you explain it, I can only tell you I sat there and realised how my sin, my pride, my selfishness and my ill-will, had eclipsed me from God in Christ. I was in Christian work, I had given my life to those poor boys and many people might have said 'how wonderful', but I did not have victory because I was not in touch with God. My work had become my idol (Buchman cited in Lean, 1985, p.30).

Tom Driberg, who appears to have been intent on denigrating MRA wherever possible, interprets the visit and the spiritual experience quite

17

differently to Buchman. He suggests that Buchman had gone through 'an emotional crisis — indeed what is usually called a nervous breakdown' because of the dispute at the hostel in America (Driberg, 1964, p.32). He goes on to question 'how stable his mind and personality were' at Keswick and 'indeed how authentic and objectively real the Keswick incident was' (Driberg, 1964, p.33). However, the event is of great significance to followers of MRA who regard Keswick as the birthplace of the movement. After the service, Buchman wrote letters of apology to those he felt he had wronged. This method of atonement, along with adherence to the four absolute standards, became a key requirement for MRA followers. Buchman returned to America and became YMCA secretary at Penn State University. During this time he began to develop regular morning meditations which involved listening to God for guidance. Eventually he left America once more to support YMCA missionary work in Asia and worked with the YMCA evangelist Sherwood Eddy in Sri Lanka, India, China, Korea, Japan and the Philippines between 1915 and 1919. Throughout the rest of his life Buchman maintained close ties with Asia and in the twenty-first century the movement still has particularly strong links with India where it runs a large conference centre.

During the 1920s, Buchman became a frequent visitor to Oxford University where he promoted his ideology and trained men for 'leadership work in many lands' (Howard, 1945, p.86). His meetings attracted thousands of people and his work became so popular that, in 1928, Buchman and his supporters became known as the Oxford Group (Boobbyer, 2013, p.2). According to Walter Clark the movement saw its world mission as changing people rather than changing political regimes. Clark comments, 'This helps to explain why the Oxford Group readily finds a warm spot in the hearts of many conservatives and those whose vested interests lie in the preservation of the status quo' (Clark, 1985, p.27). Although to the establishment the movement may have appeared no threat, because it was supportive of the dominant culture, its activities were beginning to attract media attention. In 1928 Driberg was sent to investigate 'this strange new religious group' whilst a reporter on the *Daily Express* (Driberg, 1964, p.16). Twelve years later *Daily Express* political journalist Peter Howard interviewed leading supporters of the movement following allegations of pro-German support; he subsequently wrote that there was no truth in the rumours. While Driberg became MRA's most vocal opponent, Howard eventually became unofficial leader of the movement and its chief propagandist playwright.

In 1938, as the Second World War loomed, the Oxford Group realised that it needed to introduce a new initiative, Moral Re-Armament, to reflect the mood of Britain and its allies and to widen its appeal. Boobbyer says Buchman's aim, at that time, was to 'generate a worldwide movement of moral and spiritual renewal that would avert war and bring a new spirit into national and international life' (Boobbyer, 2013, p.132). The location for the launch of MRA, East Ham Town Hall, was a tactical one, aimed at appealing to the working-class as well as the upper echelons of Oxford University. Howard claims that Buchman did not think in terms of social class divisions, believing instead that there were just two classes in the world 'men who change and those who refuse to do so' (Howard, 1961, p.16); in other words, those who abided by MRA guidelines and those who rejected them. Here is an example of Alan Sinfield's 'exclusive validity', referred to in the Introduction to this book. The way in which Buchman deliberately targeted academics, Hollywood celebrities and the unions, described later in this chapter, indicates that he was well aware of class divisions as was Peter Howard, who portrays East Ham Town Hall, in his book *Ideas Have Legs* as being 'packed by hundreds of dockers, shopkeepers, railwaymen, and the ordinary people who, under God, could become re-makers of the world' (Howard, 1945a, p. 88). The emphasis was always that for any change to be successful it had to be underpinned by a belief in God and this would have met with widespread approval at that time. Sinfield states: 'Until the mid-fifties surveys showed nine out of ten people said they belonged to a church or sect, seven to eight out of ten said they believed in God' (Sinfield, 1983, p.87). Driberg, an Anglo-Catholic, appreciated the significance of that launch saying that, by this point, MRA had gone from 'a simple revivalist movement – the experiment in individual Christian evangelism' to a 'high-powered ideological crusade, with apparently limitless funds' (Driberg, 1964, p. 120). He adds that MRA was intent on capturing influential figures from both the political right, 'the pillars of British establishment' (Driberg, 1964, p. 120) and the Labour and Trade Union movements.

While Buchman targeted the academics of Oxford, he also took every opportunity to associate himself with the working class, but always with those of influence, using carefully chosen terminology. Addressing a meeting of the National Trade Union Club in London in 1938, he declared:

> The Oxford Group is a revolutionary movement. That is the reason Labour understands it. That is why the Oxford Group understands Labour. They are both out for revolution ... British Labour and MRA have the same birthplace – East Ham. And that same spirit that cradled British Labour has cradled MRA and it too has caught the imagination of the world (Buchman, 1947, p.92-93).

The word 'revolution' was no doubt designed to attract the trade unions and those influenced by the language of communism. The movement consistently used the term when referring to the aims of the Westminster Theatre. Howard maintained that, through his plays, he wanted to 'enlist everybody, everywhere in a revolution to remake the world' (Howard cited in Wolrige Gordon, 1970, p.270). According to Richard Palmer, MRA's rhetoric was deliberately chosen to reflect that of the communists in order to appeal to them: 'Many of the techniques and much of the rhetoric of MRA seems designed to answer the communists in kind' (Palmer, 1979, p.185). As indicated later in this chapter, there were rumours that communists were infiltrating the Labour party and this would have been of huge concern to Buchman. By suggesting that the working class and MRA had the same 'birthplace', Buchman was implying brotherhood, solidarity and a bond with workers that went beyond the superficial. The message to the communists was that MRA understood their aims and could offer them a new and more effective ideology. Howard quotes Hans Bjerkholt, a founder of the Communist Party in Norway in 1923, as claiming that when he met Buchman he realised it was possible to find an ideology relevant to all — which 'unites everyone above class, above race' (Bjerkholt cited in Howard, 1961, p.69).

MRA's desire to appeal to all sections of the community caused widespread debate and suspicion. At the height of the Second World War, the movement came under fire equally from both ends of the political spectrum:

> In Britain MRA was accused by some of being a brilliantly clever front for Fascism; in Germany and Japan of being a super-intelligent arm of the British and American Secret Service. One day a section of the Press would announce that MRA was defunct and the next that it numbered nearly the entire membership of the British cabinet at the time of Munich and was responsible for engineering Hitler's attack upon Russia (Howard, 1945, p.89).

Richard Palmer states that in the post-war era 'The ultimate antagonist to the MRA disciple was communism, which epitomised the immoral society and MRA was indelibly stamped with a cold war outlook' (Palmer, 1979, p.173). However Howard claims Buchman believed both the non-communist and the communist worlds had failed because 'Neither has succeeded in creating a new type of man, free from selfishness, who is fit to carry humanity forward into the dangers and opportunities of the atomic age' (Howard, 1961, p.68). Both Buchman and Howard maintained the greatest enemy of all was materialism. They considered materialism to be when the human will or the party line had the ultimate authority and the basis for change was force; by contrast, 'In a moral ideology the ultimate authority is God's will and the basis for change is consent' (Buchman cited in Boobbyer, 2013, p.134). In a speech in 1939 at Oglethorpe University, Georgia, Buchman warned against materialism, suggesting that some people had been 'dishonest in gaining war contracts' (Boobbyer, 2013, p.143). Materialism, in this instance, is defined by Buchman as those who care more for money and possessions than they do for integrity rather than its specific meaning in Marxism that consciousness is shaped by material conditions.

Although MRA had to cope with allegations of being pro-Nazi during the war years, such accusations proved to be unfounded and these charges are investigated in more detail in chapter three. What is clearly evident is that the movement made an effective contribution towards the unification of France and Germany once the war was over. In the final weeks of the war, a group of Swiss residents told Buchman about a place where 'people from shattered countries could meet' (Dilly, 1995, p.29). That place was the near derelict Caux Palace Hotel overlooking Montreux and Lake Geneva.

A number of Swiss families and individuals raised money, through selling their homes or cashing in savings, to buy the building (Dilly, 1995, p.29). Since it opened as a conference centre, Caux has been visited by leading figures from around the world including Konrad Adenauer, the West German chancellor 1949-1963, who visited in 1947; Kofi Annan, secretary general of the United Nations 1997-2006, who attended in 2007 and 2013 and Robert Schuman, foreign minister of France in 1948 and president of the European Parliamentary Assembly from 1958-1960, who was at Caux in 1953. Edward Luttwak points out that MRA's work on unification, despite being acknowledged by Adenauer and Schuman, has largely gone unrecognised:

> The history of the Franco-German reconciliation has naturally attracted a great deal of scholarly attention. Yet no contemporary student of the published sources can be faulted for ignoring the role of MRA in that momentous evolution from hostility to cooperation because there is simply no mention of MRA in the huge academic literature on the subject (mostly in French and German). These matters would stand for all eternity but for the existence of both unpublished documents and indirect evidence that prove beyond all doubt that MRA played an important role at the very beginning of the Franco-German reconciliation (Luttwak, 1994, pp 38-39).

In the pre- and immediate post-war years MRA's work had a positive impact in many areas. An example of the movement's success can be found in its involvement with Alcoholics Anonymous, or AA as it is commonly known. Buchman stressed the need for discipline over alcohol, which he had given up in his early working life (Boobbyer, 2013, p.25). He had worked with a number of alcoholics in the early 1900s and his emphasis on daily meditations and atonement led to The Oxford Group playing a key role in the founding of AA in the 1930s. Daniel Sack writes:

The recovery movement's work — particularly the twelve steps6 and the group model — has its roots in both the group's [The Oxford Group] ideas and its people. While AA was never formally linked with the Group and has downplayed the historical connection on occasion, Buchman's influence nonetheless is central to the twelve steps method ... Alcoholics Anonymous and other recovery organisations are probably the most vital religious movements of the late twentieth century and form the Oxford Group's most long-lasting legacy (Sack, 2009, pp 81-84).

In the years after the Second World War, Buchman was decorated by a number of governments including France, Germany, Japan and the Philippines for his 'contribution to post-war reconciliation' (Boobbyer, 2013, p.3). In 1956 General Ho Ying-chin, adviser to President Chiang Kai-shek, told Buchman on a visit to Taiwan, 'If we leaders of China had had the unity of Moral Re-Armament, the history of our country would have been different' (Ying-chin cited in *New World News*, 1956b, p.40). Buchman was nominated on several occasions for the Nobel Peace Prize, albeit unsuccessfully. Some current IofC supporters believe that it was distrust of MRA that prevented him getting the prize but Buchman was quite pragmatic about it. Garth Lean, an author and leading figure within the movement, writes,

He was short-listed but the Prize went elsewhere, as it did in 1952 when parliamentary groups from Japan, the United States, Italy, Holland and Switzerland added their voices to the others. Buchman's comment on one occasion was, 'But I haven't made peace between nations. Let's get on with the work' (Lean, 1985, p.393).

Because MRA did not have an established structure or a membership list it has never been easy to classify and its motives have therefore frequently

---

[6] The 12 steps are aids to assist alcoholics in overcoming addiction and are core to the AA programme. The steps include developing a relationship with God through prayer and meditation and atoning for past transgressions — both also key requirements within MRA.

been misunderstood. It has attracted suspicion over its finances, its political persuasions and its religious standpoint. Its message — that everyone should live by the four absolute moral standards and listen daily in silence to the word of God — has been both too simplistic and too rigid for many to accept at face value. Boobbyer writes, 'The idea that the world could be transformed through the agency of changed individuals was rejected as simplistic by the American theologian Reinhold Niebuhr' (Boobbyer, 2013, p.6). Some have even regarded the movement as dangerous. Driberg, for instance, hoped that MRA would 'fail in its apparent main task of perpetuating the Cold War and the tragic division of mankind' (Driberg, 1964, p.304). Suspicion over the financing of MRA arose because it was renowned for its wealthy supporters. J. Hodgson emphasises that MRA was initially financed in Britain chiefly by individuals working full time for no wages: 'There are no millionaires with bottomless pockets behind MRA. Nor has the British government, the American government or the CIA ever given a penny to this work' (Hodgson, 1980, p.12). However, it should be noted that many supporters were able to work for no wages because they came from wealthy families, such as the industrialist Farrar Vickers of Vickers Oils, Leeds, who could also donate to the cause. A report on *The Finances of MRA* by J. B. Meakins, a Member of the House of Laity of the Church Assembly, reads: 'MRA is largely sustained and expanded not out of people's surplus but by sacrifice, the sacrifice of convinced and committed citizens' (Meakins, 1955, p. 203). These people included the family of Fiona Daukes, whose father was posthumously awarded the George Cross and whose mother gave a large part of the gratuity she received from the RAF at the end of the Second World War towards the purchase of the Westminster Theatre. Mrs Daukes says, 'Later, when funds were needed, I sold my mother's engagement ring and my grandmother's engagement ring. Not huge sums, but special to me to give' (Daukes, appendix 4 p.296). That kind of sacrifice was difficult for many, and particularly MRA's critics, to understand. Driberg devotes a whole chapter of his book to 'Where does the Money Come From?' In it he writes, 'It is a question that could be answered in comprehensive detail only by those — the MRA people themselves — who prefer to answer it in general terms' (Driberg, 1964, p.139). He refers to MRA's claim that it got its funding through donations, admitting, 'there is no reason to think that this is untrue' but adding, somewhat caustically, that MRA had thousands of supporters in Britain and the United States and 'all, we can be sure, are Guided to give what they can to the cause (and since they are also Guided not to drink or smoke or use cosmetics they have the more to give)' (Driberg, 1964, pp. 139-140).

There is no evidence to suggest that Buchman profited personally from MRA. According to Howard, 'For the last forty years of his life he had no salary and no assured income of any kind. He spent nothing on himself except for essential service ... he never owned a motor car ... the only property that was his was the family home in Allentown, Pennsylvania, where his mother and father lived and died' (Howard, 1961, p.16). Buchman believed implicitly that, if a project received God's blessing, the necessary funds would be provided:

> Buchman was meticulous with money, accounting for every penny, never letting a letter be posted if it could be delivered. He hated waste. But he would never let the cost of a venture be the deciding factor. He would carefully test whether it was right and if so go forward in faith. He would send two hundred and fifty people, with equipment for two plays, on a 35,000 mile journey round the world, even though he did not have the resources to finance them, strong

in the faith that God would provide for every need as they went (Howard, 1961, p.17).

Buchman may have believed that God would provide but he was shrewd enough to know that attracting the wealthy could only be beneficial to the movement. Anne Evans, grand-daughter of Farrar Vickers, confirmed, in a conversation with the author of this book, that Buchman would stay at Brown's Hotel in the West End when he came to London and court the rich and titled (Evans, 2012). Palmer says one of the strategies of the movement was to 'influence modern "princes" – industrialists, politicians, the wealthy, the wielders of power' (Palmer, 1979, p.174). Clark highlights the fact that Buchman had 'great political ability and ambition' and selected 'the most socially prominent colleges as the core for launching his movement' (Clark, 1985, p.99). This, according to Clark, was a tactical ploy because not only did 'wealthy contacts ease the financing of the enterprise', there was also no doubting 'the political and strategic soundness of converting first those members of the community whom others look up to' (Clark, 1985. p.102). Despite their influence however, Boobbyer argues that attracting the rich and famous was not Buchman's primary aim. He claims that although, in the Western world, the leadership of the movement was in the hands of university-educated people of middle, or sometimes upperclass backgrounds, there was also 'a solid sprinkling of working class supporters and a serious outreach into poorer areas' (Boobbyer, 2013, pp. 121-122). While MRA did reach into the working-class areas of Britain in the 1940s and 1950s, with plays being performed within the industrial and mining communities, such initiatives declined in later years and the works of Peter Howard, discussed in chapter three, show a lack of understanding of working-class culture. MRA did make a concerted effort to involve the unions in its work but it concentrated more on appealing to the union leaders than the workers, thereby continuing Buchman's strategy of addressing those with influence.

Most of the movement's original followers, including Buchman, were Christian, and it is therefore understandable to assume that it was a Christian organisation. Howard, however, argues, 'It is not an organisation, a sect or a religion. It is an ideology. It is the way men live and what they live for. The Catholic priest understood this when he said: "The church does not need Moral Re-Armament, but the Catholics do"' (Howard, 1961 p.119). The implication here is that individuals could practise the four absolute standards regardless of their religious beliefs and that, if there were failures within the Catholic Church, the faults lay with individual worshippers rather than with the Christian doctrine. The Catholic Church had not always looked favourably on MRA. In 1951, to MRA's great surprise and consternation, the Holy Office of the Vatican issued a three-point warning to Catholics stating that it was improper for priests and clergy to attend MRA meetings and no Catholic should accept any office within the movement (Lean, 1985, p.442). Lean claims the Catholic Church had received distorted information which gave the wrong impression of MRA's structure. He says the Vatican was 'convinced that behind the lack of organised framework, which Buchman had always encouraged, there was a carefully concealed hierarchy, similar to that of various secret societies it had encountered in the past' (Lean, 1985, p.444). The Vatican may also have been disturbed by the fact that MRA was open to all faiths. Belden explains: 'Buchman never soft-pedalled his own Christian faith but he respected theirs [other faiths] and anticipated the highest from them' (Belden, 1979b, p.60). A movement encompassing all religions was highly unusual in Britain in the early and mid-twentieth century. Boobbyer says 'MRA was not unique in emphasising the accessibility of divine wisdom and the importance of moral absolutes. However, the fact that it increasingly embraced people from diverse faith traditions was an innovation ... It generally avoided theological disputes and stressed the importance of moral and spiritual experience' (Boobbyer, 2005, p.209). In his latest book Boobbyer expands on this: 'It is not easy to fit Buchman's ideas into a defined theological system ... he had no difficulty combining an emphasis on the cross of Christ with an appreciation of other religions' (Boobbyer, 2013, p.159).

In addition to encompassing all religions, reconciliation and conflict resolution played a major part in the work of MRA, both during the Second World War and in the subsequent Cold War. Boobbyer argues that MRA, and Peter Howard in particular, saw the latter from a spiritual perspective: 'Both sides in the Cold War faced a common need for spiritual renewal' (Boobbyer, 2005, p.205). Howard epitomises MRA's thoughts on both the left and right of politics when he writes, 'We need an honest look at Britain. It is not honest to say that all the past was bad, that everything left is right or that everything right is wrong' (Howard, 1963, p.17). He was concerned that those supporting democracy had not got the enthusiasm and focus of the communists and claims:

> The real danger if the present drift continues is a situation patterned on the 1926 General Strike but with more disastrous consequences. Marxist dialectics is as much double-Dutch to the working class as it is to the rest of the British electorate. The unofficial strikes are not Communist but unconscious tools ... The Red men are few. But they are formidable in their Marxist faith. They succeed because they are red-hot where so many democrats are lukewarm (Howard, 1963, p.20–21).

The movement always made a concerted effort to remain neutral in areas of conflict, believing that in order to inspire individuals to listen to each other, it was essential to remain impartial. This created much antagonism and suspicion, however, and J. S. Hodgson questions why those on both the far right and far left of politics were united in their opposition:

> MRA is not political. It has nothing to do with party politics ... MRA has nothing directly to do with trade union negotiations but there are thousands of workers who have become more loyal and effective trade unionists because of their touch with it or people committed to it ... Some of our colleagues have been violently opposed to MRA. Coming in many cases from the extreme Right or the extreme Left they were united in one thing – a furious and curious campaign against it. Why should this be? ... Why should people oppose something so patently genuine when they remained completely ignorant of even its basic concepts and motivations? They retained a stubborn, prejudiced and closed mind to the truth (Hodgson, 1980, p.6-7).

Hodgson goes on to state that MRA is not 'anti anyone ... does not adopt policies or take up positions' (Hodgson, 1980. p.17) but is 'opposed to all forms of exploitation' (Hodgson, 1980, p.17). It was his belief that some politicians and trade unionists had been misled by Driberg's criticism of MRA and he claims Driberg's book *The Mystery of Moral Re-Armament* 'bristles with bitter innuendo and misinformation' (Hodgson, 1980, p.19). While it is possible some people were influenced by Driberg, it would be unfair to suggest that he was solely responsible for the antagonism and 'misinformation' surrounding the movement. Hodgson's assertion that MRA was not 'anti anyone' is unrealistic and would inevitably have created suspicion, as would its insistence that it did 'not adopt policies' and was not an organisation. It is hardly surprising that those outside the movement 'remained completely ignorant of even its basic concepts and motivations' because it was difficult to pinpoint exactly what these were. By making statements that it was unable to quantify, MRA was self-perpetuating the suspicion surrounding it.

MRA supporters claim Driberg's attacks were relentless and that he was intent on destroying them. Christine Channer, an actress in numerous MRA plays for more than sixty years, says 'Tom Driberg was very against MRA. He was a number one enemy. He would turn up all over the place' (Channer, appendix 3, p.292). MRA believed he was a double agent and this was later proved to be correct. Chapman Pincher states that Driberg was recruited by MI5 while a pupil at Lancing College, an Anglo-Catholic foundation near Worthing in Sussex. Driberg later reported to MI5 that the KGB had asked him to provide inside information on the Labour Party and for some time he was paid by both MI5 and the KGB. However, Pincher writes 'As with many double-agents, Driberg was becoming increasingly under MI5 suspicion that he was doing more for the Soviet bloc than he admitted at his regular debriefings' (Pincher, 1981, p.204). Pincher goes on to state that the KGB had incriminating photographs of Driberg, later to become Lord Bradwell, caught in homosexual situations with the British KGB spy Guy Burgess in Moscow: 'Inquiries after Lord Bradwell's death in 1976 convinced MI5 that he had been controlled primarily by the KGB since the end of the war, partly because he may have been blackmailed but mainly because he had moved further to the left ... eventually he betrayed everyone' (Pincher, 1981, p.205). Driberg's politics and his sexuality would have been anathema to MRA whose definition of its own moral standard 'absolute purity' meant that it was opposed to homosexuality as well as to any sexual relationships outside the confines of marriage. It is therefore not surprising that each was equally scathing of the other. MRA's view on morality is highlighted in this excerpt from a full-page announcement by

Howard in *The Daily Express*, 22 December, 1964. It is quite possible that Howard had Driberg, as well as the Profumo scandal, which is referred to in chapter four, somewhere in mind when he wrote it. The announcement also evidences that, whilst MRA considered itself to be an international movement, its leaders were still in the grip of British imperialism:

> No country in history has been greater than our own. The image of no great country has been dragged so low so swiftly by such petty men. Today our country is regarded as a humbug and fraud by millions of people in other countries. Surely we have enough men free from the problems of adultery, homosexuality, viciousness and drunkenness left in our society to govern us and govern us well? (Howard cited in Wolrige Gordon, 1970, p.300).

Howard believed that theatre, along with other forms of public entertainment, was a powerful tool for good or evil and that, if exposed to immoral or violent ideas, an audience could go out into the streets 'more animal like than when they went in' (Howard cited in Boobbyer, 2005, p.210). He claimed that Oscar Wilde's 'descent into homosexuality began by reading books about vice' (Howard, 1963, p.32). He blamed radio and television for 'pushing acceptance of the unacceptable on us ... neither prison[7] nor praise seem a suitable remedy for a moral condition that can be cured' (Howard, 1963, p.33). Howard believed the popular misconception that homosexuality was an 'indulgence' and was vitriolic in his criticism. He writes:

> Once upon a time homosexuality was in disrepute in Britain. Men going with men, women with women, were thought queer. Today, some say it is queer to be normal ... The habit of homosexuality spreads from the top of the nation. Public schools and universities foster it. Men who have it stick together and entrench themselves in

---

[7] Oscar Wilde was sentenced to two years hard labour in prison for gross indecency

positions of power. They work in press, politics, theatre, radio ... It is almost dangerous to lift a voice against it (Howard, 1963, p.31).

Figure 1: Four searchlights representing absolute standards of honesty, purity, unselfishness and love, illuminate the sky over a packed assembly of 30,000 people for an MRA rally in 1939 in the Hollywood Bowl, California. Photo: Arthur Strong/MRA Production

MRA's views on homosexuality represented mainstream opinion in Britain at the time Howard was writing in the early 1960s. Peter Hennessy quotes Conservative minister R.A. Butler as saying, in the late 1950s, that public opinion was not yet ready for legalisation of homosexuality 'so deeply did emotions and instincts run, not just within the late fifties Conservative party but through society generally' (Butler cited in Hennessy, 2007, p.502). Howard was clearly worried, however, that the dominant culture MRA represented during the first half of the twentieth century was being eroded by an emerging culture that the movement could not, or would not, understand and was therefore unable to influence. MRA called for change, but change on its own terms, believing that 'adoption of MRA philosophy resolves all problems' (Palmer, 1979, p.182).

While it is important to understand the ideology of MRA, it is the way in which the movement used theatre to publicise its message that distinguishes it from other religious and political organisations of the twentieth century. And the man responsible for putting MRA on the stage was Buchman, who exerted a huge influence over the movement even after his death in 1961. During the 1930s Buchman unashamedly pursued the rich, the famous and the celebrities of America, through mass meetings at the Hollywood Bowl, with four huge beams of light shining into the sky to indicate the four absolute standards (fig. 1).

There is a similarity here with the Nazi Nuremberg rallies of the 1930s where searchlight beams were used to create a theatrical atmosphere in which to promote propaganda. It is possible that just as Buchman used communist rhetoric to attract the left-wing, he used fascist theatrical techniques to appeal to the right. Andrew Rawson in his book about the Third Reich writes that the Nazis used rallies to get their message across to their supporters 'face to face in an age before television and the internet'

(Rawson, 2012, Introduction, e-book). Paul Roland observes that one hundred and thirty anti-aircraft search lights at the 1937 Nuremberg rally created a 'Cathedral of Light in which Hitler assumed a messianic stature in the eyes of his fanatical followers' (Roland, 2012, Cathedral of Light, e-book). Buchman discovered, through his large dramatic gatherings, that he could speak to individuals *en masse*, in real time, achieving an immediate response that other media such as the cinema could not match. The left-wing theatre practitioner John McGrath echoes this view, describing theatre as 'the dimension of one person communicating through the work with one other person, the writer-creator communicating with each individual in the audience' (McGrath, 1984, p.94). Louis Fleming, former stage manager and director of the arts centre at the Westminster Theatre, indicates an additional reason for the Hollywood Bowl events, claiming Buchman 'wanted to change the views of the actors in Hollywood. He knew a lot of Hollywood producers and actors who supported MRA. He believed if people like them could change, then the world could change' (Fleming, appendix 8, p.301).

Shortly after the launch of MRA in the UK in 1938, the movement in America began developing the concept of using plays and musicals to promote its ideology. Buchman's decision to introduce theatre as a propagandist strategy came at a crucial time for the United States. While Europe was involved in fighting the Second World War, America was suffering from strikes which threatened the entire economy. In the late 1930s, with the introduction in the United States of the Labor Relations Act, unions became stronger. The Act stated that if the majority of a workforce wanted a union, management must recognise it and negotiate with it in all matters. In 1935, several union leaders created the Committee for Industrial Organisation (CIO). However, according to Thomas Reeves, the organisation found involvement with the steel and automobile industries was 'especially difficult and dangerous. In 1937 ten workers died in a clash with police outside Republic Steel' (Reeves, 2000, p.111). There were a number of sit-down strikes where workers refused to move until they had won collective bargaining. It was in this environment that Buchman called his first Industrial Round-Table Conference of MRA in America in 1940. Heads of industry and trade union leaders met together and among them was former Oxford don and theologian the Rev Alan Thornhill, who had been introduced to Buchman in Oxford and subsequently invited to join him in America. The conference inspired Thornhill to write his first and most successful play *The Forgotten Factor*, which was based on some of the conversations that took place at the initial conference and subsequent meetings. Thornhill and other MRA supporters also devised a review with songs and sketches to provide entertainment at the conferences. This eventually became a full-scale musical which took to the road, travelling around America.

Thornhill states in the forward to his play *The Forgotten Factor* that, for an academic like himself, the Round Table Conferences were remarkable because, for the first time, he met labour leaders and discovered they were 'very human' (Thornhill, 1954, p.7). Thornhill's comment is illuminating; a theologian who had spent much of his life within the cloistered confines of academia in Oxford was unlikely to have come across union officials on either side of the Atlantic. His first play was a success because it identified with both the workers and the management, something he can only have done through close observation of those attending the conferences. In the forward to his play, he states that he came to the conclusion that 'a great deal of the history of the world is made at millions of breakfast tables ... for the way that a man leaves his breakfast table often determines what he will do at the office or the factory bench, in the vital interview or around the conference table. You will notice that every scene of *The Forgotten Factor* takes place at breakfast' (Thornhill, 1954, p.7). The play premiered in Washington, in 1943, where Senator Harry Truman headed the list of sponsors and announced that he wanted it shown at every works plant in the country: 'There is not a single industrial bottleneck I can think of which could not be broken in a matter of weeks if this crowd [MRA] were given the green lights to go full steam ahead' (Truman cited in Buchman, 1947, p.152). The play went on tour from Europe to India and was performed for mineworkers in South Africa where it was reviewed by Manilal Gandhi in *Indian Opinion*, the newspaper founded in Africa by his father Mahatma Gandhi (Thornhill, 1954, p.10). One London performance was filmed and translated into sixteen languages. The popularity of the play did not, however, come about without some imaginative marketing methods by Buchman. He believed implicitly in having regular Quiet Times, where he would listen to God for guidance; at the same time, however, he was convinced it was important to be in the right place at the right time. Boobbyer describes Buchman's tactics, during a UN conference in San Francisco in 1945, when he took a table near the door of the restaurant of the Fairmont Hotel, where a number of delegates were staying. After meeting many people of influence over lunch, or even in passing, Buchman managed to arrange for a performance of *The Forgotten Factor* to be included in the schedule of events. As Boobbyer remarks 'good timing and obedience to the Spirit were clearly linked in Buchman's mind' (Boobbyer, 2013, p.120).

Figure 2: Dedication of the Westminster Theatre on Remembrance Sunday in 1946. At the front is Mrs Bremer Hofmeyr (née Agnes Leakey) reading the last letter from her brother Sgt Nigel Leakey VC. The Book of Remembrance is being signed by Mr and Mrs Herbert Hayes who lost two sons in the Second World War. John Caulfield is standing on the right and is a full time MRA worker. David Hassell, who remains an active supporter of the movement in the twenty-first-century, is in the front row, left, in naval uniform aged 21. The photo was taken by his sister Kay Hassell, who also remains active within the movement

Just as Buchman was developing the use of theatre in America to promote the MRA message, leading supporters of the movement in Britain decided, in 1946, that they would set up a Memorial Fund to commemorate those within MRA who had lost their lives during the Second World War. Belden writes that the supporters had 'the unusual and far-sighted idea of seeking to purchase a West End theatre to provide not only entertainment but a constructive drama of ideas, relevant to the post-war world and based on Christian faith and moral values' (Belden, 1965b, p.23). Their aim was to reshape the cultural landscape of post-war Britain through the staging of specially written musicals and plays advocating MRA ideology. That re-shaping, however, was to be carried out within the dominant culture of the time and to be led by the ruling class, as evidenced by the twenty married couples who launched the fund to raise the finance that was needed. This core group featured leading businessmen representing a variety of industries. Senior forces personnel were also involved, including Rear Admiral Sir Edward Cochrane and Major General George Channer. Buchman's strategy of attracting the wealthy appears to have been the right one because without influential backers, in addition to the many individual small donations, MRA could not have purchased the Westminster.

Among the core group were Gordon and Gladys Hassell, whose children, David and Kay, have both been interviewed for this book and have devoted their entire lives to MRA. The whole family was at the opening ceremony (fig. 2) and Kay, who was eighteen at the time, recalls that, 'the thought was to give people a purpose for the peace. We knew what we had been fighting for. How were we to carry that spirit of unity into the rebuilding of war-torn Britain when the devastation lay around us, most foods were still rationed and returning ex-service men and women had little to look forward to?' (Hassell, appendix 10, p.308).

This was an opportune time for MRA to re-launch its message of conflict resolution, personal responsibility and high moral and ethical standards. However, Britain was poised for a new kind of modernity. The Empire was disintegrating, following the financial and economic effects on Britain of the Second World War; the concept of a National Health Service was emerging; the 1944 Education Act introduced state education for all until the age of fifteen; the Arts Council of Great Britain was formed towards the end of 1946, enabling arts organisations to receive funding from the Government for the first time, and social and class patterns were changing. When MRA purchased the Westminster Theatre it was not merely to provide entertainment but, in the words of a statement set out by the original fund raising team, to present plays that would dramatise 'the spirit that can meet the tasks of peace ... which alone can secure freedom in Britain and brotherhood between nations' (Belden, 1965, p24). Such an aim, emphasising the need for peace and a new way of thinking, appeared to be in tune with the country as a whole as it set about rebuilding after the war. Alastair Davies and Peter Saunders state that the prolonged misery and deprivation of the 1930s had created 'a widespread feeling in Britain in the early 1940s that a new start would need to be made once the war was over' and when the war did finally end 'the popular mood for change proved irresistible' (Davies and Saunders, 1983, pp 13-14). The General Election of 1945, resulted in the defeat of Winston Churchill's Conservative government by Clement Attlee's Labour Party, at a time when communist electoral victories were forecast in France and Italy. The prospect of a rise in communism in Europe must have caused MRA some considerable concern and, coupled with the possibility of another General Strike in Britain at time of austerity, may have spurred the movement on to launch its own theatre a year later. The movement's vision of a new start however was in connection with spiritual rather than political change.

As has been stated previously, although the rich and influential were at the heart of MRA, the organisation went out of its way to attract and publicise its connections with ordinary men and women. In a letter in the archives of MRA dated 28 April, 1946, announcing that the Westminster Theatre had been purchased for £132,500, George Gee emphasises that the money was raised as much by the working-class as the elite. He writes, 'Money was raised without any need for public appeal, in some cases workers in factories and housewives who heard of the "Memorial Theatre" idea, coming forward to offer small and large amounts ... a group of Yorkshire mill girls clubbed together and sent a donation ... the widow of a fighting man sold her only house property in order that she could endow five seats' (Gee, 1946). MRA's decision to highlight the contributions from those of the working-class emphasises its desire to identify with them and vice versa. A report on the original donations to the Westminster Memorial Trust Fund states that from 11 February, 1946 to 31 July, 1947 there were 1,797 donors. Of that number, 1,565 were individual gifts ranging from £1 to £100 and three were of £10,000. The Fighters' Fund of serving soldiers contributed more than £2,000 from pay whilst serving. Many serving forces personnel gave all their gratuities on demobilisation. Some of the larger individual gifts commemorated individual men who had been killed: Hayes, Skillington, Everard, Sitwell and Beresford[8]. Other gifts represented sales of jewellery and some insurance policies were surrendered. This report also emphasises that 'mill girls made collections in their shops and miners' representatives sent gifts', yet again highlighting the support of the working-class, who had traditionally not been associated with theatre audiences (MRA, 1947b, report). The fact that MRA received numerous donations was difficult for some to understand. An article in *The Daily Worker* asks,

---

[8] It was usual in the 1940s to refer to servicemen by their surname only. The first names of these men are not known.

'Where did the money come from? Well the only answer I could get was "mostly from groups of factory workers"' (*Daily Worker*, 1946). However, with three donations of £10,000, it is clear that it was not only 'factory workers' who had donated.

The aim of MRA theatre was to create a new society based on its own ideology. Stuart Sanderson, a retired woollen manufacturer from Galashiels, Scotland and chairman of the committee which purchased the theatre on behalf of MRA, explains in a statement to supporters: 'Our idea is that at the Westminster Theatre we should show plays which will perpetuate the wartime spirit of sacrifice and team work of British men and women. Certainly today, as never before, democracy needs an inspired and Christian theology. This theatre, we hope, will help to create it' (Sanderson, 1946). MRA hoped that by staging moralistic, Christian-influenced plays and aligning itself with the wartime philosophy of 'everyone pulling together' it could create a new kind of ethical and moral society. Although MRA had noble ambitions, its purchase of the theatre caused considerable controversy. *The Daily Mirror*, unenamoured by the prospect of MRA owning a theatre, printed the headline 'Theatre Sold to Group is "Lost to us", actors say' (*Daily Mirror*, 1946). The article quotes Lewis Casson, a vice president of Equity: 'I deplore its use as a means of propaganda for one particular group' and Firth Shephard, a theatrical promoter: 'In these days of great theatre demand and shortage, it seems a pity that the industry has lost another stage' (Casson and Shephard cited in *Daily Mirror*, 1946). Meanwhile *The Manchester Guardian* quotes Stuart Sanderson in defence of MRA, 'Almost all the members of the committee have lost sons or comrades in the war and they wish to perpetuate the spirit of sacrifice and teamwork. They believe democracy needs an inspired ideology and the Moral Re-

Armament plays will help to create it' (Sanderson cited in *Manchester Guardian*, 1946).

MRA knew, when it launched the Westminster Theatre, that in order to have a major impact on society it needed to have the support of the working, middle and upper classes, the armed forces and politicians. This is reflected in a brochure celebrating the commissioning of the theatre, which also alludes to fears that communism, in the guise of 'militant organised materialism', was trying to take over the newly-elected Labour Party. MRA is no doubt referring here to the hard-line domestic, military and foreign policies of Joseph Stalin and not, as referred to earlier, the Marxist term for 'materialism'. In the commemorative brochure one of the many servicemen invited to the dedication ceremony, Staff Sgt Manson of the Royal Armoured Corps, is quoted: 'I was one of the thousands of servicemen who voted Labour in the last election. I believe that Labour led by God can lead the world. I have seen through this theatre the leaders of Labour getting a whole new ideology, a Christian ideology which is making Labour proof against the ideology of materialism that is trying to dominate it' (Manson cited in Commemorative Brochure, 1946). Capt. W.L.M. Conner, who commanded a leading tank at El Alamein, writes in the same brochure: 'There are two forces bidding for the heart and mind of this country. One is a militant organised materialism. But it was not for materialism that thirteen thousand men gave their lives in a few days at Alamein. The other force is Moral Re-Armament. It is the answer to materialism and it is the spirit for which these men died' (Conner cited in Commemorative Brochure, 1946). James Haworth, Labour MP for Walton, Liverpool, promises, 'Today means for me a re-dedication of my life, heart and soul to the work of winning the House of Commons and this country to the inspired ideology of MRA' (Haworth cited in Commemorative Brochure, 1946). By associating itself with the recent deaths of thousands of servicemen, MRA was ensuring that it reflected the spirit of the nation in 1946.

Buchman, who was always keen to promote the use of theatre, realised that Britain faced huge problems, both economically and politically, in the aftermath of the Second World War and felt *The Forgotten Factor* could contribute to the country's regeneration. As a result, he transported his cast from America to Britain for the inaugural production at the Westminster. The play's emphasis on the battle between the ideologies of Moral Re-Armament and materialism accentuated MRA's belief that theatre should be used to influence culture and society in Britain. Having defeated the Nazis, the new threat to Europe was communism. Ray Merrick writes, 'In both the Foreign Office and the British Embassy in Moscow, early 1946 was a time of anxious questioning concerning Soviet behaviour and ultimate objectives' (Merrick, 1985, p. 453). *The Forgotten Factor*'s emphasis on dialogue between management and unions would have appealed to both the Civil Service and the leaders of industry who were no doubt uneasy at the Labour government's apparent reluctance to acknowledge the rise of communism in neighbouring countries. Andrew Defty writes that, whilst the British Foreign Office and US officials were worried, in 1947, at the prospect of communist electoral victories in France and Italy, UK foreign secretary Ernest Bevin 'maintained his resistance to a global campaign against communist propaganda' (Defty, 2013, p.47). There was also concern about the possibility of another General Strike, similar to that called by the Trades Union Congress in 1926 in support of the miners. Both the Labour Government, which was elected in 1945 and the Conservatives, who replaced Labour in 1951, wanted to avoid another major confrontation with trade unions. As Chris Wrigley states, 'During Churchill's post-war government, ministers appointed even more trade unionists to consultative committees than had been the case under Attlee' (Wrigley, 1997, p.6). It is clear that the necessity to appease the unions and prevent major strikes was the policy of both major political parties. Britain was also faced with serious economic difficulties in the immediate post-war period. One third of the City of London had been destroyed and other cities had been decimated, industrial plants were run down and the country was deeply in debt. According to Lean, 'Buchman felt the answers lay with the coal mines where absenteeism had risen from 6.4 per cent in 1939 to 16.3 per cent in 1945' (Lean, 1985, p.331). With Britain on the brink of an industrial disaster, 'Buchman believed that he had, in the play *The Forgotten Factor*, a weapon which could be useful' (Lean, 1985, p.340).

The play proved to be a huge triumph for MRA and the Westminster Theatre and a detailed account of its success is provided in chapter two. However, rather than concentrating on developing its work at the Westminster, MRA spent the next decade taking its plays across the world. Vincent Evans writes in 1955:

> One Saturday evening twenty six MRA plays were produced at the same time on five continents in nearly a dozen languages ... plays were also produced in Washington, Tokyo, all over Africa, most European capitals, India and Australia ... six of them and three musicals are in current production ... They are not amateur efforts produced with enthusiasm but little knowledge of the theatre. They are theatrical achievements in their own right. Elizabeth Bergner has helped produce them. Marion Anderson, Phyllis Konstam, Ivan Menzies and others, whose names have been boldly billed in New York and Paris, act in them (Evans, 1955, pp 193-194).

The concentration on overseas work meant that by the mid-1950s, less than ten years after its opening, the future of MRA's London base was in doubt. Founder member of the Board of Trustees, Gordon Hassell, in a report believed to have been written in 1954, states that 'due to a lack of decisive policy', the theatre had been let on a play-by-play basis with an average loss of £3,000 a year (Hassell, c.1954). From 1952 to 1954 the theatre was leased to London Mask Theatre Ltd at a rental of around £7,800 which, after expenses and repairs, produced a net income of £3,500 a year. This company had been unsuccessful, however, in making a profit and, according to the report, decided not to renew its lease, leaving the Westminster Memorial Trust with an overdraft of nearly £7,000 and no source of income. Options listed by Hassell included selling the building or rebuilding to include administrative offices as well as a restaurant and theatre. He writes: 'This would involve a heroic venture of faith and might cost at least £250,000' (Hassell, c.1954). Twelve years later MRA did in fact carry out a rebuild at double the cost envisaged by Hassell.

Just two years after Hassell published his report, John Osborne's play *Look Back in Anger* opened at the Royal Court and this was to have a major effect on MRA theatre strategy. Osborne's play received mixed reviews, but it was not the sight of a woman doing the ironing on stage or the regional and working-class accents of the cast, so unlike the carefully modulated tones of those featured in Thornhill and Howard's plays, which disturbed MRA; it was the anarchy and the anger of Jimmy Porter and the general despair of the piece that proved to be the impetus the movement needed to re-evaluate its objectives at the Westminster. Michael Billington describes *Look Back in Anger* as 'an eloquent testament of alienated youth' reflecting 'the sense of a country stifled by an official establishment culture'

(Billington, 2015, online). Although, in an article in the *Westminster Theatre News*, MRA acknowledges the play's 'profound effect on theatre and on society', it does not appear to have understood the reasons for Porter's anarchy and anger. The article continues, 'In 1961, seeing the way things were going, we at the Westminster decided to launch a continuous series of plays expressing a different view of life' (*Westminster Theatre News*, 1986, p.6). MRA's 'view of life' centred around overcoming conflicts, both politically and in the home environment, through adherence to the four absolute standards. Those standards did not, however, address the alienation highlighted in *Look Back in Anger*, appearing instead to represent the 'establishment culture' Jimmy Porter was rebelling against. Nonetheless, the emergence of kitchen sink[9] and avant-garde drama led to a new beginning for MRA theatre. Although its theatrical origins in Britain date back to 1946, the movement did not begin to make full use of the Westminster to promote its message until the start of the 1960s. One of the plays that the Westminster hoped would provide an antidote to Osborne and the 'kitchen sink', was Peter Howard's *The Diplomats*. The following chapter analyses both *The Forgotten Factor* and *The Diplomats* and investigates why the former was able to successfully put across the MRA message and bring about positive change in the lives of those who saw it, while the latter appears to have had little impact outside the realms of the movement.

---

[9] Kitchen sink drama emerged in Britain in the late 1950s and focused primarily on the struggles experienced by the working class living in urban areas.

2

MRA Propaganda Theatre
–Success and Failure

Propaganda is the dissemination of ideas intended to convince people to think and act in a particular way and for a particular persuasive purpose ... propaganda, power and persuasion are all about winning hearts and minds, and that remains as relevant today as it always was
–(Welch, 2013, pp 28 and 200).

For any propagandist theatre company to be a success it must not only present plays that are relevant and entertaining, it must understand the audience that it is trying to convert and the society at large that it is aiming to change. In this chapter I analyse the first MRA play to be performed at the Westminster Theatre, in 1946, *The Forgotten Factor* by Rev Alan Thornhill and compare it with *The Diplomats*, by Peter Howard, performed nearly twenty years later in 1964. I investigate each play against the cultural and political background in which it was performed, giving an insight into why the movement was unable to maintain its initial ability to inspire and influence its audience.

Buchman arrived in Britain with the American cast of *The Forgotten Factor* on the *Queen Mary*, which docked in Southampton on 30 April,

1946. Among those travelling with him was Ray Purdy, who was thirteen at the time. He recalls:

> We came by train to London and then drove through the streets in buses to the MRA headquarters in Hays Mews, London ... All through the winter of 1946–47 the play was performed. Night after night busloads would come from collieries, factories, schools, farms and towns all over the country. It was an amazing winter (Purdy, appendix 20, p.344).

The play was performed at a time when Michael Woolf describes theatre in Britain as being 'in a state close to stagnation' (Woolf, 1997, p.104). He highlights the fact that war, and the subsequent reconstruction, imposed constraints on public entertainment and as a result limited its development. Woolf quotes the theatre critic Kenneth Tynan as claiming, in the early 1950s: 'There is nothing in the London theatre that one dares discuss with an intelligent man for more than five minutes' (Tynan cited in Woolf, 1997, p.104). Tynan ignored what was happening at the Westminster entirely. *The Forgotten Factor*, about conflict between management and unions, was performed in Britain at a crucial time in the country's history. It had a major effect on both workers and management in a range of industries when it toured industrial areas of Britain, in addition to being performed at the Westminster. Raymond Williams claims that 'literature, the art of writing and creating performance, is central to articulating the dominant culture' (Williams, 2005, p.45). As will be shown in the analysis of this play, it reflects both the dominant and the emerging cultures of the immediate post-war era.

A detailed examination of *The Forgotten Factor* is needed to determine exactly why it was so successful with management and workers alike. The play represents the dominant culture of 1946, when there were clear divisions between the classes and when men and women had very different roles. Even after the Second World War, during which women played a pivotal role, it was expected that the man would be the breadwinner and the woman bring up the children and look after the house. Cynthia White writes that once the war was over women were expected to return to their pre-war roles and 'their "proper" business of running a home' (White, 1977, p.10). However the play shows glimpses of a new society emerging not only in the workplace but also in the home. The opening scene takes place in the living room of Richard Wilson, president of Wilson Consolidated, where Thornhill describes Mrs Wilson as 'coping single handed with the family breakfast' (Thornhill, 1954, p.15) as if this were a herculean task and certainly not one she was used to. He goes on to explain that 'the latest in a series of maids has suddenly left' (Thornhill, 1954, p.15) adding that Mrs Wilson's 'rather luscious négligé suggests that she is better at planning colour schemes than preparing meals' (Thornhill, 1954, p.15). Immediately a picture is created of a 1950s' upper-class woman, unable to function properly without servants. Wilson comes down the stairs shouting 'Myrtle, where's my breakfast? Myrtle!' (Thornhill, 1954, p.15) signifying that he is a man used to being waited on, but Mrs Wilson's reply, that she cannot find maids because 'they are all getting jobs in your factory' (Thornhill, 1954, p.16), indicates that society is changing. Women, however, are clearly still considered to be inferior. Wilson tells his wife, 'How do you expect me to keep a thousand men at work if you can't keep one cook ... suppose we are without a maid for a couple of days ... I should have thought any housewife could provide a simple breakfast' (Thornhill, 1954, p.16). The dynamics between husband and wife have been clearly defined and Thornhill goes on to demonstrate Wilson's obsession with work. Mrs Wilson asks him to talk to their son, before he returns to college, saying 'he's been so queer and moody lately' (Thornhill, 1954, p.18) but Wilson has no time for family matters because the possibility of a strike at the factory must take priority. He blames the Government for the introduction of new piece rates, which are the subject of the impending strike, stating that both Government and unions are at fault. Meanwhile, Mrs Wilson is absent-mindedly talking about redecorating the living room, implying that women are not interested in politics and serious affairs. Thornhill demonstrates in this exchange his knowledge of the difficulties facing management and unions in Britain in the immediate post-war era, as highlighted by Alec Cairncross:

> Faced with labour shortages and lacking the necessary staff for care-
> ful planning and supervision, British managements tended to rely on
> piece rates to provide their workers with the necessary incentives and
> to surrender them the power to plan their work in detail. The en-
> hanced bargaining power of the workers then either blocked the pro-
> cess of innovation or exacted a price that slowed it down. Manage-
> ments in turn shrank from conflicts that change and innovation re-
> quired (Cairncross, 1991, p.33).

Thornhill chooses to set the conflict between management and unions against the background of a school play to show that, while the men in power – the factory boss and the union leader – refuse to negotiate, their daughters can separate the personal from the professional and have no problems working together in a play. The girls, Betty, who is the daughter of Wilson, and Polly, who is the daughter of union boss Rankine, refuse to allow their friendship to be affected by their respective fathers' disputes and eventually bring about a resolution. While the older generation is continuing to maintain the class divisions and the roles of controlling husband and subservient domesticated wife, the younger generation is demonstrating that women can assert themselves and have their own opinions. When Wilson says, 'I don't want a daughter of mine mixing with that crowd. They'll use everything they can against me. Besides, people may talk', Betty retorts 'Well, let 'em talk' (Thornhill, 1954, p.19). Wilson's son Dick has gone to college and has begun to appreciate the plight of the workers. By mixing with the working class, Wilson's children are beginning to appreciate their struggles and are an example of the emergence of a new society. Wilson complains to his son that the trade unionists are being unreasonable: 'I've got to step up production, satisfy seventeen different bureaux, keep the shareholders happy – yes and plan how to keep those same fellows on the payroll. Don't they realise we've all got to make sacrifices?' (Thornhill, 1954, p.32). However Dick challenges his father and the following conversation, about the union leader Rankine, highlights the gulf that still exists between the classes:

Dick: What kind of guy is he anyway?
Wilson: Crooked and pig-headed like all the rest of that bunch.
Dick: I know, but as a man what's he like? In ordinary life I
mean?
Wilson: How should I know, I never met him in ordinary life.
Dick: Couldn't you make friends with him?
Wilson: What do you mean?
Dick: Well, take him to a ball game or something.
Wilson: Look here, Dick, I'm not in a mood for joking
(Thornhill, 1954, p.33).

Dick then begins to deliver the MRA message: talk about problems, listen to each other and practise absolute unselfishness. He tells his father about a family he has got to know who have rows but know how to work out their difficulties, 'instead of just jumping on each other when things go wrong ... their idea is to get rid of selfishness ... how can you change a world that's selfish as hell when you're selfish as hell yourself?' (Thornhill, 1954, p.33-34). The common thread running through all MRA plays is that, in areas of conflict, both sides are usually in the wrong. The first act ends dramatically with Rankine's daughter Polly running into the Wilson household saying she has been forced to leave school and resign from the play because her father thinks 'they're a lot of damned snobs' (Thornhill, 1954, p.37). Rankine is shown to be just as bigoted as Wilson. Polly tells Dick the police are at the factory gates with guns, 'They're going to kill us, all us workers... They'll kill my father ... your father's living off us ... do something, do something' (Thornhill, 1954, p.38). The phrase 'your father's living off us' indicates that Thornhill is sensitive to the resentment of the working class.

The second act begins in the Rankine household and the setting clearly shows the difference between the classes. Thornhill describes a horse-hair couch and wooden rocking chair that belong to a family who have 'been through hard times' (Thornhill, 1954, p.39). The factory chimneys and walls of high buildings block out the sunlight but there is a shelf of modern books on current affairs and a globe in one corner of the room. There is an indication here of the rise of the working class through education, through books, through knowledge of the world. Food is scarce and Rankine spends all his time on union business. He warns his wife that life is about to get much tougher; they will all have to cut back on food and clothes and prepare for a long strike. The family is shocked by the arrival of Dick who tells Rankine, 'We're all shot to pieces among ourselves. We've got to get together' (Thornhill, 1954, p.48). When Rankine replies that the bosses can have co-operation on the workers' terms, Dick counteracts with, 'You know, you and my dad are a lot alike' (Thornhill, 1954, p.48). He then, once again, introduces the MRA ideology by saying that he has been listening to God in quiet and as a result believes he should have breakfast with Rankine

(Thornhill, 1954, p.50). The two begin to communicate but they are interrupted by the entrance of Polly with a gash across her forehead, received while she has been demonstrating at the plant. Rankine ends the scene: 'She wouldn't ever have been there if I hadn't taken her out of school. My god! If anything happened to her, I'm the one that's done it' (Thornhill, 1954, p.52). The next scene begins with Polly recovering and discussing with Dick the similarities in their families. 'You know Polly,' says Dick, 'if our two families ever get fighting on the same side, then Lord help the enemy' (Thornhill, 1954, p.54). Rankine arrives, with a change of heart, to tell Polly she can go back to school and to the play. Dick and Rankine begin to converse and Dick discovers that Rankine had a serious head injury in an industrial accident fifteen years earlier, caused by negligence on the part of the management. The depression and lack of food contributed to the death of Rankine's eldest child. Dick assures Rankine he is not trying to change his political opinions and invites him to the Wilson home for breakfast the following day. Yet again Thornhill has highlighted the MRA message, that faults exist on both sides and that non-judgemental listening is important in order to discover the causes of what might initially appear unreasonable behaviour.

The morning of the breakfast dawns and Wilson is furious at the arrival of Rankine. Betty and her mother calm the situation but, just as a breakthrough is about to happen, union activists force their way into the house. Rankine tells the men he has seen a change in the boss's son which has led him to decide that, 'We've got to do things different ... these days it's not a question of who's right but what's right ... let's get honest for a change ... we're all of us to blame' (Thornhill, 1954, p.77). The MRA ideology is reinforced; all sides are to blame for conflicts and are equally responsible for

54

what takes place in the future. Wilson is impressed by Rankine's words, telling him that he has shown trust, honesty and 'something I'd forgotten … I guess most of us have … It's the forgotten factor … It's …' and Dick interrupts: 'It's God isn't it?' (Thornhill, 1954, p.79). The climax to the play is the delivery of the message that is at the core of the movement: the way to individual change and adherence to the four absolute standards is through belief and trust in God – and, in this case, it is God that is the 'forgotten factor'. The play ends with Wilson and Rankine shaking hands and their wives bringing in the coffee. The women have briefly been shown as peacemakers, but have now reverted to housewives. Thornhill incorporates in this play some of the cultural changes taking place but at the same time recognises that his audience also needs the security of a comfortably familiar ending. The various aspects of the MRA message have all finally been delivered: listen to each other and listen in silence to the word of God for the solution to problems; those with the power should not be complacent because the 'answer' to difficulties is often delivered through the mouths of the least likely candidates, which, in this case, are the women and children. The fact that these two groups could help to resolve the conflicts between the menfolk would have been revolutionary in the late 1940s when society was dominated by the upper and middle classes, and women and their offspring played subservient roles. As stated in the first chapter, religion played an important part in the lives of the British people in the 1940s and 1950s so the emphasis on belief in God would have been welcomed and understood. The play also reflects the emergence of a new culture in which class divisions are lessened and the role of married women begins to alter. Referring to the effects of the Second World War, Harold Smith states, 'It is generally believed that one of the most significant lasting changes was the acceptance of married women working outside home' (Smith, 1986, p.218). He goes on to add that this could also have been due to a campaign by the Labour government to encourage more married women into the workplace. That campaign, however, was no doubt initiated by the effects of the war. The lives of so many men had been lost that women were needed to boost the work force and inevitably society's view of women began to alter.

On 22 October, 1946, *The Forgotten Factor* opened at the Westminster and Garth Lean states that initially Buchman sat in a box at the theatre each evening 'watching the audience not the play' (Lean, 1985, p.342). Buchman's aim was to convert people to the MRA ideology of living by the four absolute standards, therefore what was happening on stage was secondary to what was occurring in the audience. Lean adds that in just one week a thousand miners saw the play and 'The ensuing campaign in the coalfields, initiated by management and trade unions, centred on performances of *The Forgotten Factor*, was to continue for the next four years' (Lean, 1985, p.342). The audiences were specifically targeted; coaches were arranged to transport them to London from a variety of industries. In a ground-breaking move for British theatre at that time, *The Forgotten Factor* toured the mines and industrial heartlands of Britain emphasising the need for management and unions to work together in order for both to survive. Thornhill says the early performances of *The Forgotten Factor* lacked scenery, equipment and experience, but adds: 'we banked everything on one quality – reality' (Thornhill, 1954, p.5). The actors were all unpaid, untrained MRA supporters, but according to Thornhill: 'There was no need to act. We only had to be real,' adding that the actors were 'living on the stage what they know in real life.

Figure 3: Union officials and their families from Staffordshire at the Queen's Hall, Burslem, in 1947, watching *The Forgotten Factor*. MRA had been invited by the president and secretary of the North Staffs National Union of Mineworkers

They are not play-acting. They are fighting for the hearts and minds of men. The real drama is not on the stage, it is happening in the audience' (Thornhill, 1954, p.6). While it is unlikely that, when the play was performed at the Westminster Theatre, the actors had an in-depth knowledge of the managers and union officials they were playing, they had enthusiasm and absolute belief in the MRA message they were portraying. Where the greater impact no doubt came, however, was after the performance when the union officials, workers and managers in the audience would talk with the actors playing their roles on the stage (figs. 3 and 4). Those conversations would have given the actors an insight into their roles that was unlikely to have happened at any other theatre of the time and was a true example of art mirroring life.

Figure 4: The presentation of *The Forgotten Factor* at Tamworth in the Warwickshire coalfield in 1948. L to R Eric Bentley, who played the employer; G A Mawbey, manager of Kingsbury Dexter Colliery; Frank Painter, president of the NUM Warwickshire; Paul Campbell, who played the union leader and Alderman G H Jones, labour director of the West Midland division of the National Coal Board

Mahala Menzies, daughter of English professional opera singer Elsie Griffin (1895-1989), understudied the role of Polly Rankine and, although she never actually got to perform on stage, toured Britain with the company working back stage. She highlights the effect the play had on the audiences:

In the Midlands in the coal fields, where the battle for communism was taking place, we put on the play and it did change the atmosphere in the mines. The play was a focal point. There is something about a group of people sitting in a darkened room watching a story unfold in front of you that makes you want to see it through to the end. There is just you and what is going on on the stage. In the end you are left with making your own decision (Menzies, appendix 18, p.341).

Kay Hassell also recalls the early performances of *The Forgotten Factor*:

> Night after night the play was shown to packed audiences, many staying on after the show to meet the cast and talk about how their lives could be changed and entrenched positions between Labour and Management could be resolved. Entrance to the theatre was free. We relied on the collection and on gifts to cover the costs. Of course, all the cast and back stage people gave their services voluntarily (Hassell, appendix 10, p.308).

The play is an example of successful propaganda: its message was received and understood by those within the community that it most wanted to influence. One thousand men from Woolwich Arsenal, eight hundred from Siemens' Electric, six hundred from Chatham Dockyards, two thousand from Ford's Dagenham, one hundred and fifty from General Electric Laboratories and hundreds from other industries saw *The Forgotten Factor* at the Westminster in just two months (MRA, 1947a). Tributes poured in from union leaders and management and leading professional actress, Dame Sybil Thorndike, announced, 'I was completely captivated by the play and the players. Here was genuine theatre – it had something to say and expressed it well. It was very well acted by players who believed what they were saying. Their keenness, humour and characterisation made the play alive and true' (Thorndike cited in Report, 1946). The success of the play is highlighted in a report of an industrial conference held at the Westminster Theatre on 27 March, 1947. This event was organised by MRA and attracted around four hundred company directors, labour leaders and businessmen and women indicating the respect and influence the movement had at all levels of industry. In that report, Farrar Vickers is quoted as saying: '*The Forgotten Factor* brings to the problems of industry the explosive force of a new spirit – it sets men free from fear and greed, turning individual goodwill into a national and international force' (Vickers cited in MRA, 1947a). He adds that he sent his son, who was also his works manager, and his daughter-in-law, to an MRA centre for training based on the spirit of the play. In that same report, Blyth Ramsay, a shipyard worker from the Clyde, describes the response from trade unionists:

> Sixteen thousand Trade Union officials and shop stewards, four hundred representative delegates from the London Trade Councils, labour parties and national trade unions have been to the Westminster to see *The Forgotten Factor*. From eleven coal fields have come five hundred miners and they are still coming. Sometimes you see four buses at a time arrive outside the theatre. Out come the miners, pouring into the theatre. And they pay their own expenses. One hundred and fifty MPs have been to the play. Two labour delegations from Holland and Sweden were sent over for a week. As a typical example, one shop steward has already had six hundred of his workers here. Another one hundred come tomorrow night (Ramsay cited in MRA, 1947a).

Duncan Davidson, Associated Pattern Makers Union at Ford Motor Company, states: 'Three thousand men from Ford's have already been to see the play with their families. In that three thousand we have had forty shop stewards, also high management and departmental management. It used to be a daily occurrence to have to report trouble to the management but the new spirit and the new vision of the people who have seen the play has had a practical effect ... for the shop steward now knows how to deal with human nature' (Davidson cited in MRA 1947a). Bill Slater, branch secretary of the National Union of Mineworkers, who had just completed his thirty-fourth year in the pits, reports that, after seeing the play, 'Everyone agreed that this is the thing we want. This is the spirit needed in the mining industry' (Slater cited in MRA, 1947a).

There is evidence that the impact of the play was felt far beyond the confines of the Westminster and was achieving even more than conflict resolution between workers and management. A letter to the *Yorkshire Evening News* signed by councillors and aldermen claims the play would help unions to fight communist infiltration: 'We would like to congratulate and thank the miners and officials who were responsible for getting the industrial drama *The Forgotten Factor* shown in the Yorkshire coalfields ... The Forgotten Factor may well prove the decisive factor in strengthening every constructive and democratic element in our Labour and Trade Union movement against the encroachment of anti-democratic and totalitarian ideas' (Burton, Nicklin, Quince, Webster, Wilson, 1946). A review of *The Forgotten Factor* in *The Motor Trader* November 1946 comments, 'The play points the only practical way to the solution of many of the world's problems. As to the "forgotten factor" which enters in to make this possible, my advice to traders and industrialists is to see the play and find it' (*Motor Trader*, 1946). In a letter to *The Weekly Scotsman*, 14 December, 1946, Thomas Gunn, a Prestongrange Miners' delegate, states, 'The Midlothian miners spoke from the stage before the play and I am proud to say their call for teamwork made a deep impression on the distinguished audience ... I would have walked to London to see the play. It is what I have dreamed of all my life' (Gunn, 1946). When *The Forgotten Factor* visited Staffordshire in 1948 for a month of performances at the invitation of five Cannock Chase collieries, the cast was introduced by Jack Ashley, Coal Board Labour Officer for the area, who later became a Labour MP before entering the House of Lords and by Frank Smith, secretary for 7,500 Leicestershire miners. Smith, who had been active in the Communist Party, told the audience, 'Here we see the solution to the problems we meet in the manager's office, the union office, local government and the Labour party' (Smith cited in *New World News*, 1948, p.7). The tours continued for several years. Dan Hurley, of the National Amalgamated Stevedores' and Dockers' Union, describes the effect performances of the play had on audiences at Poplar Civic Theatre in the early 1950s:

> It is certainly a play with an answer. There is a good deal of suspicion in the minds of the folk of Poplar and it has been implanted by the ruthless actions of certain individuals right down through the industrial age. But many of our friends came along and saw the play and their reactions were so favourable that they themselves convinced other people to attend the play. On the final day hundreds were standing in the aisles and stairs ...Naturally it would be foolish to state that all who have seen the play have left the theatre accepting the philosophy that is so convincingly imparted by all the players on the stage. Nevertheless it would be true to state that a considerable number came along to criticise, stayed for a friendly discussion and invariably agreed that their outlook had certainly been changed by what they had seen and heard (Hurley, 1952, p. 4-5).

While the play appears to have been universally welcomed by many unions, this was not always the case within the church. The Moderator of the Church of Scotland Rev G. Johnson Jeffrey wrote to 1,560 Scottish Ministers, who had welcomed the play's visit to Glasgow in 1953, describing it as 'a venture of faith which deserves the closest attention of all church leaders' (Johnson Jeffrey cited in Lean, 1985, p.435). However, in Sheffield, in the early 1950s, Canon E.R. Wickham, leader of an industrial mission, disapproved of MRA intervention and regarded *The Forgotten Factor* as 'a hindrance rather than a help' (Wickham cited in Lean, 1985, p.435). The Bishop of Sheffield Rev L.S. Hunter, addressing the Convocation of York shortly after the visit of *The Forgotten Factor*, dismissed the play as pure propaganda. He described it as 'glib emotionalism and shallow psychology' adding 'it is frightening how easily some industrialists and others fall for the salesmanship of MRA' (Hunter cited in Lean, 1985, p.436). The ideology MRA was advocating could hardly be described as being in opposition to

Christianity. Perhaps the Bishop believed that promoting a belief in God was the prerogative of the established church and not of a propagandist theatre movement. It is clear that there were those within the Protestant church who, like the Roman Catholics referred to in chapter one, were highly suspicious of a movement that accepted other faiths and promoted an ideology alongside Christianity.

Raymond Williams states that while the art of writing and creating performance is central to articulating the dominant culture, literature also embodies some residual meanings and expresses some emergent practices which, when incorporated into society, cause the dominant culture to change (Williams, 2005, p.45). Whilst, as has been demonstrated, *The Forgotten Factor* in the 1940s and early 1950s, did incorporate some emerging practices, the situation was very different twenty years later. MRA restaged the play at the Westminster Theatre, in the summer of 1970, at a crucial point in trade union history. It was just a few weeks after Edward Heath won a surprise victory for the Conservatives in the General Election in a turnout that was the lowest since the 1930s (Pelling, 1992, p.283). During the run of *The Forgotten Factor*, from July to December, Heath introduced the controversial Industrial Relations Bill, aimed at legally restricting trade union affairs. Alan Thornhill, writing about the play in the *Westminster Theatre News*, quotes the London *Daily Telegraph*: 'nothing could be more topical than the theme' and adds, 'Industrialists and union leaders who have seen the play in the first week agree with this view. Some who saw it in 1946-47 consider that this play was never more timely than today' (Thornhill, 1970, p.1). While some may have thought it topical, the play did not have the same influence as in the immediate post-war years. This was no doubt due, in part, to the fact that the play was no longer culturally breaking new ground and the priorities of the unions were changing. Class was no longer such an issue, the views of young people were being given more respect, the feminist movement was aiding the emancipation of women and audiences could no longer easily identify with the characters. Christianity was not so widely practised. Sinfield states that, until the mid-1950s, surveys showed nine out of ten people belonged to a church or sect, but this was not the case in the 1970s. He claims 'Christianity's grip weakens not when its improbabilities are exposed but when, because of changes in the world, it is no longer relevant' (Sinfield, 1983, pp. 87-89). Callum Brown asserts, 'British people since the 1960s have stopped going to church, have allowed their church membership to lapse, have stopped marrying in church and have neglected to baptise their children' (Brown, 2001, p.1). Belief in God – the 'forgotten factor' – was crucial in Thornhill's play, but changes in culture made this less relevant by the time *The Forgotten Factor* was revived in 1970.

Perhaps most important of all, however, in explaining the lack of interest in *The Forgotten Factor* is the fact that the National Union of Mineworkers had radically altered. Two months after the play opened at the Westminster, in 1946, the National Coal Board (NCB) was formed leading to hopes of a new beginning. A period of industrial nationalisation followed and the play complemented the aspirations of the unions. In 1970 the political situation was quite different, particularly in relation to the unions who felt threatened by the Government's proposed pay restraint policy and price rises. Although the miners were amongst the highest paid workers in the country, nationalisation had not brought them the power they had hoped for: 'The primary objective of the NCB was to make a profit, not to meet a social need' (Working Class Movement Library, online). Chris

Wrigley, referring to the introduction by Edward Heath's government in 1971 of the Industrial Relations Act, maintains, 'The trade union movement saw the Industrial Relations Bill (and then the subsequent act) as a massive attack on itself' (Wrigley, 1997, p.16). There was not the same will amongst the miners to listen to management because, while 1946 had been a victory, 1970 was the start of a battle. Heath's attempts to control the unions resulted, in 1972, in the first national miners' strike since 1926, which eventually led to a state of emergency, three-day working week and the defeat, in 1974, of the Heath government. *The Forgotten Factor* lost its propagandist power because it did not reflect the mood or the dominant culture of the time.

One such play, which was heralded a success by MRA supporters but received very mixed reviews in the press and created controversy before it even reached the stage, was *The Diplomats* by Peter Howard. Howard, whose life and work are described in detail in the following chapter, was hailed by those sympathetic to MRA, including French philosopher and playwright Gabriel Marcel, as comparable to Brecht but by leading theatre critics as an over-simplistic preacher. This huge difference of opinion may in part be related to the transitive nature of what people "value" in literature, as Terry Eagleton observes:

> Just as people may treat a work as philosophy in one century and as literature in the next, or vice versa, so they may change their minds about what writing they consider valuable ... There is no such thing as a literary work or tradition which is valuable in itself, regardless of what anyone might have said or come to say about it. 'Value' is a transitive term: it means whatever is valued by certain people in specific situations, according to particular criteria and in the light of given purposes (Eagleton, 1983, p.11).

The Diplomats was first performed in 1963 but was originally written nearly ten years earlier when it was called The Man with the Key. Both versions contain the same characters, the same plot and almost the same dialogue; Howard has merely included, in the later version, specific references to current political situations in the early 1960s. Thomas Postlewait states that, while it is possible to study plays purely for their dramatic content, 'theatre also takes its meaning from the social milieu, including the political conditions, influences and controls that operate at any historical moment' (Postlewait, 2002, p.9). Howard made the mistake, however, of believing that all he needed to do to make a play relevant was to include some current political situations, without taking note of the changes in society and culture. The play includes references to the Polaris missile and McCarthyism[10], but its language, the class divisions and the role of women remain firmly entrenched in the 1950s. While The Forgotten Factor reflects the culture and society in which it was written, The Diplomats proved, in the 1960s, to be neither historical nor contemporary and this did not escape the notice of the critics. A review in Theatre World in 1964 claims that Howard's play could not be considered as a contribution to contemporary drama because it did not reflect the current social order. The writer states: '"below stairs" characters discuss their superiors and vice versa that fairly whirl us back to the thirties' (Theatre World, 1964). Theatre critic J.C. Trewin writes, 'I remain unsure of the value of such a play as The

---

[10] The Polaris missile was designed to be used by the United States as a tripartite nuclear deterrent. Its first flight was 7 June, 1960. McCarthyism was named after US Senator Joseph McCarthy who launched a vociferous campaign against alleged communists between 1950 and 1954.

Diplomats. It is idealistic but it makes the problems of our time seem all too easy' (Trewin, 1964).

MRA was particularly concerned in the 1960s with what was happening in the rest of London's West End and in the country at large. The establishment was still reeling from the effects of the 'Profumo Affair' which contributed to the downfall of Prime Minister Harold Macmillan's Conservative government. In 1963 John Profumo resigned as Secretary of State for War after being forced to admit to having had a relationship with call girl Christine Keeler; an affair that he had initially denied in the House of Commons (Sandbrook, 2011, pp.657-659). At the same time the Cold War was creating paranoia throughout the Government, which was not helped by the revelation that British intelligence officer Kim Philby had defected to the USSR. He followed in the footsteps of his fellow Cambridge graduates, Donald Maclean and Guy Burgess, who were discovered to have been spying for the Russians a decade earlier (Sandbrook, 2005, p.668). Howard was inevitably influenced by these events when revising his original script as will be seen in the following analysis. In addition to the political situation, MRA was concerned, on moralistic grounds, by the new writing that was being performed at the Royal Court; plays such as the 1967 production of *A View to the Common* by James Casey, described by theatre critic Milton Shulman as involving 'a collection of neurotic deviates masquerading as characters and a string of sexual fantasies pretending to be a plot' (Shulman, 1967). Sinfield maintains that the work of playwrights such as Arnold Wesker, John Arden, Harold Pinter, David Mercer and Edward Bond proved to be vehicles in the 1960s for debate and discussion about social issues (Sinfield, 1983, pp.190-192). These were the writers that MRA was trying to counteract but Sinfield fails to mention the movement's own plays which, as will be seen from reviews of *The Diplomats*, also stimulated debate.

Howard's daughter, Anne Wolrige Gordon, claims, in an interview for this book, (appendix 26, p.365) that her father always surprised people with his plays and *The Diplomats* does have an unusual twist. This is a play about a meeting between four diplomats, British, French, American and Russian, who each accuse the other of leaking secrets. In the 1950s and 1960s Britain was gripped by fear of a communist takeover and if Howard had wanted to align himself with the culture of the times he would have demonised the Russian. This would have fitted comfortably with the populist view that MRA was a right-wing movement fiercely opposed to communism. However, the Russian ambassador and his wife are portrayed as sensible people who do not drink or smoke and are therefore at an advantage at cocktail parties when Western government officials get drunk and reveal more than they should. The wife of the Russian ambassador, Mme Zenofors, tells the assembled company 'My husband says drink makes people talk silly ... My husband brings home very funny stories from these drinks parties ... The people who say them forget. But my husband, he always remembers. He writes them down and sends them to our Government. My husband says he gets most of his news out of other men's bedrooms and bottles' (Howard, 1964, pp 51-52). Howard is no doubt referring here to the tactics of the KGB for obtaining secrets. Istvan Deak says: 'Official Russian receptions ... whether at Yalta or in Moscow, aimed at getting the guests drunk, presumably in order to coax from them their secrets' (Deak, online, 2013). Although it appears that the Russians were being duplicitous, it was the personal responsibility of those guests to remain sober. MRA ideology is about individuals taking responsibility in order to change the world and the Russians, in this instance, appear to have had the moral high-ground. The sympathetic portrayal of the Russians is significant because, just five months before the play's debut at the Westminster Theatre, Howard took out a libel action after being called a communist. The *Evening News* of 11 July, 1963, reports that Howard's counsel took action in the High Court following statements by Albert Cooper, Conservative MP for Ilford South, to three of his constituents. Cooper was alleged to have told the constituents that 'Mr Howard was or had been a Communist or that it was said by some Members of Parliament that he was or had been a Communist' (*Evening News*, 1963). The court was told that Cooper now accepted the assurance of Howard that 'he differed from communism on moral, political and many other grounds and that any suggestion that he is or has ever been a Communist was wholly without foundation' (*Evening News*, 1963). Cooper apologised, Howard agreed not to proceed with a claim for damages and the judge approved the withdrawal of the record. By showing understanding for the Russians in *The Diplomats*, Howard re-enforced the MRA belief that neither capitalism nor communism had the answer to the world's problems and that the only way to resolve conflicts was through change in the individual. The play's message, as with all Howard's plays, is that everyone should listen to each other and appreciate opposing viewpoints. And, as with Thornhill's *The Forgotten Factor*, it is the least likely people – in this case the servants – who bring about resolution. Boobbyer suggests that Howard's reason for doing this is to imply 'that even the most ordinary person in the audience might be the catalyst for bringing change into a difficult situation' (Boobbyer, 2005, p.215).

The cast consists of Sir Malcolm Wisdom, a top British civil servant; Sam Trumper and Mrs Trumper his loyal servants; Irene, Sir Malcolm's daughter; Bob Babcock, his confidential secretary and the fiancée of Irene; Abraham Hardwood, an American diplomat; Comte De Grossac, a French diplomat; M Zenofors a Russian diplomat and Mme Zenofors, his wife. The choice of names for the characters is significant. Sir Malcolm represents the British establishment and Howard is no doubt showing a touch of irony when he calls him 'Wisdom' for it is clear that Sir Malcolm, like the ruling class he represents, frequently lacks perception. Sir Malcolm is portrayed as a stereotypical upper-class Englishman of the period, refusing to acknowledge that the British Empire has lost its power and confident that he can unite nations. When Howard was just twelve years old, in 1920, the British 'held sway over more than one-fifth of the world's entire land surface ... they also governed the lives of more than 410 million people' (Sandbrook, 2011, p.278). By the time *The Diplomats* was performed, the decolonisation of British Africa was almost complete. Dominic Sandbrook writes that in 1964 'the overseas population governed from London had fallen to scarcely fifteen million people. There could be no disguising the fact that the age of the Empire was over' (Sandbrook, 2011, p.282). Grossac, or gros sac, means 'big bag' in English and the Comte De Grossac is portrayed as 'a big bag of air' – a larger than life character with little substance. The American, Hardwood, is shown to have a tough exterior and an inner vulnerability, not unlike Hardwood trees which produce seeds with a protective covering. Zenofors sounds suspiciously like xenophobia – a fear of foreigners – which, in this play, is symptomatic not only of the Russians but of all four diplomats.

Figure 5: Scene in 1964 production of The Diplomats

The Diplomats begins with a rather pointless exchange between Mr and Mrs Trumper about sandwiches, in which Mr Trumper tells his wife, 'I'd sooner have sandwiches from you than sex on celluloid' (Howard, 1964, p.8). This appears to be an attempt by Howard to incorporate 1960s' language and is not part of the original version. In all the early MRA plays written by both Thornhill and Howard, there is emphasis on the importance of both family and world peace and a correlation drawn between the two. Boobbyer says 'international tension is found to be rooted in family conflict and the failings of character' (Boobbyer, 2005, p.214). This is illustrated in the following exchange between Irene and Bob: Irene urges Bob to inform her father that they are engaged but Bob, who is preparing for a crucial meeting between the diplomats and Sir Wisdom, tells her 'Your father's doing something very brave tonight, Irene. He's asked men here who, if they really decide to do it, can pull something off. Literally they may save nations from catastrophe. Maybe save millions of lives. I just can't bother him with us tonight' (Howard, 1964, p.13). When Irene protests he tells her condescendingly 'My dear girl, I forbid it' (Howard, 1964, p.14). This is the first of many examples of Irene being patronised by the male characters and is symptomatic of the way Howard portrays women. Anne Wolrige Gordon insists, however, that far from being sexist, her father was highlighting how women should not be treated. She recalls, 'I remember my father discussing the role of women with my mother. His portrayal of women was showing how they should not be treated. He believed women were equal to men' (Wolrige Gordon, appendix 27, p.368). While Howard may have thought he regarded women as equal to men, the way in which women were treated in the MRA family – having to dress modestly and being given administrative tasks rather than leadership roles – indicates that Howard, and the movement as a whole, had not appreciated

Figure 6: Bob helps Sir Malcolm enter via the window in 2013 staged reading

the way in which the role of women had changed significantly from the 1950s to the 1960s. Thornhill portrays Betty and Polly in *The Forgotten Factor* as young girls preparing to be independent and have their own careers. However, more than a decade later, Howard's Irene appears to have no job, to be still living at home and to be completely reliant on her father for financial support. A popular 1960s BBC sitcom *Take Three Girls* features three middle-class young women sharing a flat in 'swinging London' — a life far removed from that of Irene and of those living in the MRA houses.

Sir Malcolm makes his entrance on to the stage scrambling through a window, (fig. 6), telling Bob 'A bit undignified but it's a habit ... saves Sam opening that wretched door with all its bolts and chains' (Howard, 1964, p.15). The entrance is amusing and designed to show not only that Sir Malcolm is just as human as everyone else, despite his elevated position, but that he also cares about his servants. Both versions emphasise the frequent locking and unlocking of doors and the need for security, highlighting the paranoia of the 1960s, epitomised by the popular phrase 'reds under the bed'. There was a widespread fear that communists were lurking somewhere, in disguise, in order to obtain the secrets of the West. Sir Malcolm begins to discuss his view of the world with Bob and is clearly expressing the concerns of MRA when he complains:

> If you dare to suggest that people who play the fool in private with whores, or drink, or other men, are not the most suitable people to trust with secrets, you're accused of intolerance or lack of charity or witch-hunting or some much nonsense. It's McCarthyism in reverse. It's hounding down everybody who has the common sense to prefer purity to perversion when it comes to positions of responsibility' (Howard, 1964, p.20).

This speech is omitted in the earlier version suggesting that Howard was motivated in 1964 by both the Profumo and the Cambridge spy scandals. It also highlights MRA's sense of righteous indignation that its four absolute standards were becoming increasingly marginalised by the new liberalising trends.

Figure 7: De Grossac greets Irene in the 2013 staged reading

One by one the diplomats begin to arrive and each is a caricature of his nation. The American, Hardwood, is portrayed as brashly confident, particularly in relation to his country's part in the Second World War. The Frenchman De Grossac is a smooth talking womaniser, paying special attention to Irene and Mme Zenofors (fig. 7). He subtly ridicules British imperialism whilst highlighting both the pomposity of Sir Malcolm and the naivety of Hardwood. A conversation between Hardwood and de Grossac indicates the animosity between the French and the Americans after the Second World War. De Grossac tells the American:

We have had two world wars in Europe this century and the blood
of my country is always the first to be shed. Your people, Hardwood,
have had a habit in history of encouraging us Europeans to do what
you call the right thing and then let us pay in blood for your encouragement if fighting begins ... my people are sensitive, perhaps over-
sensitive, to the risk of being left alone to fight another war (Howard,
1964, pp.28-29).

Hardwood replies 'Don't forget it's my country's money that puts the
weapons in the hands of your boys. And don't forget too that if things go
badly wrong, the sons of my country will be forfeit too – in millions' (Howard, 1964, p.29). Howard has touched here on a subject that has been contentious from the Second World War onwards – the perceived role of the
Americans in world conflicts. The fact that the Americans played a key role
in the Second World War is not disputed; it is the American perception of
that role that has created controversy. Michael Adams says that while combat in World War Two was 'a horrible experience and left lasting physical
and mental scars on many combatants' (Adams, 1994 p.xiv), for the American people it became more Hollywood movie than truth. For many Americans, the war years had become 'America's golden age ... the best war ever'
(Adams, 1994, p.2). Predictably, it is the British whom Howard portrays as
the peacemakers. Sir Malcolm intervenes between the Frenchman and the
American, with a word of support for the Russians: 'Zenofors and his crowd
spend both blood and money. Perhaps they may be as sincere as any of us
in a strange way in the desire for peace' (Howard, 1964, p.29). There is an
acknowledgment here of the loss of life endured by the Russian army in the
Second World War and it is another example of the MRA ideology – listen
to both sides, no-one has the complete answer. The message is re-empha-
sised during another conversation between the American and the Frenchman, with each accusing the other of being responsible for the leaking of

75

information. Sir Malcolm tells them: 'Your governments can't both be right. But of course they might both be wrong' (Howard, 1964, p.27).

The arrival of the Zenofors provides Howard with a vehicle for criticising capitalism rather than denigrating communism. The following conversation illustrates the hypocrisy of the West:

Zenofors: There is one big difference between the lies I tell and the lies you tell.
Sir Malcolm: And what is that?
Zenofors: I know I'm a liar. You don't. You just lie because you cannot help it ... It's all the things you say about your love of liberty, your way of life, your idealism. You really think you mean them. They are all untrue
              (Howard, 1964, p.46).

Boobbyer highlights the desire of MRA not to be seen to be taking sides in the Cold War: 'Whilst warning of the spiritual dangers of communism, Howard's writings were also an attempt to point the West away from arrogance and decadence towards a humbler and more wholesome version of democracy' (Boobbyer, 2005, p.214). An example of this is given in the following speech by Zenofors, highlighting the hypocrisy of the West:

> You have preached to us about God. Now even some of your bishops and clergymen seem to say we were right all the time, that there is no God. You've preached to us about purity. Now your literature, your radio, your television screens are full of the sort of dirt we long ago discarded. You preach to us about peace and unity but your whole society and civilisation is divided. Your home life, your industrial life, your political life, your national life. It's a landscape of division. We are not impressed (Howard, 1964, p.48).

As all sides continue to accuse each other of deception, a twist emerges. Irene reveals that she has become friends with the Zenofors, visiting them at their hotel. While De Grossac, Hardwood and even Sir Malcolm now believe that unwittingly Irene is the source of security leaks, it is left to the audience to decide if this is the case or if, in fact, the Zenofors are simply befriending Irene with no ulterior motive. The second act ends with the Zenofors being asked to leave and Irene running from the room in tears.

Figure 8: Mrs Trumper and the teapot in the 2013 staged reading

The final act brings resolution to the conflict through the MRA message delivered by the 'humble' servant Sam and his wife Mrs Trumper. Irene and Bob have escaped the clutches of the diplomats and retired for a 'below stairs' conversation with the Trumpers who describe their experience of dealing with Mrs Trumper's difficult mother-in-law. Mrs Trumper says, 'We decided that though she was ninety-nine per cent wrong, we'd put our one per cent right first. We went and told her we were sorry we'd been so much against her' (Howard, 1964, p.72). Howard is not content with just one very obvious stab at the message, however, and uses Irene to emphasise the world view:

Surely we don't have to go on and on hating each other because we are different colours, or talk different languages or went to different schools? Surely some nation or group of nations could start to offer the right revolution to everybody – the sort of revolution the Trumpers started with Sam's mother – where the world began to live like a real family? (Howard, 1964, p.73).

The rest of the act veers towards a 'Whitehall-style' farce with the diplomats appearing one by one in their dressing gowns, beginning with Sir Malcolm. Mrs Trumper rushes on and off stage with a teapot, suspecting that each diplomat is a spy before they appear (fig. 8).

With the arrival of each new character, Howard reiterates the importance of not only listening to each other but of listening to God – a key element of the MRA message – in order to bring about changes in attitudes and beliefs. An example of this is in the following exchange between Sam and Sir Malcolm:

Sam:	You just have to listen to the part of your conscience your brain is always trying to kill – then do what it tells you in every detail, every moment, every day for the whole of your life.
Sir Malcolm:	The part of your conscience your brain is trying to kill? What exactly is that, Sam?
Sam:	It's a word that used to be used a lot when I was first in service, Sir Malcolm, though nowadays it's gone a little old fashioned. It's God. In those days people used to think God knew better than they did on most points (Howard, 1964, p.79).

While the political situations highlighted in *The Diplomats* could easily relate to the twenty-first century, the relationship between the upper and working classes is more difficult to understand in the present day. Sam is portrayed as the loyal and faithful servant but in the current climate in Britain he seems, at least superficially, to be irritatingly obsequious. Howard obviously intended Sam to represent the 'common man', the audience member, the voice of the people, but he is far from that even in the 1960s. It is clear that Howard had little idea of how the working class functioned because the people he mixed with – academics, business leaders and MRA supporters – rarely came into contact with them. However, while Mr and Mrs Trumper are more reminiscent of the stereotypical working-class characters portrayed in 1940s British films, such as *Brief Encounter*, Howard does indicate that they are, in fact, far more astute than the ruling class. There is a clear indication of satire in Sam's final lines of the following exchange:

Hardwood: What do you say Sam? This business of believing in a God that can tell you what to do all the time. It's anti-American somehow. That sort of God must be easier for a man like you than for men like myself and Sir Malcolm

Sam: That may be true Mr Hardwood. You see I've had to do what I'm told all my life. There's nothing new in that for me. I've never had to give orders. I've always known I didn't know. I've always had to be told. I never had the experience of gentlemen like you which seems to answer every question before it's even asked
(Howard, 1964, pp 83-84).

Depending on the way in which the director wishes to interpret the play, the following lines could portray Sam as sycophantic and servile or cunningly cynical:

Sam: Personally, Sir Malcolm, I'm glad not to be too intellectual a man. Not knowing much, it means I can learn new things so often. It's such a help. It's so interesting.

Sir Malcolm: Is there no hope for fellows like us, Sam?

Sam: I didn't mean that at all Sir. Of course not. It's only a little hard perhaps for people like you to accept an answer that ordinary people understand at once
(Howard, 1964, p.84)

Howard appears to suggest that not only are those of the working class insightful, they are actually manipulating the ruling class, rather than the other way around.

The play concludes with Sir Malcolm admitting he is 'nothing but a fraud ... I haven't been able to make peace in my own family circle – until tonight ... I've put my own career and my own country first all the time' (Howard, 1964, p.87). The doorbell rings for the final time and Sam announces that the Zenofors have returned. The last line of the play belongs to Sir Malcolm: 'This time and for the first time I feel we are really ready for Zenofors or anyone else he cares to bring' (Howard, 1964, p.90). The curtain falls as those on stage look towards the front door, ready to receive the Zenofors. That final scene indicates that, while there are faults with both capitalism and communism, the Russians remain outsiders and Howard is ultimately an upholder of the democratic system. The last act, whilst being the most fast-moving and entertaining, is also the most unsatisfactory. The notion that the Trumpers' story, about making peace with their truculent mother-in-law, could unite diplomats from four warring nations is just a little too far-fetched. To those outside the movement, whom MRA hoped to convert, it would have appeared even more unbelievable because Howard has not drawn his characters in depth. If the characters appear unreal, so must their words and ultimately the message loses credibility. However, the supporters of MRA would have had no problem in accepting such a conclusion, because they were immersed in the movement's ideology.

The Diplomats was the first play at the Westminster to be directed by MRA's new artistic director Henry Cass, resident director at the Old Vic Theatre in the 1930s. However, an established director and a cast of well-known actors, including Phyllis Konstam, Bryan Coleman, Brian Hawksley and Richard Warner, could not prevent it from being savaged by the critics. Howard was used to criticism of his playwriting and to attracting controversy but rows over *The Diplomats* began before it had even reached the stage, highlighting just how contentious MRA had become. A decision to stage the play, prior to its London run, at Darlington Civic Theatre towards the end of 1963, resulted in outrage and protest from Councillor James Whelan, Independent, former Labour member of Darlington Borough Council. He tabled a motion deploring a decision by the theatre management to 'support the activities of the Moral Re-Armament Movement in a theatre which is subsidised from public funds' (Whelan cited in *The Northern Echo*, 1963). Conversely, Alderman Fred Thompson, chairman of the civic theatre, when asked if he thought using the theatre for propaganda was wrong, replied 'No it's a splendid idea. When people see such rubbish on TV it's time they got some good stuff over the footlights with a moral at the end' (Thompson cited in *The Northern Echo*, 1963). Councillor Whelan was not alone in his view however. *The Northern Echo* published a letter from John Whitley of Darlington claiming: 'I have spoken to many people – not only in the North-East – who feel as I do that no group should be allowed to use a theatre belonging to a town to put over blatant propaganda' (Whitley, 1963). Despite protests, the play had its world premiere in Darlington where Michael Morrissey of *The Northern Echo* maintained the fact that it was an MRA play 'should be stated more clearly' (Morrissey, 1963); a rather curious comment considering the pre-show publicity over the controversy. When *The Diplomats* arrived in London, Howard was subjected to a barrage of criticism which at times verged on the personal. David Pryce-Jones, in *The Spectator*, claims: 'It is soft and mushy, intellectually non-existent. Like the freak that it is, the play is tied up in its own cage at the MRA theatre, the Westminster, although properly it should go crack-potting back to Hyde Park Corner' (Pryce-Jones, 1964). The *Daily Telegraph*'s critic W.A. Darlington, renowned in the 1960s for his vitriolic comments, writes in similar vein: 'His characters are puppets; his dialogue is so amateurish that even professional actors cannot make it seem natural. He can only hope to convince an audience of wishful-thinkers. That, however, is just the kind of audience he has got. I have never known people so ready to laugh and laugh so loud at any line containing the feeblest spark of life' (Darlington, 1964c). Roger Gellert in *The New Statesman* describes the audience as 'grotesquely appreciative' and the first two acts as consisting of 'urbanely inert satire on national mentalities and diplomatic hokum' (Gellert, 1964). These comments support Sinfield's view that people interpret their world and their place in it through their own cultural codes. He maintains that literature 'is developed by certain groups in ways that enable them to identify themselves through it ... While the prevailing literary culture offers great signifying power to its adherents, those who do not share its codes may actually define themselves in opposition to it. The privilege that is claimed for literature is actually the privilege, real or aspirant, of its enthusiasts' (Sinfield, 1983, p.6). MRA plays no longer represented the 'prevailing literary culture' and while its supporters could appreciate the sudden conversion of the diplomats to their own ideology, those outside the movement viewed it as an outdated and rather naïve outlook on life. Sinfield maintains that there is 'an agreement within a community to use words in a certain way' (Sinfield, 1983, p.7) and, as long as people remain within their own cultural groups, 'we all "know what we mean" ' (Sinfield, 1983, p.7). MRA supporters welcomed

The Diplomats because they understood the language and the message that was being delivered – they 'knew what it meant'.

The critics did not confine their attacks to the playwright and over-appreciative audiences. Anthony Howard asks in *The New Statesman* 'Are the actors and actresses who have to spout these morals-without-tears required to believe it?' (Howard, 1964) and the *Croydon Advertiser* claims: 'the acting is generally deplorable' and likens MRA to 'a rich man's Salvation Army ... well-intentioned but not likely to appeal to anyone who has thought seriously and read widely on the issues it endeavours to face' (*Croydon Advertiser*, 1964). Critical reviews often met with protests in the letters pages, quite possibly from supporters of MRA. One such example comes from Winifred Tardrew in the *Croydon Advertiser*: 'You term it propaganda and liken MRA to a prosperous Salvation Army ... surely this propaganda (as you term it) is preferable to that handed out to the teenager – plays of the kitchen-sink and pre-marital sex shown as the ultimate enjoyment of life' (Tardrew, 1964). It would not be surprising if such MRA letters were the inspiration for playwright Joe Orton to create his alter ego, the infamous guardian of the country's morals, Edna Welthorpe, who frequently wrote letters of protest about Orton's plays to national newspaper editors. Although MRA plays always attracted a wealth of criticism there were also favourable reviews. Colin Frame in *The Evening News* claims the first act of *The Diplomats* is 'hilarious' and the entire play 'acted heart-warmingly well' (Frame, 1964). Another reviewer says it provides 'food for thought and raises a laugh at the same time' (*East London Advertiser*, 1964) and the *West London Press* describes it as 'an exceedingly well written play [which] scores because of the light handed touch of the author and some good team work by the experienced cast' (*West London Press*, 1964). Such contrasting opinions support Eagleton's view that 'value judgements are notoriously variable' (Eagleton, 1983.p.13).

Regardless of the positive comments, *The Diplomats* was unable to repeat the success of *The Forgotten Factor*. The earlier play conveys the MRA ideology in a relatively subtle way, whilst *The Diplomats* leaves nothing to chance and repeats its message many times in ways that appear far too simplistic and leave nothing to the imagination. It is difficult to assess just what impact *The Diplomats* had on the general theatre-going public in the 1960s. It achieved good houses but MRA was adept at pulling in the people; its supporters literally knocked on doors to publicise the plays. As with *The Forgotten Factor*, the movement laid on coaches and combined the theatrical experience with meals and meetings to encourage visitors to the theatre. Whether or not these visitors actually enjoyed what they saw cannot be assessed as the only evidence is in the reviews, which, on the whole, were not favourable but cannot be said to represent the opinions of all the audience members. For example, journalist Bill Boorne claims Joe Orton, Bertolt Brecht and Samuel Beckett 'have done as much damage to the theatre as anyone' (Boorne, 1964, p.8), but this was not a universal opinion; in 1969 Beckett was awarded the Nobel Prize for Literature. What can be assessed, however, is the response that *The Diplomats* received when I directed a performance, nearly fifty years later, in 2013, at the headquarters in London of Initiatives of Change (IofC). The audience was equally divided between those who had supported the movement for most of their lives and those with no prior knowledge of IofC. At the end of the performance the audience was invited to give both verbal and written feedback and a brief selection of comments is provided in appendix 25, p.363. I deliberately selected actors who were unfamiliar with the movement to ensure their approach to the play was an objective one. Whilst most of those present regarded *The Diplomats* as simplistic and overtly propagandist, many also thought it was entertaining. In 1963 the play reflected the 1940s and 1950s – an age that was fast disappearing; it was therefore neither contemporary nor historic. However, in the twenty-first century *The Diplomats* was viewed by the audience as historical, whilst also featuring elements – particularly the behaviour of the diplomats – that could be re-interpreted in the current political climate. A review of the play, published in the newsletter of the *Friends of Renewal Arts*, a group of artists from all over the world who support the movement's ideology, has the headline 'Fifty years after first performance *The Diplomats* is still as relevant as ever' (fig. 9). An analysis of the feedback forms indicates that a number of those not involved in IofC believed the play was still relevant and could be a success in 2013, whereas many supporters of the movement disagreed with this statement (fig. 10). What is important to establish here is the concept of 'success'. To IofC supporters the success of *The Diplomats* meant the message being favourably received and acted upon. It was clear to many people in the audience that the way in which the message was portrayed was too obvious and simplistic, therefore it is understandable that the supporters of that message would consider the play a failure today. The majority of the non-IofC supporters considered the play to be an amusing farce and believed it could be a success in that context. They were viewing it purely as a piece of theatrical entertainment and not as a propaganda play. It does have elements about it that are reminiscent of the popular television comedy series *Yes, Prime Minister* and this could have had an influence on those not concerned with whether or not it successfully promoted a message. Terry Eagleton says literary works are constantly being revaluated by those who read them. He claims all literary works are:

> 're-written', if only unconsciously, by the societies which read them; indeed there is no reading of a work that is not also a 're-writing'. No work, and no current evaluation of it can simply be extended to new groups of people without being changed, perhaps almost unrecognisably in the process; and this is one reason why what counts as literature is a notably unstable affair (Eagleton, 1983, p.12).

The graph below shows that none of the IofC supporters thought the play was poorly written, although a number admitted they found the characters stereotypical and the message over-stated. It appears, therefore, that there could have been a reluctance to criticise such a key figure within the movement as Peter Howard and suggests that those closely involved with a specific group are unlikely to 're-write' work that promotes their own belief system. The differing receptions to both versions of *The Forgotten Factor* and to *The Diplomats* are due, in part, to audiences interpreting the text in the light of their own personal knowledge and the culture in which they live. What is seen as preaching propaganda in one era can be regarded as amusing satire in another and unless the message is not only relevant but transmitted effectively it will be 're-written' and the original meaning lost. Peter Howard had been a successful political journalist before becoming MRA's most celebrated playwright but his plays lacked the verve, acidity and intellect that had gained him the respect of his peers in Fleet Street. As will be seen in the following chapter, Howard was the driving force behind MRA's campaign to halt the rise in kitchen sink theatre but he made the fatal mistake of thinking that it was enough to promote a message and that the vehicle — the play itself — was of secondary importance.

Figure 9: A review of *The Diplomats*, staged by the author of this book at IofC headquarters in 2013

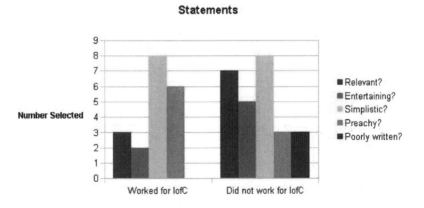

Figure 10: Audience reaction to *The Diplomats* in 2013

3

Peter Howard – the Propagandist Playwright.

I write to preach. I write for the sake of propaganda. I write with a message and for no other reason. Do not believe those who say the theatre is no place for a man with a message of some kind.
–(Peter Howard cited in Wolrige Gordon, 1970, p.270).

Frank Buchman and Rev Alan Thornhill instigated the use of theatre to promote the work of Moral Re-Armament, but it was Buchman's successor, former Fleet Street political journalist Peter Howard, who transformed the Westminster from its somewhat amateur origins into a new and controversial professional performance venue. The following chapter examines the way in which Howard's cultural roots influenced his work and compares him with another propagandist playwright, Bertolt Brecht. Although Howard and Brecht were of vastly differing political persuasions their aims for the theatre were similar – both wanted their plays to change society.

Howard, who became unofficial leader of MRA following Buchman's death in 1961, was a prolific playwright, who, according to his daughter

Anne Wolrige Gordon, 'did not write to amuse himself. He wrote because the plays were required for a reason, for a specific purpose' (Wolrige Gordon, appendix 27, p.368). Howard was intent on ridding the world of what he considered to be the dangers of communism and the arrogance and greed of capitalism. He considered both to be equally in need of moral and spiritual renewal but also wanted to create an antidote for what was happening in British theatre in the 1960s. Boobbyer states that in the Cold War era Howard, whilst committed to Western democratic principles, 'did not believe that good and evil could be simply identified with the policies or actions of different sides. In his view everybody and every nation needed to turn to God and absolute moral standards as a way out of the global impasse' (Boobbyer, 2005, p.205). According to Boobbyer, Howard challenged people through his work to view political conflicts as symptoms of a 'deeper spiritual battle' (Boobbyer, 2005, p.206) and he describes Howard's plays as 'campaign weapons' (Boobbyer, 2005, p.210). These 'weapons' and the way in which he attempted to challenge his audiences are examined in this chapter through critiques of Howard's plays *The Boss* and *The Dictator's Slippers*.

For Howard, the craft of playwriting was secondary to the message. Kenneth Belden's daughter Hilary likens Howard's work to that of the medieval Morality Plays, adding 'I would put his work into the area of Theatre of Debate and Theatre of Discussion. What made him a good playwright was his instinct for where the fault lines were and where the controversy was' (Belden, 2013, appendix 1, p.284). Howard saw himself as a revolutionary. He had a mission to convert everyone to the MRA ideology of living by the four absolute moral standards and listening daily in silence to the word of God. Boobbyer believes Howard wanted to 'subvert and redefine the concept of revolution. The revolutionary, in Howard's terms, was someone who was ready to embark on the road to personal change' (Boobbyer, 2005, p.213). 'Personal change' for Howard meant abiding by the absolute standards but 'redefining the concept of revolution' through his plays would have been difficult for him at a time when theatre in Britain was undergoing a rather different kind of revolution with a shift in emphasis and form. Howard's plays reflected the rapidly disappearing culture of 'Aunt Edna' — the middle-class, middle-aged woman that playwright Terence Rattigan created to epitomise the typical theatre-goer of the 1950s. The following excerpt from an article in the *West London Observer* could almost have come from the mouth of the fictional Aunt Edna instead of a Peter Howard supporter:

> Parts of the London theatre seem to be sinking pretty low, always encouraged of course by the pseudo-intelligentsia ... sex seems to have no box office attraction unless it is perverted to the final degree ... How Peter Howard manages to write play after play in addition to the full life he leads is a matter of mystery but we know that he does care very much about the landslide in public morals that has taken place over the past years and which finds its virulent nadir in the filth of which I have been writing (V.C., 1963).

Aunt Edna's days, however, were numbered. The English Stage Company's search for new writers, who would appeal to the younger generation and make theatre accessible to the working class, resulted in the historic 1956 Royal Court production of John Osborne's *Look Back in Anger*. It should be noted, however, that neither the Royal Court, nor the Westminster, from the 1960s onwards, could attract the elusive working-class theatregoer. Despite their efforts, theatre remained the province of the intelligentsia. Left-wing theatre practitioner John McGrath says 'the language the Royal Court spoke was the language of a small metropolitan cultural group with developing, but essentially bourgeois, values' (McGrath, 1984, p.18). A more detailed examination of the work of the Royal Court and the left-wing theatre of the mid-twentieth century is given in chapter four.

Howard's plays toured the world and Wolrige Gordon claims that, when relating to individuals, her father 'had the gift of putting himself at once in the framework of the person next to him ... When he put foot on Asian soil he did not arrive with a British point of view' (Wolrige Gordon, 1969, p.265). It is difficult to know exactly what is meant by the 'British point of view', although in true imperialist fashion, it is the British man or woman, whether it be the company director or the servant, who invariably delivers the MRA message in his plays. British or not, however, Howard certainly arrived on Asian soil with the MRA point of view. Wolrige Gordon quotes from a letter written by her father stating that 'Moral Re-Armament is for everyone, everywhere ... absolute moral standards represent a common battleground and a common step for the whole of humanity' (Howard cited in Wolrige Gordon, 1969, p.264). This seems to emphasise the fact that, while Howard might have been prepared to 'put himself in the framework of the person next to him', he clearly wanted conversion to MRA ideals. He did however acknowledge that others might also have solutions – providing belief in God was at the core: 'I do not believe that Moral Re-Armament has the monopoly for rebuilding the world ... I do believe that the spirit of God in the hearts of men is the one force that will shift humanity forward' (Howard cited in Wolrige Gordon, 1970, p.278).

Howard appears far more dogmatic in his beliefs than his more pragmatic predecessor, Buchman. The latter was a Christian and promoted

Christian beliefs to atheists but, as Boobbyer states, Buchman treated people from other faiths differently 'not expecting them to convert to Christianity but suggesting that they take their own religious traditions seriously' (Boobbyer, 2013, pp.85-86). Howard however claimed, at a lunch in his honour, that the purpose of MRA was to 'enlist every political party and every voter in the supreme task of making Britain Christian ... and if MRA wins, Britain will lead the whole world in every sphere of human progress' (Howard, 1964c). By the 1960s the British Empire had all but disappeared, but Howard seems to imply that the country could regain its power as a world leader if it took the moral and spiritual high ground of Christianity. His call to 'make Britain Christian' contradicts his earlier statement that MRA is for everyone. However, MRA supporters who knew him maintain Howard would adapt his speeches to suit his audiences. This was a ploy which, whilst common amongst public speakers, was not quite in keeping with the moral standard of absolute honesty. The lunch in Howard's honour was in Newcastle-upon-Tyne, in November 1964, and was given by Alderman N. Garrow, chairman of Northumberland County Council and Sir Robin Chapman, a leading member of Jarrow Conservative Association. Howard's audience was the establishment and therefore more than likely to be sympathetic towards Christianity. It is also important to read the reference to Christianity in context: at the time, Howard was countering a statement made in Edinburgh by the left-wing theatre producer Joan Littlewood that 'The theatre can be a marvellous world since God is dead and religion is dead' (Littlewood cited by Howard, 1964c). Howard told the assembled company, 'We are in the midst of a deliberate and global attempt to secularise society ... Nowadays some artists use the theatre as a means for destroying faith, traditional morality and the ancient virtues of our country' (Howard,

1964c). He went on to accuse 'cynics and satirists' of attempting to 'create the neo-fascism of godlessness' (Howard, 1964c).

Littlewood, along with Theatre of the Absurd, Theatre of Cruelty and playwrights such as Joe Orton, epitomised all that disturbed MRA about theatre in the 1960s. MRA considered that adherence to the four absolute standards was not only essential but urgent if the world was not to destroy itself through conflict and moral decline and Howard wrote his plays with that same urgency. Fellow MRA playwright Hugh Steadman Williams, who was artistic director at the Westminster 1975–1990 and chairman of Westminster Productions until a few months before his death in 2015, claims Howard's work suffered as a result:

> Lots of Howard's concepts were brilliant and parts of the plays were brilliant, but he was living a busy life. He got up at 4am to write plays before breakfast and you cannot write great works of art like that. Shaw [George Bernard Shaw] spent months on his plays. Howard did not have this leisure. They had an unfinished look about them. They were rushed. I think if he had been able to concentrate on playwriting he would have been a very good playwright (Steadman Williams, appendix 22, p.350).

Howard's plays were written from his own perspective, growing up in the 1920s when the British Empire was still a formidable force in the world. Roger Louis claims the British Empire 'reached its greatest territorial extent in the inter-war years ... in retrospect the inter-war years represented the golden age of British colonialism, at least in the imagination' (Louis, 2006, pp 44–45). After the Second World War, Howard recognised that the concept of a British Empire needed to change and suggested that the Commonwealth could become 'the pathfinder for the unity of the world' (Howard, 1945a, p.157). However, his plays situate Britain firmly in the centre of the world stage and depict the British as peacemakers, reflecting his own belief that 'with a new inspired philosophy of Empire, Britain can win the heart not only of India, but of China and the gratitude of the whole world. It is Britain's opportunity for greatness' (Howard, 1945, p.157).

Although Howard always insisted that, politically, he was neither right nor left-wing, his plays appear to show a greater insight into the habits of the ruling rather than the working classes. To understand why this was the case it is necessary to examine his background. Wolrige Gordon's book *Peter Howard: Life and letters* is the only comprehensive account of Howard's life. She writes that her father was born into a family that had farmed land at Meldreth, Cambridgeshire, for nearly three hundred years. His grandfather Eben founded a journal called *Wit and Wisdom* and was the first Mayor of Bexhill. Howard's father Ebenezer opted out of his final examination for the Bar to marry Evangeline Bohm, thereby estranging himself from his parents. However, Howard's birth on December 20th, 1908, into a modest home in Maidenhead to a father who taught at a preparatory school, reunited the family (Wolrige Gordon, 1969, p.11). He was born with the back of his foot attached to the knee joint and, after an operation to straighten his leg, wore an iron brace and had daily massage in his early years. He was determined not to let this disability prevent him from doing whatever he wanted to, however, and attributes this determination to his father, who was a headmaster by the time Howard started his education. Robert Mowat, an Oxford academic and supporter of MRA, describes how, when studying Latin and Greek, Howard was told by his father, 'No translation, no tea'. Mowat quotes Howard as saying: 'I have been immensely grateful for that discipline my father built in me.' (Howard cited in Mowat, 2000, p.2-3). Howard went up to Wadham College, Oxford, in 1928, with a Government grant, on the understanding that he would become a teacher after obtaining his degree. According to Wolrige Gordon, however, he had little intention of pursuing that profession; his aim was to play rugger for Oxford and gain a Blue which he did just a year later (Wolrige Gordon, 1970, p.40). Despite having a limp Howard played rugby for England, eventually becoming captain of the team. He also got a taste for the theatre, acting alongside Peggy Ashcroft and George Devine (later to become his nemesis as artistic director at the Royal Court) in an Oxford University Dramatic Society production of James Flecker's play *Hassan: The Story of Hassan of Baghdad and How he Came to Make the Golden Journey to Samarkand* (Wolrige Gordon, 1970, p.54). In addition, Howard became a regular contributor to the university magazine *Isis* and embraced Oxford life. Sadly, however, he could not keep pace with the costs. In April 1931 Howard decided to leave Oxford without a degree believing that with 'unpaid bills amounting to over one thousand pounds' (Wolrige Gordon, 1970, p.55) a job was more important.

After leaving Oxford, Howard was introduced to Oswald Mosley by a mutual friend, the politician and author Sir Harold Nicholson, and was urged to join the New Party. Mosley was something of a political maverick, entering politics as a Conservative MP in the 1918 General Election, but defecting to Labour in 1924. He was a key figure in the Labour party during the 1920s before forming the breakaway New Party in 1931, which at that time was opposed to fascism. Luisa Passerini outlines the party vision:

> The Mosley Manifesto, a mixture of planning and laissez faire, proposed a new approach to the economy through a complete reorganisation of industry and agriculture as well as institutional change, the creation of a cabinet of five ministers with the power to carry through emergency policies, subject only to the general control of parliament (Passerini, 1999, p.234).

Mosley was a charismatic character appealing to the young who wanted a different style of British politics. Nigel Copsey writes that the image Mosley cultivated was of 'a dynamic, passionate and confident young man, selflessly foregoing the interests of his own class in order to defend the working classes especially the massed ranks of the unemployed' (Copsey, 2009, p.463). Here was a character Howard could look up to: son of the affluent Staffordshire landowner Sir Oswald Mosley, educated at public school, graduating as an officer from Sandhurst and sharing a disability – Mosley had a limp, after crashing a plane he was piloting. Howard was offered a paid position at £650 a year, as National Secretary of the New Party Youth Movement: 'I was flattered to imagine that men of the standing of Nicholson and Mosley should select me as a member of the patriotic band to save Britain' (Howard, 1941, p.11). The New Party appears to have appealed to a wide range of people. According to Dominic Sandbrook, even former Prime Minister Harold Macmillan 'thought about joining Oswald Mosley's New Party before Mosley went over to fascism' (Sandbrook, 2011, p.72).

Robert Row, a Mosley activist for most of his life, writes in *The Journal of Historical Review,* that the New Party 'had been at least an attempt to save Britain from the mass unemployment that followed in the thirties' (Row, 1984, p.193). Howard and Mosley shared a desire to control and change society and the prospect of 'saving Britain' would definitely have attracted the former. Later, as a political journalist, Howard exercised considerable influence over the elite of British society; within the realms of MRA his talk was of revolution and changing the world. The New Party appeared to offer fresh ideas on solving the poverty crisis in Britain and this would undoubtedly have appealed to Howard. Initially he was responsible for the organisation of youth clubs and also writing for the New Party paper *Pioneer*, but he became a candidate for the party in the October 1931 General Election and it was whilst campaigning that Howard observed, at first hand, the plight of the poor. Wolrige Gordon says that in South Wales, during the election campaign, her father witnessed 'the torment of unemployment for the first time' (Wolrige Gordon, 1969, p.56). He saw children playing in the street and 'almost every one of those children had misshapen legs or ankles. They had felt the weakening drag of malnutrition' (Howard cited in Wolrige Gordon, 1969, p.57). Howard describes a visit to a Glasgow basement: 'I found a man living in a single room with five children ... there was no window at all in this dug-out. The place stank. On the faces of the children, except the smallest, there were sore scabby places, looking like scrum pox' (Howard, 1941, p.12). Howard was convinced that the New Party alone could save the poor from destitution but mentions little of how it planned to achieve this. His passion for power and a cause is emphasised in his book *Innocent Men* where he writes, 'I began to envisage myself as a sort of latter-day Lenin, inflaming the country by my voice and pen, getting power with public acclamation and at once by drive and initiative righting these shameful wrongs' (Howard, 1941, p.14)

At the same time as his New Party involvement, the Howard family insisted their son should read for the Bar and he began to study, whilst supplementing his income with tutoring. One tutoring position took him to St Moritz, Switzerland, where the summer tennis tournament was taking place. It was there that he met his future wife – falling in love with her whilst watching her play tennis. She was Mlle Doris Metaxa, the junior tennis champion of France, known to her friends as Doe. Howard proposed three days after meeting her and although at first she refused and her parents were not initially pleased at Howard's attentions as 'they had no idea who he was, or whether he had any prospects' (Wolrige Gordon, 1969, p.48), the couple were married just over a year later in 1932. They went on to have three children, Anne, Philip and Anthony. Between meeting and marrying Doe, Howard wrote her numerous letters, many of which are published in Wolrige Gordon's book. One, written in August 1931, replies to Doe's concerns about his involvement with Mosley and provides an insight into Howard's attraction for both the man and the party:

> You are by no means alone in disliking Mosley's face ... He is probably the most unpopular person in England today. But you have to be a rather big person to be as hated as that especially in England ... He is very courageous ... he is alight with his own cause ... He really does believe he can save the British working classes and no-one else can. And I think you would like this part of him as much as I do (Howard cited in Wolrige Gordon, 1969, p.51).

Howard's letters to Doe reveal his excitement at being part of a volatile election campaign and a member of a controversial political party. He tells her that, at various meetings, communists 'tried to kill us with chains and bottles and I got cut on the head' (Howard cited in Wolrige Gordon, 1969, p.59). His description of speech-making indicates a man enjoying a brief starring role in a drama rather than someone with serious political intent:

> I have just come in from making a speech to the miners at Treharris as they came up out of the ground from their work in the pit. It was rather wonderful, a thing I won't forget. I was standing on a heap of slag making my speech and the sun was going down very red and splendid behind the pithead and the other black slag heaps. All the miners came pouring out of the shaft with coal-black faces, tired from their work and looked up at me and listened. It was strange and wonderful. My body was the only white thing and everything else black, except the red sun (Howard cited in Wolrige Gordon, 1969, p.56).

Here is a hint of the character of Howard – a man who relished being the centre of attention, a man who enjoyed power. It is not surprising therefore that he went on to become a journalist with a reputation for being provocative and the leader of an international movement that attracted controversy. The election was a disaster for Mosley; none of his candidates were elected and the party was dissolved. Howard writes, 'Funds were declining. Mosley's thoughts began to turn to fascism, which Harold Nicolson and I detested ... Mosley's shirt darkened as day followed day. Presently Nicolson picked his hat off the peg. I was handed mine. And we both walked out of the New Party together' (Howard, 1941, p.15). Richard Thurlow says Mosley justified turning to fascism as a result of the disruptive tactics used by opponents of the New Party. He adds, however, that Nicolson had noticed other fascist traits emerging in 1931 such as 'Mosley's adoption of a more authoritarian manner and the increasing importance he gave to developing the youth organisation as a relatively disciplined defence force' (Thurlow, 1998, p. 64).

Howard continued with his legal work but having reported on some rugger matches for *The Sunday Express* and meeting its owner Lord Beaverbrook at his political club, the Empire Crusade Club, Howard was invited to join the newspaper and give up the law (Wolrige Gordon, 1970, p. 92). Wolrige Gordon says it was a hard decision for him to make but he 'took a calculated gamble' (Wolrige Gordon, 1970, p.92). The gamble paid off because within five years of joining *Express Newspapers*, in 1934, he had become one of the highest paid political journalists in Fleet Street. He wrote not only for the *Express* but also for the *Evening Standard* under a variety of pen names including Adam Bothwell, John Hampshire, Brent Ely and Captain Barnabe Rich who was 'rude to all the people you had to be very polite to.

Beaverbrook knew I was writing this stuff but nobody else knew' (Howard cited in Wolrige Gordon, 1970, p.119). Mowat describes Howard as one of London's 'most aggressive and hyper-critical journalists ... with an acidity that few could rival' (Mowat, 2000, p.1). Howard may have given up on Oxford but he says he took a degree at the 'Fleet Street University' (Howard, 1945a, p.20). He relished life as a national newspaper journalist declaring, 'For seven long years I have given Fleet Street my life. In return Fleet Street gave me three F's, Fun, Fame and Fortune' (Howard, 1945a, p.18). He adds, 'There is a sense of power in the knowledge that the words you write late at night will affect the thinking of millions of homes on the morning after' (Howard, 1945a, p.20). These sentiments were no doubt the inspiration for

Figure 11: Peter Howard, the writer

him becoming a propagandist playwright – he clearly recognised the power of the pen (fig. 11).

Howard's claim to be neither left nor right-wing is illustrated in some of his articles in the *Express*. In a report, entitled 'Four things to kick up a row about', he castigates the Socialists for not being an effective opposition party. Referring to a couple of forthcoming by-elections he tells the left-wingers:

> Fight the by-elections. Fight for sound principles and good policies. Scan the conduct of the war, criticise the deficiencies of the Government. Complain with enough strength, with sufficient power, with a display of public approval – and if you do not put this Government out, you will certainly push them on. Your message to them will be: Get on – or Get out (Howard, 1940, p.6).

However, there was no doubt in the minds of many politicians that Howard was a Tory. In another article he clearly revels in his own notoriety, stating that the executive of the Socialist Parliamentary Party devoted one of its meetings to 'abuse of my writings. I take the view that the Executive of the Opposition would be better occupied discussing Mr Neville Chamberlain than debating Mr Peter Howard' (Howard, 1940, p.6). In the same article he writes: 'Mr A. V. Alexander, the Co-op boss, is after me. He says I gave him the black spot. He complains that I praised him in my column. And he expresses the opinion that it is damaging for a Socialist to be praised by me' (Howard, 1940, p.6).

The 'three F's' of Fleet Street, that Howard so enjoyed, were to be relatively brief however. At the beginning ofis parents could not afford to send him to un iverfsity and it was only through the grant that he was able to go (EWol the Second World War he teamed up with Michael Foot, future leader of the Labour party and Frank Owen, a former Liberal MP, to write the book Guilty Men under the pseudonym Cato. The book placed the blame for the defeat in France, which led to the evacuation at Dunkirk in 1940, squarely on the shoulders of Neville Chamberlain and others in the cabinet and proved to be a journalistic bombshell (Wolrige Gordon, 1970, p.135). The publication of Guilty Men not only embarrassed the Government but infuriated Lord Beaverbrook, who was in the war cabinet. Howard was called into the office of the newspaper's general manager and told he could no longer write articles about politics (Wolrige Gordon, 1970, p. 137). This was a massive blow to a political journalist of his stature and soon afterwards Howard was to receive yet another setback to his professional career. Edith Duce, secretary to the general manager of the Daily Express, was a supporter of MRA, also still referred to at the time as The Oxford Group, and suggested he meet one of its leading members Garth Lean. Howard was aware that MRA was being criticised by many Fleet Street reporters for being 'racketeers and pro-German' (Wolrige Gordon, 1970, p. 140). He writes, 'In Britain MRA was accused by some of being a brilliantly clever front for fascism; in Germany and Japan of being a super-intelligent arm of the British and American Secret service' (Howard, 1945a, p. 89). Fellow Daily Express journalist Tom Driberg had earlier launched an attack on the movement after Buchman was quoted in the New York-World Telegram in 1936 as saying that Adolf Hitler 'built a front line defence against the anti-Christ of communism' (Buchman cited in Boobbyer, 2013, p.137). Boobbyer says Buchman later denied any sympathy with the Nazi cause, claiming instead that he had hoped to be able to 'change' Hitler. Boobbyer adds: 'He was concerned about the communist threat and thus picked on Hitler's anti-communism as something to build on' (Boobbyer, 2013, p.138). Here is an example of MRA's inability to understand the culture, society and politics of the time, which indicates a degree of naivety. That naivety is also illustrated in Buchman's reference to the persecution of the Jews. In the same New York-World Telegram report Buchman announces: 'Anti-Semitism? Bad naturally. I suppose Hitler sees a Karl Marx in every Jew' (Buchman cited in Boobbyer, 2013, p.138). Howard felt impelled to investigate MRA and was enthused by the prospect of a scoop, claiming that if he found proof of pro-Nazism he would disclose it in the Daily Express and give details to the Home Office (Wolrige Gordon, 1970, p.145). He found no such proof, however, and wrote a 'Reply to Hickey' aimed at the *Express*'s William Hickey column, which at that time was being written by Driberg. In what appears to be a personal attack on his fellow journalist Howard writes, 'It is a real sadness to me to see a man with the power and ability of William Hickey spending his forces in hatred of the Oxford Group' (Howard cited in Wolrige Gordon, 1970, p.145). Howard goes on to explain exactly what he did discover about the movement:

> Thousands of Oxford Group men and women belong to the fighting services. Many of them are in the fighter squadrons at present engaged against the Nazi bombers. The Oxford Group people in factories engaged on war production are striving to lessen friction between employers and employed, to settle disputes by friendly negotiation instead of by strike action, and to increase production ... I place on record my considered view that the Oxford Group are exerting all their efforts to increasing the unity, strength and abilities of the country (Howard cited in Wolrige Gordon, 1970, p.145).

To Howard's surprise that article did not appear in the newspaper. Wolrige Gordon claims *Express* editor Arthur Christiansen told her father he thought it would be 'better journalism to attack the Oxford Group' (Wolrige Gordon, 1970, p. 146) and when Howard wrote a book entitled *Innocent Men*, in which he claimed to set out the truth about MRA, the Express refused him permission to publish. Howard concluded, in the spring of 1941, that he had no other choice but to leave.

> It was a big decision to make. But there was that in me which said that publication of the truth about a great world movement was of more importance than the fate of one journalist, even a journalist so important to myself as me. So with regret, I picked my hat off the peg and said au revoir to Fleet Street. I wrote and published my book. It is called Innocent Men. Its sales swiftly rose above six figures; it still sells steadily, four years after publication in Britain and in other parts of the world (Howard, 1945a, p.131-132).

It must have been a hugely traumatic decision for Howard. Here was a man who described journalism as 'my breath, blood and bones ... You are of the world and in the world and yet above the world. Life in Fleet Street

Figure 12: Peter Howard the farmer

is a bug. It burrows beneath your skin and into your blood stream' (Howard, 1945a, pp 131 and 19). His decision to leave was ridiculed by his fellow journalists. 'Cassandra' of *The Daily Mirror* said he had turned into the 'Reverend Howard, throwing his soul on the counter where it stinks like a codfish that's been too long out of water' (Cassandra cited in Wolrige Gordon, 1969, p.122). Howard's parents wrote to him saying 'The Buchmanites have absorbed you, but before you are entirely lost, can we do nothing to rescue you?' (Wolrige Gordon, 1969, p.123). The only member of the family who appeared to support Howard was his grandmother Gracie who wrote to him 'Perhaps you have received a special call from God and if so you must obey it and go wherever He bids you' (Wolrige Gordon, 1969, p.123).

Figure 13: Peter Howard the family man with his wife and three children

Having given up his work as a journalist Howard began devoting his life to his family and their farm in Suffolk containing a run-down farm house (figs. 12 and 13).

He describes his fear at facing a complete change in his circumstances overnight:

> There is a big difference between a man in a highly-paid job on Fleet Street who owns a farm and has plenty of money to spend on it and an ex-journalist with an old farm that is losing money and which is the only means of livelihood for himself and his wife and children ... I knew a little of the theory but next to nothing of the practice of farming (Howard, 1945a, p.133).

Howard and his family gradually began to make the farm pay and he also became increasingly involved in the work of MRA. He discovered that the 'war of words' he used in Fleet Street could be turned into another kind of battle – the spur for a revolution to change the world, a revolution that ensured everyone lived by the four moral standards. It would appear that the failed politician and frustrated journalist had found salvation in an entirely new direction. Supporters of MRA give differing accounts of Howard; some found him kind and empathetic, particularly those who knew him when they were children, others found him distant, intimidating, forceful, bad tempered and a workaholic. Anthony Thomas, who has been involved with MRA for more than fifty years and knew Howard well, says,

> I firmly believe in theatre to bring about a change in society for the better ... Peter's was a committed life, given to changing the world, whether it was youth or elderly. He was funny, yet deadly serious, not afraid of rebuking when necessary, but always concerned with the lives of those he touched, and he touched the lives of many, not only in life but through his books and especially his plays (Thomas, appendix 26, p.366).

Thomas is representative of many MRA supporters throughout the twentieth century. They felt the world was being destroyed by conflicts and that the only way to 'change society for the better' was to adopt the four moral standards and listen daily to God for guidance. They would meet at the Westminster Theatre every Sunday morning to have group 'quiet times' in which they would listen for guidance, write down their thoughts and then discuss them with each other. Wolrige Gordon claims those meetings were 'incredibly stodgy – all gloom and doom with people with notebooks taking things down' (Wolrige Gordon, appendix 27, p.368). Her admiration for Howard is clear in the following description:

> When my father was there he would gallop down the aisle and on to the stage and you could feel the windows open. He would say: "Put away your notebooks, don't listen to me, think for yourselves". It was like an electric shock. He lifted it all. That's what I loved about him. It was like fresh air, vigour; he wanted people to think for themselves (Wolrige Gordon, appendix 27, p.368).

However, one of the faults in his playwriting, highlighted by many theatre critics and examined in this book, is that he did not allow his audiences to think for themselves and make up their own minds.

While Howard was concerned at what he felt were negative aspects of theatre and new writing in the 1960s and thought many plays of that era were destructive and decadent, he often visited the Royal Court – renowned as a hot bed of left-wing experimental theatre. Wolrige Gordon would frequently accompany her father to plays and says:

> He told me: "If you don't know what is going on you don't have the tools to answer it. You need to know what is going on in other people's lives." I don't think my father felt theatre censorship was realistic. He didn't think much of the kitchen sink drama but he thought there was an answer to it. He felt that the theatre could get the mes-

sage across ... it could give people a picture. They had drama unfolding before them. In a theatre, regardless of what the play is, there is a direct engagement with the audience and you have to win them. That really interested him (Wolrige Gordon, appendix 27, p.368).

Howard aimed to provide an alternative to the work of Joan Littlewood and the Royal Court Theatre, by presenting moralistic plays demonstrating that all conflicts could be resolved through adopting the MRA ideology. However, his plays reflect his upbringing – son of a teacher, an Oxford University education, trainee lawyer, journalist and, following his introduction to MRA, Christian. As has been seen in the analysis of his play *The Diplomats*, he could not relate to the working class, whom he genuinely wanted to include in both his plays and the movement. MRA was run largely by the middle and upper classes and while Howard was anxious not to be seen as right wing, because he wanted to appeal to all sections of society, his plays represent the environment in which he lived.

Howard was not only clear about the message he wanted to portray in his plays and the audience he wanted to attract but also about the type of actors and actresses he wanted to tread the boards at the Westminster:

What is in my mind is to create in the world of theatre a group of actors and actresses who will fearlessly, constantly and with all their professional genius and flair carry a new spirit into the heart of the stage and screen world ... I am asking for people who will actually understand the need of a regeneration of art in modern England and be willing to play their part in creating the plays, producing the plays, acting the plays and winning the nation (Howard cited in Wolrige Gordon, 1969, p.240).

As part of his campaign to 'win the nation' and appeal to the entire theatre-going public and not merely MRA converts, Howard introduced a new professionalism. In the immediate post-war era, MRA supporters, many of them theatre novices, acted in the plays and carried out technical and stage management tasks but Howard was determined that the Westminster should compete with other West End theatres. He began hiring professional actors, technicians and the film director Henry Cass, who had directed at the Old Vic prior to the Second World War. Louis Fleming, former director of the Westminster's Arts Centre, is critical of Howard's decision to make the MRA theatre a professional commercial enterprise claiming 'All the creative people who had given freely of their knowledge and services felt, when it became professional, there wasn't a part for them' (Fleming, appendix 8, p.301). That may have been so, but Howard had no doubt realised that society was changing and a London theatre could not survive financially unless it was competing on the same professional level as other theatres in the capital. Whilst he was opposed to the greed that accompanied capitalism, he recognised the need for the Westminster to at least break-even if it was to survive and be competitive. In addition, he no doubt realised that the more accomplished the actor and director, the more effectively the MRA message could be delivered. Fleming does admit that Howard's dynamism and focus on the theatre were such that 'had he not died the Westminster would definitely have carried on putting on MRA plays' (Fleming, appendix 8, p.301). Howard wanted to ensure that those MRA supporters who remained working for the theatre had professional training. Wolrige Gordon, at the age of eighteen, was the youngest member of the cast of Howard and Thornhill's musical *The Vanishing Island* when it toured North America. It was performed in New York and Detroit, to great reviews, but when the company arrived in Hollywood, Howard called in top Hollywood actors, choreographers and directors, who were supporters of Buchman, to improve the production. His daughter recalls:

They tore it to strips. We were told to improve one hundred per cent and my father said "Hooray, well done". These top choreographers and musicians gave their services free. It was phenomenal. We had the most rigorous training and what a transformation. We went on to tour the world including Japan, the Philippines and Manila (Wolrige Gordon, appendix 27, p.368).

Back in London, with professional actors such as Phyllis Konstam, Bryan Coleman and Nora Swinburne taking on the leading roles, the Westminster became renowned, during the 1960s for its controversial, propagandist plays. When it came to promoting its own ideology, this was the most productive decade for MRA. Howard wrote fourteen musicals and plays, some in collaboration with Thornhill and his pantomime *Give a Dog a Bone* was performed for thirteen successive years, launching the career of musical theatre actress Elaine Page and seen by thousands of schoolchildren. The public packed the theatre – due in part to the vociferous dedication of MRA supporters who arranged coach parties, pre-theatre suppers, and post-theatre conferences and literally knocked on doors of London homes to invite people. A more detailed examination of these and other ventures in the 1960s and 1970s is given in chapter four.

Howard wrote his plays very quickly, with the first draft often completed in as little as three days. His works were structured around a crisis or conflict with personal lives mirroring business lives. Much of his playwriting, like his journalism, targeted political, civic or labour leaders. However, he was also keen that his work should appeal to the ordinary man and woman in the street so while many of his characters were members of the establishment, the answers to conflict in the form of the MRA message were usually delivered by the lower classes and the women. Nevertheless, while the 'answers' might have been delivered by the workers, the upper classes remained in control. Women in Howard's plays were always seen to be 'serving' the men as home-makers and the working classes, even if they were enlightened, were always subservient to their masters, indicating that Howard wrote about the culture and society that he knew and had experienced in the pre-war years.

Although calling his form of theatre 'revolutionary', his plays do not appear to challenge the structure of society or theatrical conventions. Billington refers, in *The Guardian*, to the original negative response in 1958 to Harold Pinter's *The Birthday Party*, claiming, 'The visionary artist is always ahead of the critics and to some extent the public. There is a consistent pattern in post-war theatre in which ground-breaking works are greeted with initial incomprehension' (Billington, 2008, online). While Howard's plays were certainly not incomprehensible, MRA would have regarded them as 'ground breaking' because of the ideology they were promoting and might therefore have considered the negative response of some theatre critics as merely reflecting a lack of understanding of the message. Howard's theatre always divided opinion and was criticised by some for being too simplistic — 'it is soft and mushy, intellectually non-existent' (Pryce-Jones, 1964) — and hailed by others as having 'reached heights which set him on the level of the most significant poets and philosophers of the world' (Karter cited in *Westminster Theatre News*, 1977, p.2). Many theatre critics were irritated by Howard's bombastic, propagandist style of writing which, unlike Pinter's, left nothing to the imagination. One reviewer described Howard's *The Diplomats* as 'nothing short of a half hour sermon' (*Evening Gazette*, 1963). Howard hoped he could provide an alluring alternative to kitchen sink drama but the response to his work depended largely on whether or not those watching it were MRA converts. Mowat describes Howard's plays as 'a new way in English theatre of developing themes of spirituality and morals re-lated to the social and political context of the time' (Mowat, 200, p.51) but, for J. C. Trewin, reviewing *Happy Deathday*, a play begun by Howard and finished by his daughter after his death in 1965, there was nothing original about MRA theatre: 'The morals of these Westminster plays are impeccable but I have to court the usual polite rebuke by asking again why the dramatic form must be so elementary' (Trewin, 1967).

Throughout his playwriting years, Peter Howard was compared by a number of people to another propagandist playwright, Bertolt Brecht. *Tele-graph* theatre critic W. A. Darlington appears to have had little time for ei-ther, claiming that Howard had become the resident dramatist at 'the play-house of wishful thought' (Darlington, 1964c) while Brecht's *The Good Woman of Sezuan* had resulted in 'one of the dullest evenings I have had in the theatre ... three hours by the watch (but they felt like six)' (Darlington cited in Shellard, 2000, p.74). Darlington describes Brecht's plays as 'soused in Communist propaganda and I find them easy to admire but impossible to like' (Darlington, 1964b, p.15), adding that an exception to this was *Mother Courage* where, although the propaganda was present, 'it is not crammed down your throat' (Darlington, 1964b, p.15). In what is no doubt a veiled reference to MRA theatre, he continues 'Direct propaganda, the naked, undisguised attempt to convert people to a belief or win them to a cause, demands a conditioned audience' (Darlington, 1964b, p.15). French philosopher and playwright Gabriel Marcel believed that Howard's work could be compared with that of Brecht because for both 'it is a matter of forming a new type of man, the one Marxist, the other trained to the dictates of a Christian conscience' (Marcel cited in Wolrige Gordon, 1970, p.271). Professor Theophil Spoerri, Rector of the University of Zurich from 1948 to 1950, also compared Howard's work favourably to Brecht. In an article for the *Westminster Theatre News* he writes:

> What gives Brecht his influence on modern theatre, from Sartre to Durrenmatt and from Osborne to Albee can be summarised in three points:
> - The theatre is meant to change the world.
> - The force of inspiration comes from a faith incarnate in a militant group of people.
> - The technique of the theatre transforms the spectators into participants.
>
> On all these three points Peter Howard's plays go more deeply into the reality of life (Spoerri, 1966, p.1).

Brecht and Howard both came from the same era and from Christian backgrounds but they developed opposing political viewpoints. Howard initially told an MRA supporter, 'I am not a religious person, I am an agnostic' (Howard cited in Wolrige Gordon, 1970, p.140), but he later became thoroughly immersed in Christianity and its values. Brecht, whose father was a Catholic and mother a Protestant, showed no interest in communism until he was nearly twenty-nine and began to study Marxist theory. James Lyon and Hans-Peter Breuer reveal that, following his introduction to Marx, Brecht 'devoted the larger part of his life to the cause of communism, offering much of his work as a playwright, poet and essayist to the Party and later to a state that appeared to be working towards the realisation of socialism on German soil' (Lyon and Breuer, 1995, p.20).

Brecht's theatre first appeared in England prior to the Second World War, between 1926 and 1936, at a time when there was a rise in the Workers' Theatre Movement. The Movement performed anti naturalistic sketches and made use of music hall traditions but its work on class struggle was superseded by Unity Theatre in 1936. For Unity, opposition to fascism took priority over the class struggle and it performed Brecht's *Senora Carrar's*

Rifles, about a mother who decides to kill the fascists who shot her son for being a communist (Thomson and Sacks, 2006, p.xx). Ewan MacColl and Joan Littlewoods's Theatre of Action began experimenting with Brecht's ideas in 1934 but with the onset of World War Two the Brechtian influence disappeared. His work began to reappear in England in the mid-1950s, at a time when MRA was still presenting Thornhill's *The Forgotten Factor* to unions and management around the country. The Berliner Ensemble visited London in 1956 and performed *Mother Courage*, *The Caucasian Chalk Circle* and *Drums and Trumpets*, but, according to Maro Germanou, their reception was not as Brecht would have wished. 'Spectators and critics noticed more the way things were said and acted in the plays and less, if at all, on what was said' (Germanou, 1982, p.212). This was hardly surprising however as the performances were in German. Germanou quotes theatre critic Harold Hobson as saying of the Berliner Ensemble 'it does not seek emotion it seeks understanding' (Hobson cited in Germanou, 1982, p.212) but Hobson adds that he does not think theatre is the place for 'thinking': 'I do not believe that fundamentally there is any more rational illumination in *Mother Courage* or the other plays of Brecht than there is in *Uncle Tom's Cabin*' (Hobson cited in Germanous, 1982, pp. 212–213).

The driving force for both Brecht and Howard was in getting their message across. Steadman Williams' view is that Howard and Brecht were both didactic playwrights; for them, the message was all-important and their aim was to spread that message as far as possible. Boobbyer, too, says Howard's plays are 'best located in the tradition of didactic theatre' (Boobbyer, 2005, p.210). Like Howard, Brecht was looking for a 'theatre that would help change the world' (Rorrison, 1983, p.xxviii). Roswitha Mueller says Brecht's focus was on audience reception: 'the insistence that the audience develop an altogether different attitude' (Mueller, 2006, p.102). However, the two playwrights differed radically over the way in which they believed society could be changed and the use of theatre to bring about that change. Brecht declares: 'We who are concerned to change humans as well as ordinary nature must find means of shedding light on the human being at the point where he seems capable of being changed by society's intervention' (Brecht, 1964, p.235). Howard, however, believed that it was up to the individual to intervene in order to change society. While Howard aimed to inspire individuals to adopt the four absolute standards and belief in God, Brecht promoted communism as the way forward, emphasising the importance of the party over the individual. Palmer explains: 'The communists believed that change is accomplished by a dialectical process which demands revolution and clear defeat of its antagonists, whereas MRA promised the eventual abolishment of the conflict by the conversion of all parties to MRA ideals' (Palmer, 1979, p,.183). Kenneth Belden emphasises that change has to start with the individual and not with political systems: 'In the past many people sincerely believed that to change conditions, to get the structure of society changed, would lead to a change for the better in people. But sixty years of Russian revolution, if nothing else, have shown this to be unfounded' (Belden, 1979, p.5).

Both Brecht and Howard took their plays out of the traditional theatre setting and into the workplace. They also blurred the dividing line between spectator and actor. Brecht developed the Lehrstücke or 'learning plays' with the aim of getting them performed in schools by students. The audiences at such performances were handed questionnaires after the show 'so people could write their opinions' (Mueller, 2006, p.112) and Brecht changed some of his plays as a result. He also worked outside the theatre with a small staff of collaborators: 'We tried a type of theatrical performance that could influence the thinking of all the people engaged in it. We worked with different means and in different strata of society. These experiments were theatrical performances meant not so much for the spectator as for those who were engaged in the performance' (Brecht, 1964, p.80). Mueller, referring to Brecht's learning plays, claims, 'the insistence that the audience develop an altogether different attitude is at the core of Brechtian theory ... the historical basis for the Lehrstücke is a society in transition to socialism' (Mueller, 2006, pp.101 and 104). Like Brecht, Howard's plays were taken out of the theatre and into industry. His play *The Boss*, about conflict between management and unions, was performed in key steel and coal centres in Europe (Howard, 1954a, p.5). Audiences were often specifically selected to see the plays such as miners from the Midlands, schoolchildren from London, visitors from around the world and leading politicians, including Sir Winston Churchill. Howard's plays, like those of Thornhill, were usually followed by discussions and forums involving actors, director and audience — very often those audience members whose roles in real life were being portrayed on the stage.

Although both playwrights wanted to involve the audience, they had completely opposing views on how to write and stage a play. Wolrige Gordon says her father read a lot of plays by Brecht and met him in Switzerland in the early 1950s, basing his play *The Dictator's Slippers* on what Brecht had said to him. She explains: 'Brecht was very avant-garde in those days. The establishment in Britain didn't like Brecht's plays but they were accepted by the left-wing radical element. My father was not interested in Brecht's politics but in his playwriting and the way he introduced ideas on stage. My father really liked him' (Wolrige Gordon, appendix 27, p.368).

Howard may have admired Brecht's stage craft but he does not appear to have sought to emulate it. His plots are formulaic, dealing with conflicts, whether they be between world leaders, management and unions or parents and children. Arguments are always resolved following the delivery of the MRA message and good not only overcomes evil but replaces it entirely; by the end of the play all characters are MRA converts. His productions always featured an historically accurate stage set, observed through the absent 'fourth wall' – a device abhorred by Brecht. Martin Esslin states that Brecht was a 'rebel' and his rebellion was against the theatre in Germany in the 1920s – a theatre very similar to that in Britain at the time – which he describes as:

> A theatre in which bombastic productions of the classics alternate with empty photographic replicas of everyday life, whether in melodrama or drawing-room comedy, a theatre which oscillates between emotional uplift and after-dinner entertainment (Esslin, 1980, p.111).

Brecht did not want his audience to empathise with his characters; in fact he believed that doing so prevented them from analysing and coming to conclusions about his work. In order to encourage the audience to evaluate his plays without emotional involvement, he developed 'epic' theatre, aimed at transforming the audience member from 'a spectator into an observer' and 'forcing him to take decisions' (Brecht, 1964, p 37). Devices he used included storyboards, musical emblems, visible use of lighting equipment, communist workers' choirs and the requirement of actors to perform with a detachment that many found extremely difficult. In spite of all his efforts to 'distance' his audiences, Brecht discovered they often misinterpreted his intentions. Writing in 1954, he refers to productions of *Mother Courage*:

I do not believe and I did not believe at the time, that the people of Berlin – or of any other city where the play was shown – understood the play. They were all convinced that they had learned something from the war; what they failed to grasp was that, in the playwright's view, Mother Courage was to have learned nothing from her war. They did not see what the playwright was driving at: that war teaches people nothing (Brecht, 1972, p.389).

What Brecht failed to understand was that his audience would inevitably have become emotionally involved in the plight of a woman whose children had been killed during a war, especially as the early performances were in the immediate post-Second World War era, when many had lost their own children. Brecht was not only misinterpreted, he became known and admired for the way in which he staged his plays rather than for their political content. Germanou states that, following the visit of the Berliner ensemble to London in 1956:

Brecht and his company came to stand for the potential for aesthetic plurality and novelty in the theatre. The disregard of the significance that Brecht's theory and politics had for his theatre practice and their absence from the evaluation of his artistic work, gave rise to the intrinsically aesthetic framework within which Brecht was placed and on the basis of which he was going to be read, seen and directed (Germanou, 1982, p.213).

While Brecht's message appears to have been too subtle for his audiences to grasp, they could not fail to have understood the meaning Howard was trying to convey in his plays. Howard took the view that his writing ability was not as important as getting his message across and there is no doubt that he succeeded in his aim – often in ways that infuriated critics such as Michael Morrissey of the *Northern Echo* who complains that the message is 'overdone' with 'too much lecturing and later preaching'(Morrissey, 1963). Anthony Howard in the *New Statesman*, writes of Howard 'Are the actors and actresses who have to spout this morals-without-tears required to believe it?' (Howard, 1964). As always, however, art is subjective, with audiences interpreting what they see in the light of what they know and have experienced, and Howard had his admirers. A reviewer for the *Kentish Times* writes: 'The task of the theatre is to hold up the mirror to life and this Peter Howard achieved both ably and wittily in his new production' (*Kentish Times.*, 1964). A critic with the *Bromley and Kentish Times* claims, 'Mr Howard is no preacher. He takes the rise out of politicians, the conditions under which we live and most of all human beings in general' (T.F., 1964). MRA actress Christine Channer recalls a fellow cast member in Howard's play *The Ladder* telling her: 'This play is just the bare bones, there's nothing there', but Channer's view was 'It is a wonderful challenge to give it flesh and blood' (Channer, appendix 3, p.292).

The involvement of both playwrights in their own productions was as different as their message. Brecht was director as well as writer, adopting a hands-on approach with his actors. John Fuegi explains: 'His usual practice during rehearsals was to sit or stand in the middle of the third row or so of seats. From this position he would then run up the small flight of stairs to the stage and would demonstrate how he wanted something done' (Fuegi, 1987, p.23). Howard, however, handed his plays over, usually to the MRA resident director Henry Cass and took no part in the rehearsal process, believing his message was clear in the writing. The differences between the two can be seen most clearly through an examination of their work. Howard hoped to convert communists to MRA's philosophy with his play *The Boss*, first performed in the early 1950s, which also warns of the dangers of capitalist extremism. It is so similar in structure and content to *The Forgotten Factor* that it is highly likely Howard was influenced by Thornhill's play and hoping to emulate its success. *The Boss* makes clear from the very first page that the lead character, industrialist Daniel Ironbank, chairman and managing director of Ironbank's Ltd, is a workaholic. His wife says 'You haven't stayed away from the plant since that time six years ago when you fell downstairs and broke your ankle' (Howard, 1954, p.12). The subservient role that women take in all Howard's plays is indicated from the very beginning in the stage direction: 'As the curtain rises, Mrs Ironbank is seen arranging the tie of the great man himself' (Howard, 1954, p.11). Ironbank announces that he has to lay off one thousand men because of a decision by the government to cancel contracts for war equipment. The son of Ironbank, Peter, returns from the war with the news that the son of trade union organiser Coolcreek sacrificed his life to save that of Peter. When the union threatens strike action Peter decides to join them — a move that would have been quite revolutionary in the early 1950s when the class divide was rarely breached. Arguments and threats ensue between management and unions and the play follows a similar path to *The Forgotten Factor*, with the MRA message being delivered at every opportunity. Ironbank tells his butler Biggs, 'I have been surrounded for so long by people who all know their place that I have been too damn certain I knew mine' (Howard, 1954, p.49). The play ends with everyone changing their views and becoming MRA converts. Ironbank announces that no-one will lose their jobs and Coolcreek tells Mrs Ironbank 'You see, your husband and men like him have spent the last fifty years thinking of little except Capital. I and my friends have thought of little except Karl Marx. If men like Mr Ironbank take on a responsibility for putting the nation and the world right, then both of us are out of date together' (Howard, 1954, p.73). Coolcreek's final line is that he must now re-consider his views on God whom he hasn't 'much liked up til now' (Howard, 1954, p.75). Howard's message reflects that of MRA itself: neither the left-wing and Marxist ideas of the workers and unions, nor the capitalist ideas of the management have the answers to the world's problems. The solution lies in living by the four absolute standards and listening to the word of God. Boobbyer says 'The essential idea of the play is that the underlying tensions in industrial relations are rooted in the character flaws of those involved. Public unrest is rooted in private unrest; there is a seamless continuity between the public and the private' (Boobbyer, 2005, p.211). The play's message may seem naïve in present day culture but when it was performed in Delft in 1954 the Dutch Invitation Committee said: 'This play demonstrates in an impressive way the solution to the ideological struggle in the world. It is a positive contribution to the unity of Europe' (Howard, 1964, pp.5-6). An MRA report in December 1953 claims that 16,000 attended the French and German versions of *The Boss* in Switzerland (Report, 1953). The play was also performed by a German cast in Aachen, in French at Firminy, in English in the former Rhodesia – now Zimbabwe – and also in London and Edinburgh (Report, 1953). The report quotes an article in *The Gazette de Lausanne* claiming, 'An evening like this confronts Marxists and Capitalists as well as everybody else with questions which cannot be easily evaded' (*The Gazette de Lausanne* cited in Report, 1953). In April 1954, the play was performed in the Midlands and a letter addressed to 'Frank' – believed to be Buchman – and signed 'Hugh' says 'They came from the automobile factories of Birmingham, the lace and engineering factories of Nottingham and Lincoln, the hosiery factories of Leicester and the coalfields and potteries of Stoke on Trent' (Hugh, 1954). Just as the play was similar in style and content to *The Forgotten Factor*, so, it appears, was the response from the workers.

The message in Howard's play *The Dictator's Slippers* is even more obvious in its warning of the dangers of communism and capitalism. There is no conflict between families or between unions and management; instead this is a fantasy about what will happen to the world if it continues on its path of decadence. The setting is a fictitious country ruled by a dictator Adamant, who is never seen but who dominates the play. As usual the names for Howard's characters are euphemistic. The Minister of Interior and Chief of Police is called Saturn, which could be construed as the Russian dictator Stalin; Adamant's personal physician is Dr Hippocrat; Bullbluff is from Britain; Irasca from Africa; Desstani from India and Polyglot has eighteen passports and is 'at home in many lands' (Howard, 1956). The play was one of Howard's earliest and first published in 1954 when The Asian Conference, the Conference of the International Labour Organisation and the World Assembly for Moral Re-Armament were taking place at venues around Lake Geneva, Switzerland. It was clearly written with these events in mind and was performed at the conferences with simultaneous translation in Chinese, French, German, Italian, Russian and Spanish. An introduction to the play in the 1954 edition quotes the Ethiopian Delegate to the Asian Conference: 'It carried the conviction of truth ... it brings a new language to Geneva that speaks to the hearts of all' (Howard, 1954a). The introduction continues with a comment from Congressman R.T. Lim of the Philippines at the International Labour Organisation conference, stating that *The Dictator's Slippers* is 'a wonderful play ... while we are caught between the two ideologies, communism and democracy, fighting one another, many of our purposes in the ILO will be defeated. Our only hope is in the Moral Re-Armament programme' (Howard, 1954a). *The Dictator's Slippers* emphasises the communist belief that the party is more important than the individual. Dr Hippocrat tells Saturn he is well aware that, because of his intimate knowledge of the country's leader, when Adamant dies 'you will have to get rid of me ... they [doctors] can't be allowed to survive their patient when their patient happens to be the dictator of a nation' (Howard, 1956, p.9). Bullbluff, Irasca, Desstani and Polyglot arrive for a meeting to discuss who will take over when Adamant dies and the ensuing conversation demonstrates that the driving force amongst all nations is love of power, regardless of political persuasion. In the second act a prisoner appears, who is the voice of MRA and has attended a 'revolutionary training centre' in Geneva, which appears to represent the MRA training centre at Caux, near Montreux. The prisoner describes how, at the centre, he met 'people who are changing the world ... They seemed determined to revolutionise the world economically, socially, politically ... They were out for a change in human nature' (Howard, 1956, p.41). Saturn then puts forward the communist view, 'Human nature can never change until economic conditions change' but the prisoner disagrees: 'It took me seven years of my life to master scientific dialectic materialism. It took less than seven days for these ideas to master me ... They said that nobody is more reactionary than the person who wants to see the world different but is unwilling to be different himself' (Howard, 1956, p.41). The prisoner is highlighting the MRA message that change has to start with the individual. He goes on to describe how he has adopted the four standards – beginning with absolute honesty – and reveals that Adamant agrees with this ideology and has allowed the prisoner to be incarcerated for his own safety. The doctor then tells the assembled company that he has kept secret the fact that Adamant died a year earlier and Saturn admits that he suspected Adamant was dead and has been working to succeed him. The prisoner's story transforms all those present into agreeing to find a new way of working. Saturn is nominated to attend a conference of major world powers, on behalf of Britain, Africa and Asia, and all decide that the way forward is not through imperialism, communism or materialism but through adherence to the four standards. The prisoner announces:

> We've learned how to break a man's will and leave him like a jelly in a vacuum. We've never learned to replace it with a superior will – the will for what is right. If we take this secret to the conference table it will revolutionise the situation in the world (Howard, 1956, p.56).

The play concludes with Saturn recommending putting people before pride, prejudice and political ambitions and the doctor replying 'When men like you change, the whole world can change' (Howard, 1956, p.58). The message from Howard to Brecht has been delivered: society cannot change unless people change and people can only change when they relinquish the desire for power and listen to the viewpoints of others. As is the case with the majority of Howard's plays, the message is a reasonable one but the simplistic way in which it is delivered and the sudden conversion to MRA ideology, result in an unsatisfactory piece of theatre that was unlikely to achieve its aim of getting support from Brecht.

In Brecht's learning play *The Measures Taken*, the revolution is taken to the masses through education, aided by books and other literature, rather than through weapons. The aim is for the party to succeed rather than the individual and when the Young Comrade objects to the party line and wants to 'fight for power instead of better wages' (Brecht, 1977, p.23) his life is sacrificed. He is killed by his colleagues because the plight of the masses is more important than one individual and the Party supersedes all else. The

Young Comrade announces 'I can see with my two eyes that misery cannot wait' but the Chorus replies 'The individual has only two eyes. The Party has a thousand eyes. The Party can see seven lands. The individual a single city' (Brecht, 1977, pp.28-29). Brecht emphasises that the misery of the few is nothing compared to the revolution which will change the world, whereas for Howard and MRA the individual is crucial and all important. MRA believed that if the leaders of industry and unions could see a play at the Westminster they would be inspired, as individuals, to go back to their workplaces and bring about change in the hearts and minds of others.

Despite their various efforts, neither Brecht nor Howard managed to create the changes in society that they had hoped for and both had a greater appeal amongst the middle rather than the working classes. Germanous says:

Figure 14: Audience at the Westminster in the mid-1960s

Deprived of their political dimensions Brecht's "novelties" were treated as isolated artistic devices that could be incorporated unquestioningly into the dominant bourgeois theatre in order to revitalize it, while originally they were meant to work against it (Germanou, 1982, p.213).

MRA made sure that Howard's plays were watched by working class audiences, particularly when the plays were touring, but, as can been seen from this photograph taken in 1965, the audiences at the Westminster, wearing dinner jackets and evening dress, were of a different class to those pictured in Staffordshire in an earlier chapter (fig. 14).

Brecht's plays may not have achieved the response he wanted but he is now regarded as one of the leading playwrights of the twentieth century who revolutionised the concept of theatre. Howard did not convert the masses to MRA but, despite being savaged by some of the leading London theatre critics, his plays were popular with many people and he inspired supporters of the movement to carry on his work at the Westminster for many years after his death. Howard was well-aware that his plays lacked finesse but it appears that, apart from Thornhill, there was no-one else within the movement with the same creative zeal. He wrote to one of his children whilst on a South American tour:

I am a shabby fellow. My handwriting is hard to read. My books and plays are second-rate. I do my work in MRA in a way that is far from what would satisfy me. My failure is apparent. But God loves me and He even uses me and though I should not be, I am happy. My eyes are sore and my heart aches from many hours of toil .. (Howard cited in Wolrige Gordon, 1970, p.395)

That last sentence, written on the day he landed in Lima, Peru, 21 February, 1965, indicates that he was beginning to feel unwell. On 23 February he was taken to hospital with viral pneumonia but even then he demonstrated the iron will and perseverance that he had shown throughout his life. Wolrige Gordon describes how, in an ambulance on the way to hospital, he dictated the outline for the final act of a play he had been writing in the early mornings during his tour; ironically it was named *Happy Deathday*. On 25 February, two days after being taken to hospital, he died. The president of Peru arranged for Howard's body to lie in state at City Hall, Lima, before it was brought back to his family home in Suffolk for the funeral (Wolrige Gordon, 1970, p. 395 and 397).

A year earlier Howard had written that he wanted his funeral to be 'merry, militant and many voiced. Let my enemies have their whack also' (Howard cited in Wolrige Gordon, 1970, p.397). And he had his wish. Wolrige Gordon says the man the BBC chose to provide the tribute was none other than his arch enemy, Tom Driberg. Messages received by the family after his death indicate that, although he might not have entirely understood the changes in society that occurred during his lifetime, he did have widespread appeal. Tributes came from a huge variety of people and organisations including the US House of Representatives, the Prime Minister of New Zealand, the *Scottish Daily Express*, a soldier, an eight-year-old boy, a physically handicapped man from Kerala in South India, a housemaster at Eton College and the miners of the Ayrshire coalfields (Wolrige Gordon, 1970, pp 405–407).

Many who knew Howard claim that, although the diagnosis was viral pneumonia, he actually died from overwork. At a memorial service in St Martin-in-the-Fields, London, on 12 April, 1965, the Rt. Hon. Quintin Hogg, Q.C., M.P., told the congregation, 'No-one now, reflecting upon his early death, can fail to speculate how far his resistance to infection may have been undermined by the tremendous impetus he maintained year after year'

(Hogg cited in Wolrige Gordon, 1970, pp 401–402). Howard was driven by a belief that the world was teetering on the edge of a precipice, facing catastrophe and that it was up to him and his fellow MRA supporters to save it. He was desperate to get the support of men and women throughout the world and wrote what could be said to be his epitaph, twenty years before his death, in his book *Ideas have Legs*:

> Many plan for the future. But you and I live the future. We are the future ... We stand on the threshold of a new age. A new age of some kind is about to be ushered in, with all the sweat and blood and agony of new creation. It can be God's idea of a new age. If not, it will be a new age of another kind. And we, the ordinary men of our nation, sitting in our chairs today, we alone, the citizens of destiny, decide (Howard, 1945, p.189-190).

The following chapter explores the way in which one 'ordinary man' took steps to ensure that Howard's legacy lived on and the Westminster remained a bastion against what MRA considered to be the evils of the modern world. Kenneth Belden, chairman of the trustees of the theatre, was emphatic that God and not the Devil – in the shape of contemporary twentieth century theatre – should usher in the 'new age'.

4

The Westminster Fights
the Avant-Garde

The real indictment of many trends of modern theatre is not so much that they are sordid or violent or cruel or take place at the kitchen-sink. The real indictment is that so much modern theatre is socially worthless (Kenneth Belden, 1968a, p.8).

When Peter Howard died, the work of the Westminster Theatre could easily have died with him, but for the determination of a few key figures in the movement led by Kenneth Belden, chairman of the theatre's trustees. This chapter examines the development of the theatre under Belden and explores the way in which MRA attempted to adapt to the cultural shifts of the 1960s and 70s.

A letter to supporters from Belden and Roland Wilson, the first secretary of the Oxford Group, written on 2 March, 1965, prior to Howard's funeral, indicates the determination of both men that the movement should continue to use the theatre to promote its ideology:

The letters he [Howard] wrote to us in the past months constantly stressed the importance of the Westminster Theatre. He urged us to heighten and expand our use of it. With the last shreds of his strength and in a voice scarcely audible he was dictating a new play in the final days of his life. We can honour him and do what he would most wish to see by demonstrating our accelerated pace and our united conviction in the way we carry forward the theatre he believed in so much (Belden and Wilson, 1965).

While Howard was writing plays, at the same time as travelling around the world promoting MRA, it was Belden, and his team of dedicated volunteers, who ensured that the theatre continued to attract audiences. Belden believed the Westminster was, 'a theatre with a strategy' which aimed to attract an audience of 'people of all kinds whose change could affect the country. We aim to bring change and therefore hope, where change and hope are needed' (Belden, 1972, p.4). When Belden spoke of 'change' he was referring to conversion to MRA ideology. Palmer states, 'The MRA theatre existed to make a life led by moral principles attractive to an audience and to demonstrate the way in which moral conversion could solve personal and social problems' (Palmer, 1979, p.174).

Belden was not a playwright, but he was a vociferous propagandist speaker and writer of books and pamphlets, all delivered in the language of the charismatic preacher or politician in a style that was frequently more dramatic than the MRA plays themselves. In the Westminster's 1963 souvenir brochure, he accuses contemporary playwrights and their supporters of:

Looking for the exit door from the sordid bed-sitters with their confused and confusing inmates. Adultery and perversion are losing their charm — if they ever had any — dirt is as disagreeable in the theatre as in the drains, and more out of place (Belden, 1963, p.1).

This emotive statement indicates a certain lack of understanding of the life that existed outside the confines of the Westminster. There was little appreciation of the backgrounds or intentions of playwrights such as John Osborne or Harold Pinter. Belden's view reflected that of the establishment, which appeared to condemn the sexual liberation of the 1960s and was clinging steadfastly to the 'residual culture' referred to by Raymond Williams. Williams argues that, whilst 'the art of writing and creating performance is central to articulating the dominant culture' a great deal of literature is of the residual kind, reflecting the values belonging to cultural achievements of past societies (Williams, 1997, pp. 44-45). Society was changing but the 'old guard' was not going to give up without a fight. At the height of the 1960s' sexual revolution, a report in the *Westminster and Pimlico News* quotes Dr Ernest Claxton, assistant secretary of the British Medical Association, as declaring that there was a 'preoccupation with sex as a source of pleasure' and that girls who practised sex promiscuously 'cannot expect to occupy their rightful status as mothers of Britain's future children' (Claxton cited in *Westminster and Pimlico News*, 1968). Claxton was speaking at an MRA women's group luncheon where his views would no doubt have concurred with the standard of absolute purity.

MRA's theatre director Henry Cass told a meeting of the Westminster Theatre Forum, in July 1964, that the theatre should be creating 'works which show the wholeness, the completeness of life' rather than attempting to please the public (Cass, 1964, p.1). From a box office point of view the movement's plays appeared popular with the public, but the same could not be said of the theatre critics. W.A. Darlington made clear, on many occasions, his dislike of what he regarded as the movement's preaching propaganda, claiming:

A dramatist of real quality is never caught preaching. If he is a crafts-man he soon learns a technique of concealment. If he is neither artist nor craftsman enough to do this, but only a devotee of a cause, his plays will be avoided by all but his fellow-devotees. They however will think him a wonderful dramatist and if there are enough of them his play will prosper. The process may be seen in practically continuous operation at the Westminster (Darlington, 1964b, p.15).

While Howard seems to have taken criticism of his plays, and the movement as a whole, in his stride – probably because, as a former journal-ist, he was used to critical comment – Belden appears to have been both frustrated and bitter at the way in which society was progressing in the 1960s and 1970s and at his inability to stop it. He occasionally used the press as a vehicle for retaliation and, in a letter to the Editor, responds to Darlington: 'The fact that you can understand what a play is saying does not necessarily mean that it is unskilfully constructed. There is no virtue in obscurity' (Belden, 1964a). Darlington could not resist having the last word and in a reply states: 'I dislike being preached at in the theatre ... As things are, I go there [the Westminster] knowing that I shall be preached at and I enjoy neither the preacher nor the process' (Darlington, 1964a). It is worth noting however that although Darlington was no supporter of MRA theatre he was also, like Belden, no fan of the avant-garde either. Steve Nicholson quotes Darlington as claiming that 'kitchen sinks and left-wing politics' were likely to have only limited appeal to the public and that the 'better dramatists' had decided to 'abandon the contemporary and gone back into the past for themes of their next plays' (Darlington cited in Nicholson, 2015 pp. 21-22).

Belden had been recruited to MRA whilst at Oxford University in 1933 and regarded himself as one of the leaders of the movement's revolu-tion, claiming the new forms of entertainment that were emerging were not merely immoral but highly dangerous. He writes: 'One crucial test of any theatre or any culture is: Does it or does it not equip us to deal with the age we are living in?' (Belden, 1968b, p.7). However, MRA's desire to maintain an 'absolute' morality that conflicted with the sexual liberation of the latter half of the twentieth century, meant the movement's theatre would have had difficulty equipping its audiences to deal with the age in which they were living. Belden's provocative statements frequently attracted controversy. At a luncheon of businessmen he praised a headmaster who marched his pupils out of an 'undesirable play', adding 'The British theatre public has been kept too long at the kitchen sink. Now it is straightening its aching back and looking for something better' (Belden cited in *Birmingham Post*, 1963). Belden did not stop there however. He told those at the luncheon that the BBC, cinema, literature, medicine, education and even the church had joined the theatre in opposing 'any philosophy that is not bitter, cynical and materialistic ... these are the moral Hitlers of today' (Belden cited in *Birmingham Post*, 1963). Belden was concerned not only by what he considered to be the immorality in many plays but also by what he regarded as the 'theatre of pessimism and despair' and the 'theatre of diagnoses'. He describes the latter thus:

> It is often a theatre of consuming bitterness and frustration... It is not only boring – it is dangerous, because it paralyses action. It makes the world appear so impossible, so frustrating, so lost in its own selfishness, that nothing can be done about it (Belden, 1968a, p.6).

Of theatre of pessimism and despair, Belden may well have had Samuel Becket in mind when he says: 'Such theatre seems intent on creating a world without landmarks, a desolate world emptied of purpose, faith or moral standards, a world of meaninglessness, a "wasteland of nihilism"' (Belden, 1968a, p.7). Belden also attacked Theatre of Cruelty declaring, 'what such drama offers is too limited and selective an idea of reality. The reality of the sordid, the violent, the perverted and the cruel is only a part of the reality of life' (Belden, 1968a, p.8). Belden's definition of Theatre of Cruelty as: 'everything from Pinter's veiled menace at one end to the mad violence of the *Marat Sade* at the other' (Belden, 1968a, p.8) was a populist, rather than a theoretical, one and is discussed in more detail in the conclusion to this book. Belden did not confine his attacks to modern theatre. He condemned the nineteenth century naturalists, claiming Chekhov portrayed a world 'without hope and without illumination' and Ibsen exposed 'selfishness as the wrecker in human life ... what modern man needs is a way forward out of selfishness. He needs an answer as well as problems' (Belden, 1965a, p.5). As far as Belden was concerned only one type of theatre had the answer to the world's problems and that was the Theatre of Moral Re-Armament with its emphasis on the need for individuals to change. He maintains, 'in the hands of the right dramatists, good might prove even more shocking to the public than evil and a great deal more interesting' (Belden, 1968a, p.8). He was supported in this view by stage and screen actress Phyllis Konstam, who performed leading roles in many plays at the Westminster. Both Konstam and her husband 'Bunny' Austin, a Davis cup tennis champion and runner up at Wimbledon in 1932 and 1938, were concerned by what was happening in British theatre in the 1960s. At a meeting in Caxton Hall, Westminster, Konstam attacked the entire entertainment industry proving that, like Belden, she was adept at making highly charged statements. The *Westminster and Pimlico News* reports her speech:

I believe there is no more corrupting influence
at this time in history than the filth and sewage
pouring forth from the stage, screen and television ... I am absolutely certain that a great mass
of the British public really hate the kind of thing
which is now going on in the theatre, but they
are afraid to speak up because they don't want
to be thought stupid or not 'with it'. Well I am
not 'with it' I am against it (Konstam cited in
Westminster and Pimlico News, 1963).

Bill Boorne, writing in *The Evening News* in 1964, supports the MRA
view of contemporary theatre and indicates a similar lack of understanding
of the new work that was emerging. 'Would you dare to take your teenage
daughter?' he asks, referring to Joe Orton's play *Entertaining Mr Sloane*. 'This
sort of play and those of Brecht and Samuel Beckett leave audiences baffled
and bewildered. They have done as much damage to the theatre as anyone'
(Boorne, 1964, p.8). The fact that Boorne links Orton with Brecht and
Beckett makes it difficult to assess what he means by 'damage'. The article
makes it clear that he is opposed to the violence and sexuality in Orton's
play but there is little violence in Brecht and none at all in Beckett. It appears that Boorne's bafflement is more to do with the form of playwriting
than with its content and it is difficult to imagine how a change in form
could 'damage' theatre. Konstam and Boorne were not alone in their public
condemnation of the avant-garde. Steve Nicholson states that Peter Cad-
bury, chairman of Keith Prowse and Company Ltd; Peter Saunders, a former president of the Society of West End Managers and Emile Littler, on
the governing board of the Royal Shakespeare Company, all attacked the
emerging theatre with Saunders proposing an 'F for filth' label for certain
plays (Nicholson, 2012, pp. 56–57).

Steadman Williams emphasises that the role of MRA theatre in the latter half of the twentieth century was not only to provide an alternative to what it regarded as a theatre of extremes but to convert people to its ideology. His words below highlight the problems involved in trying to promote revolutionary theatre whilst clinging to the values of a disappearing age:

> The motive of MRA then was to counter the culture of the 1950s and 1960s of deliberately debunking and going against moral and spiritual values. John Osborne deliberately did that, as did Shelagh Delaney and A *Taste of Honey*. It got even more extreme with Edward Bond's *Saved*. Even the National Theatre had a season of Theatre of Cruelty. *The Romans in Britain* had one particularly violent scene of homosexual rape ... Unfortunately, the Westminster was seen as trying to perpetuate the old drawing room theatre. We were regarded as too conservative. Our revolution was for people to live the values and standards of MRA. Peter Howard said people would not survive without a change in character. Many people were aware of this alternative theatre. The Westminster was trying to give a balancing factor. Everyone was pushing the boundaries. It's difficult to say what effect we have had (Steadman Williams, appendix 22, p.350).

What MRA did not appear to appreciate was that the movement's plays, with good always overcoming evil, were no more realistic than those of the kitchen sink and avant-garde. They failed to stimulate debate on the human condition in the way that the 'veiled menace' of Pinter was able to do. Victor Cahn explains the importance of realism in Pinter's work:

> The most crucial aspect of *The Homecoming* is that underlying the play is a psychological realism, a depiction of forces that drive men and women toward authority and acceptance and sexual and emotional fulfilment. To bring these forces to light, Pinter dramatises that, without the constraints of conventional morality, certain elemental aspects of human nature inevitably manifest themselves (Cahn, 1994, p.74).

While MRA was critical of writers such as Pinter, it seems Pinter was equally critical of the type of theatre MRA was promoting. He warns:

> Beware of the writer who puts forward his concern for you to embrace, who leaves you in no doubt of his worthiness, his usefulness, his altruism ... what is presented so much of the time as a body of active and positive thought is in fact a body lost in a prison of empty definition and cliché (Pinter, 1991, p.xi).

Belden and Howard were concerned not only with the genre of plays being performed but the type of theatres promoting them – in particular the Royal Court and Joan Littlewood's Theatre Royal, Stratford. Radical Marxists Joan Littlewood and Jimmie Miller, later known as Ewan MacColl, and their company Theatre Union, had toured England between 1939-40 with *Last Edition*, part of their Living Newspapers project. The show claimed the political agenda of the British ruling class was anti-working class as well as anti-Soviet Union. Despite being staged as a club production to avoid censorship, it was raided by the police during the run in 1940. Miller and Littlewood were arrested and found guilty of giving unlicensed public performances. They were bound over and their company was thrown into disarray (Harker, 2009, p.17). Theatre Union was disbanded in 1942 but later emerged as Theatre Workshop. Initially it had no permanent base and the company rehearsed in a barn and slept in tents in the grounds of the home of MRA's arch rival Tom Driberg (Holdsworth, 2006, p.21). They eventually found a home in a dilapidated Victorian theatre in Stratford East, the Theatre Royal. Littlewood's iconic production *Oh, What a Lovely War!* premièred at Stratford on 19 March, 1963 – the same year that *The Diplomats* opened at the Westminster. While the former was politically left-wing and the latter on the side of the right, both used theatre to present a message and both plays highlight the defects of a capitalist society. Nadine Holdsworth describes *Oh, What a Lovely War!* as being 'the last in a long continuum of works in which Theatre Workshop and its predecessor Theatre Union, characterise war as inextricably tied up in capitalist profiteering, imperialism and the exploitation of the working classes' (Holdsworth, 2006, p.79).

Playwrights across the spectrum were no doubt influenced at the time by the enormous changes taking place during the 1960s. Steve Nicholson maintains 'In assessing and understanding the theatre of any period it is not enough to look only at what was occurring on the stage; we need also to pay attention to what was happening in the auditorium (and beyond)' (Nicholson, 2012, p.30). This was the decade in which authority was challenged and, in some cases, extreme violence used. The United States president John F. Kennedy and his brother Senator Robert Kennedy were both assassinated; Martin Luther King, hero of the Civil Rights Movement in America, was also shot dead; there were mass student riots in Paris; the British Minister of War, John Profumo, was involved in a sex scandal that rocked the government and the establishment to its core; theatre censorship in Britain was lifted; the contraceptive pill became widely available in the UK creating a new kind of sexual liberation; homosexual acts were decriminalised in Britain in specific circumstances and the British pop scene began to conquer America with the advent of The Beatles. *The Guardian* describes 1968 as 'the year that changed history' (*Guardian*, 2008, online). It was a time of enormous change which the Theatre Royal reflected in its experimental approach to theatre but which the Westminster appeared unable to embrace. Belden's wife Stella, a trained social and educational worker, called on women to demand more plays which reflected 'faith and purpose' saying that many modern plays were formless because 'to many life appeared to have no meaning. No-one could live forever on a diet of pessimism' (*Bucks*

Free Press, 1965). At a talk to women from church organisations in 1964, following a performance at the Westminster of Howard's play *Mr Brown Comes Down the Hill*, Mrs Belden castigated Joan Littlewood's production of *Oh, What a Lovely War!* claiming it 'blasphemously derides religion and the cross and patriotism ... Our job is to see it [the theatre] used to the glory of God ... the Westminster is truly a people's theatre' (Belden, 1964b). It is not surprising that MRA, with its close links to the establishment, was opposed to this production. Steve Nicholson writes, '*Oh, What a Lovely War!* was seen by some people as "anti-British propaganda" – and it certainly was an attack on aspects of Britishness' (Nicholson, 2012, p.44). Phyllis Konstam also condemns Littlewood's theatre:

> While Joan Littlewood in Stratford East and Arnold Wesker with his Centre 42 rightly felt the need of a Theatre for the People, the Westminster Theatre has become the People's Theatre, not in theory but in fact. Men from the mines, from the docks, and shipyards, from the railways and motor industries, from all over Britain, bring their wives and families ... The Westminster Theatre is avant-garde in the sense that it looks to the future (Austin and Konstam, 1969, p.228).

Konstam was correct in describing the Westminster as the 'People's Theatre'. MRA managed, in the 1960s, through its vigorous and somewhat unorthodox marketing campaigns, to attract the workers of Britain as well as the middle and upper classes. MRA regarded the Royal Court as just as much of a threat to society as Littlewood's Theatre Royal, although neither was as successful as MRA, during the early 1960s, in attracting audiences from across the class spectrum. This could have been due, in part at least, to the fact that, unlike MRA, the Royal Court and Theatre Royal did not offer cheap tickets, coach travel and refreshments after the shows. John McGrath observes that, despite wanting to appeal to the unconventional and the working class, the Royal Court became the home of 'the university educated, perhaps in origin non-middle class, perhaps non-public school, perhaps even from Manchester ... absorbing as many of the values of the middle class as possible' (McGrath, 1984, p.12). Although plays at the Royal Court and the Westminster portrayed very different views of society, the reviews could be surprisingly similar. While Howard was constantly chastised for being propagandist and creating stereotypical characters, Arnold Wesker at the Court received comparable criticism. Alan Brien in the *Sunday Telegraph* describes Wesker's *Their Very Own and Golden City* as a 'potted history of the Labour movement' adding that 'the programme, really a political pamphlet, is more provocative and invigorating than the play' (Brien, 1966, np.). Brien describes Wesker's characters as 'neither representative types nor unpredictable human beings but cartoon outlines, oddly shackled with occasional quirkish mannerisms or bizarre biographical details' (Brien, 1966). Two years earlier a critic had described the characters in Howard's play *The Diplomats* as being 'puppets preaching the author's views' (*Thames Valley Times*, 1964).

The Royal Court and the Westminster both attacked commercial theatre because it failed to reflect their ideologies, but, according to Palmer, 'MRA had considerably less influence on mainstream theatre than did the left-wing drama' (Palmer, 1979, p.185). While the Royal Court established itself in the 1960s as a centre for new and experimental drama, promoting the works of John Osborne, Edward Bond, Arnold Wesker and other playwrights, the Westminster did not manage to make any such inroads into British theatre. However the Royal Court had a huge disadvantage in that it was beholden to the Arts Council. Its reliance on government funding meant that it had to be accountable to a body that did not always share its views. William Gaskill, who took over as artistic director from George

Devine in 1965, was keen to develop repertory but a lack of good plays and lower than hoped for box office takings in 1966 resulted in the 1966-7 season consisting mainly of revivals (Roberts, 1986, p.46). Philip Roberts writes that funding issues forced the Royal Court to abandon its vision of repertory and claims that the management kept 'a very tight grip on the company's finances, partly because of the attitude of the Arts Council' (Roberts, 1986, p.47). Gaskill was concerned that financial restrictions were affecting artistic integrity. In May 1966 he wrote to Greville Poke, secretary of the English Stage Company, ESC, from 1955-73 and chairman from 1973-78: 'Although I am fully aware of the financial responsibility involved in running this theatre and the absolute necessity to remain solvent at all costs, I don't think that our work should be judged by the amount of profit we make ... I sometimes get the impression that Neville [Neville Blond, first chairman of the ESC from 1955-70] thinks this is a commercial enterprise' (Gaskill cited in Roberts, 1999, p.115). Henry Cass understood the pressure facing theatres like the Royal Court: 'Theatre today is in a state of flux. Management is uncertain what will please the public and much money is lost in trying to please them' (Cass, 1964, p.1). The Royal Court, like the Westminster, had its fair share of condemnation from the critics. Gaskill's production of *Macbeth* in October 1966 was greeted with 'almost total hostility ... Gaskill was simply in contempt of the play and its audience' (Roberts, 1986, p.53). So annoyed was Gaskill that he wrote to the editors of most of the major newspapers and the reviewers: 'In the circumstances we are seriously considering whether we should invite your critic to future performances' (Gaskill cited in Roberts, 1986, p.54). In this particular case he need not have worried about the critics. The production, with Alec Guinness as Macbeth, staged in modern dress with bright lighting and minimal scenery, was one of the most successful productions at the Royal Court that year. No doubt Gaskill was concerned that the critics would lose his theatre money, which could have led to reduced grants from the Arts Council. Like it or not, the Royal Court had to take into account the views of the Arts Council when planning its programme.

What the Westminster had, which the Royal Court did not, during the 1960s and 1970s, was a strong sense of identity, a unified approach to its future goals and a large band of supporters prepared to work for nothing. Its strength also lay in the fact that it did not rely on Arts Council funding but on internal fundraising, resulting in an artistic freedom which Gaskill must surely have envied. The Westminster was initially so successful in its fundraising that it was able to offer free tickets to many productions. Palmer states 'During its prosperous years MRA, so unlike the left-wing theatre, seemed able to attract large donations and function on a truly grand scale' (Palmer, 1979, p.179). This was probably due to the fact that the Westminster, on the whole, reflected the views of the establishment whereas the experimental theatre of the left was a threat to the established culture and society of the day. Until the 1970s, whether or not they received bad reviews, MRA supporters could still fill the theatre using an innovative approach to marketing that would have been impractical in a commercially led theatre. One of the volunteers was David Locke, who first came into contact with MRA at the age of nineteen in 1954 and became a full time, unpaid, worker from 1964 onwards. Even before joining the movement full-time, Locke was organising coach parties to see the plays: 'We would go up and down the street knocking on doors and inviting people to the theatre' (Locke, appendix 15, p.324). Locke went on to become part of a marketing team based in a small office in Mayfair led by Ronald Mann, a member of the World Methodist Council who had promoted MRA plays and films in post-war Italy and South America before moving to London in 1963. The team received daily reports from the box office on the number of vacant seats that were for sale at a range of prices up to £1. They then strove, by a variety of means, to fill them all. Journalist and writer Michael Henderson, who spent years travelling the world with MRA plays, says 'Like many others I signed a pledge that I would get ten people into the theatre a week' (Henderson, 2015, appendix 12, p.314). The way in which the Westminster went about marketing itself was unlike any other theatre in the country. In 1966, at a time when the Royal Court was dealing with internal disputes and 'ominous signs of a financial crisis' (Roberts, 1999, p.111), the Westminster was using somewhat unorthodox, but successful methods, to attract audiences. These included obtaining lists of voluntary organisations and contacting the secretaries. David Locke elaborates:

> Very often this would be a personal doorstep visit after a phone call. Sometimes it would be through a letter. We would use different techniques at different times. The theatre was the main weapon – the main tool to get across our ideas to people from all over the country. Each of the London [MRA] houses took a different night to host receptions. For instance people involved with MRA who were concerned about Middle East issues would invite people from the Middle East on a particular evening for a meal and then a visit to the theatre. We held special events. We noted that all the Mayors coming to Buckingham Palace garden parties in the afternoons from around the country had nothing to do in the evenings so we would invite some of them to one of the houses and then on to the theatre. We would meet every morning to look at vacant seats. If we were low in numbers we would contact nurses and hospitals nearby and discuss other places we could contact. Getting audiences was like a military operation (Locke, appendix 15, p.324).

MRA full-time worker Robin Evans was also involved with marketing and describes his strategy: 'We used to meet as a team and decide which factory could usefully be approached to take people to the theatre. I happened to have been in the army with the chief of personnel at the Firestone Factory which made tyres near Ealing. He taught me desert warfare and became my platoon sergeant. He was very helpful to us and sent a number of groups to see the plays. After the play we would talk to individuals at the theatre and they were very responsive' (Evans, appendix 7, p.300). One of those involved in marketing the theatre also worked in the travel industry and arranged for Americans booked on tours of England to have a play at the Westminster included in their itinerary. MRA also organised regular coaches for miners from the coalfields.

MRA worker Geoffrey Pugh, who lived in Manchester, was asked by the movement in 1966 to go to Stockport and get as many people as possible to travel to the Westminster to see the MRA musical *Annie*, about the life of Stockport woman Annie Jaeger who devoted herself to the movement. The part of her son Bill was played by Bill Kenwright[11], who went on to become a television 'soap' actor in *Coronation Street* and subsequently a West End impresario. A friend of Pugh's, who was also a lecturer at a further education college, decided to hire a special train from Stockport to London, at a cost of £2,000, to enable people to see the show. 'We then set about filling it,' said Pugh. 'We ended up organising three trains from Stockport and taking around a thousand people to the Westminster. People would come down to the Westminster in large numbers particularly at weekends, including people from Welsh mining villages and male voice choirs. They

---

[11] Bill Kenwright declined to be interviewed for this book and his Personal Assistant maintained his contribution to the Westminster had been minimal. However, he starred in one MRA play and directed at least one other.

would stay over in the homes of MRA activists all around London and then on Sundays the choirs would help to entertain' (Pugh, appendix 19, p.342).

An article in the *Yorkshire Post* in 1963 gives a first-hand account of reporter Campbell Page's experience on a specially commissioned MRA Yorkshire Theatre Special train taking three hundred people from Sheffield and South Yorkshire to the Westminster Theatre to see the musical *Music at Midnight*, by Howard and Thornhill, starring the professional film and stage actress Nora Swinburne. Interviews Page had with some of the trippers provide an illuminating portrait of an MRA audience member. He describes the MRA supporters on the train as being 'neatly dressed men who were impeccably courteous and undemanding ... A Doncaster member told me he was worried about pornography – about the spread of strip clubs and obscene literature' (Page, 1962). Page attended a buffet meal at one of the MRA houses after the performance, during which the day-trippers discussed the play. On the return journey he said:

> Most of the travellers ruminated quietly ... People had been challenged but not 'changed'. Some read MRA magazines. Some talked enthusiastically. Some sang *Abide with Me* with the excursionists' traditional fervour ... I shall be interested to know what their final responses are and whether a new kind of improving theatre can establish itself (Page, 1962).

Although Belden was unable to prevent the march of British kitchen sink drama down what he regarded as a decadent path, at least one leading theatre critic had an interesting observation on the Westminster's moralistic stance. Harold Hobson, of the *Sunday Times*, maintained that the West End had become complacent since the advent of John Osborne's *Look Back in Anger* and instead of being 'brave and defiant', was going through 'a period of unusual timidity' (Hobson, 1964). According to Hobson, 'brave and defiant' was now the province of the Westminster – the only theatre in London which 'would dare to suggest that homosexuality is a sin ... They [the theatres] would all, from Temple Bar to Sloane Square, be afraid of the derision with which such an unconventional judgement would be greeted' (Hobson, 1964). It would appear that the left-wing theatre of Joan Littlewood, the experimental theatre of the Royal Court, the pessimism and despair of Theatre of the Absurd and Theatre of Cruelty and the overt sexuality of playwrights such as Orton, that had seemed so revolutionary to the theatre world in the 1950s and early 1960s, had become the norm. For Hobson, the theatre of the middle class and the establishment, once the bastion of conventionality, had now become the avant-garde. W.A. Darlington, however, was consistent in his dislike of MRA theatre. Although he does not identify it by name, he is clearly referring to the Westminster in an article in 1967 on the lifting of theatre censorship. He writes that he fears a much worse form of censorship 'imposed in some way by the force of unenlightened public opinion – in other words, by the puritan element still rampant not far below the surface in the natures of most of us and implacably hostile to art' (Darlington, 1967).

Despite much criticism, the 1960s were halcyon years for the Westminster compared with other theatres, according to an article by MRA actress Nora Swinburne in the MRA publication *New World News*:

'The worst London has had since the war' are the *Daily Express* words for the 1962 season in the London theatre. Many plays did not survive more than a score of performances. The fashionable themes of perversion, decadence and class war failed to sustain the interest of theatre-goers. Meanwhile, Peter Howard and Alan Thornhill's play *Music at Midnight*, starring Nora Swinburne and Norman Wooland, ran for four months at the Westminster Theatre before accepting pressing requests for a tour of the main provincial cities of Britain. At the height of the holiday season, when many other theatres were empty, the House Full signs were out — a vindication of the Westminster Theatre's policy of presenting thoughtful and constructive plays in the West End (Swinburne, 1962, p.29).

The movement presented a continuous run of MRA plays throughout the decade and brought two of its own specially written musicals to London from Asia; *India Arise*, with a cast of sixty and *Song of Asia*. The Westminster Theatre's work with schoolchildren, described in detail in the following chapter, was both innovative and highly successful. In 1963 the Westminster became the first British theatre to introduce simultaneous translation, reflecting the fact that MRA attracted an international audience. Belden writes 'The Westminster Theatre is unique in London and perhaps the world in offering its patrons a simultaneous translation system in as many as four languages at once' (Belden, 1965b, p. 54). He goes on to describe exactly how the system worked, which, just two years after being introduced, had translated plays into languages as diverse as Arabic, Japanese and Turkish.

Each play is given 'live', not on tape. For each language a qualified actor and actress, with experience in microphone technique, speaks from the sound-proof translation cabins which have been created by transforming the boxes at the back of the theatre ... The translation is so carefully timed that theatre-goers sitting in the audience hear every word of the play on the earphones using a small transistor receiver, as if it were being spoken in their own language from the stage (Belden, 1965b, pp 54–55).

147

Belden quotes the Rome newspaper *Il Tempo* as hailing it 'perhaps the most revolutionary discovery in theatre since the revolving stage' (*Il Tempo* cited in Belden, 1965b, p.55). John Bridges, former director general of the British Travel and Holidays Association, called it 'a tremendous step forward in the theatre world, an almost unbelievable accomplishment' (Bridges cited in Belden, 1965b, p.55).

In the year before Howard's death, plans were launched to extend the theatre and build an arts centre costing around £550,000. Belden had envisioned expansion as early as 1955 when he stood outside the theatre and was 'struck with the force of revelation' (Belden, 1992, p.117). He realised that the actual theatre occupied only half the site and the remainder was taken up with a parking space, a derelict cottage, small garden and scenery store. The freehold of the site was owned by MRA and Belden commissioned architects to draw up plans to create an arts centre. However, it was not until 1964, at Howard's suggestion, that a preliminary planning application was lodged. Belden describes the urgent need for expansion, based on the MRA belief that not only were the plays important but also the discussions afterwards when there were opportunities to expand on the MRA ideology:

> We were running our own plays all through the year and it was painfully obvious that the theatre by itself was inadequate for our purposes. Two minutes after the curtain fell at the end of the play, everyone was out on the street and this was just the moment when people wanted to sit down and talk about the implications of the play for their own lives (Belden, 1992, p.120).

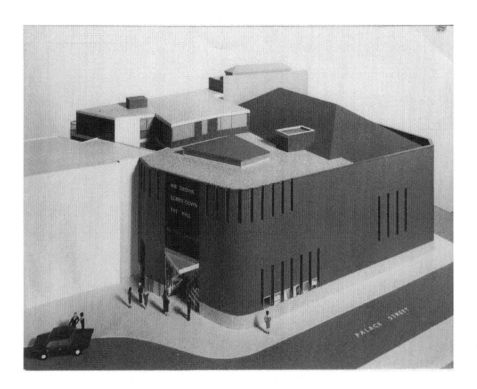

Figure 15: Architects' model of Arts Centre

Howard's sudden death gave the plan momentum and in June 1965 the Building Fund was officially launched. Plans included a new entrance and spacious foyer, a restaurant which would also double as a conference hall and cinema, a snack bar, cloakrooms, new dressing rooms and offices (fig. 15).

The Friends of the Westminster Theatre, formed a year earlier in 1964, played an important role in raising the money, most of which came from individual gifts. The very first gift was a cheque for £10,000 from Miss Margaret Lear, following the sale of her restaurant and store prior to her retirement. In a report in the *Westminster Theatre News* she writes 'I am an ordinary woman and I care about the kind of world the ordinary child will grow up in tomorrow, so I am giving £10,000, a large proportion of my capital, to forward this development' (Lear, 1965, p.3). Nigel Morshead, treasurer of the building fund, compiled a special report on the campaign to raise funds (Morshead, 1968). In it he states that a woman donated £15,000 from shares in a family business in memory of her brother, an MRA worker who was killed in the Western Desert attempting to rescue the wounded driver of his tank. Morshead continues that at the fund-raising launch sixty people undertook to raise £1,000 each and at a press conference, nineteen days after the launch, a total of £97,619 had been raised. The invaluable connections MRA had developed worldwide, with both governments and industry, were crucial to the success of the project. The Sudan Government Tannery donated leather for panels in the new foyer; the Friends of the Westminster Theatre in Sweden raised £6,000 to provide 'some of the most modern catering equipment in Europe' (Morshead, 1968, p.6). Frits Philips, chairman of Philips Electrical Industries, donated two pairs of the most advanced Philips 35mm and 15mm projectors and all the sound equipment. A seventeenth-century tapestry was presented by Mr and Mrs J. Blanton Belk on behalf of the men and women of MRA in the United States; a lady confined to a wheelchair raised money by knitting and typing; a Sheffield steel worker raised £1,000; the village of Wall in Northumberland, with a population of three hundred, collected £200 and children sold 'bricks' for the building at 2s 6d with those completing a wall of 24 bricks reserving a free seat for the Peter Howard pantomime *Give a Dog a Bone*. By the time the centre opened in November 1966 a total of £301,000 had been raised. On the first anniversary of the opening in November 1967, two and a half years after the fund was launched, the trustees announced that all the money needed to complete the work had been raised. This was an enormous achievement and all the more incredible because, according to Morshead, 'Not a penny came from any national or local authority. Not a penny was borrowed from the banks. No fees were paid for counsel or campaign advice. All those who organised the fund-raising campaign on behalf of the Trust did so without salary or payment' (Morshead, 1968, pp 14–15). This demonstrates the wide appeal of MRA and the dedication of its many full-time workers. Belden's daughter Hilary says, 'The arts centre could never have been built without dad. He was a hands-on practical man. He could see the detail as well as the bigger picture. He was also an amazing fundraiser and a great manager' (Belden, appendix 1, p.284). 'Bunny' Austin describes the arts centre project as 'a venture of faith. When Kenneth Belden signed the contract for the building operation there was no money in the bank. Yet by the time the Arts Centre had been completed every bill had been paid. More than fifty countries contributed' (Austin and Konstam, 1969, pp 237–238).

The centre was built in Howard's memory and designed by architects John and Sylvia Reid, who had been responsible for the lighting in Coventry Cathedral. A report by the Reids, in a brochure to mark the opening of the centre, describes how new techniques had been developed especially for the building: 'The method of employing slate for the external cladding for example ... The building has been conceived as a complete entity and even carpets and crockery have been designed as part of this whole' (Reid J. and S., 1966, p.37). The slate the architects chose to use came from the mountains of Merioneth in North Wales and Welsh MPs and Mayors combined to raise £10,000 to meet the cost. The centre was opened in November 1966 and a decision to ask the Bishop of Colchester to dedicate the building appears to indicate a subtle shift in ideological emphasis. When MRA purchased the Westminster, it was with the aim of presenting drama 'based on

Christian faith and moral values' (Belden 1965b, p.23). Although it was a policy of the theatre that any clergyman or minister could have a free seat for a performance, Buchman emphasised that MRA welcomed people from other faiths, wanting them to embrace MRA ideology rather than convert to Christianity. However, Belden makes an illuminating comment about the aim of the new centre:

Figure 16: Rajmohan Gandhi opens arts centre on November 26, 1966. Photo: Press Association

This is a theatre and arts centre with a unique aim. The Trust which owns it has as its objective 'the advancement of the Christian religion'. When we opened the Arts Centre a few months ago we wanted to make our position clear from the start. That is why we asked the Bishop of Colchester to come and dedicate the building (Belden, 1967).

Staging plays based on Christian values is somewhat different to staging plays aimed at actually promoting the advancement of that religion, as indicated here. Belden, unlike Buchman, appears keen to promote Christianity over MRA ideology: 'We think a theatre like this is meant to stand in the front line of the battle between Christ and anti-Christ in the modern world' (Belden, 1967). Such a statement might not have been so welcome to the Hindu, Muslim or Buddhist whom Buchman wanted MRA to accept within its fold. There is, however, no evidence to suggest that the movement was becoming less tolerant of other faiths. The new arts centre, for example, was opened by MRA supporter Rajmohan Gandhi, the grandson of India's most celebrated Hindu, Mahatma. Rajmohan Gandhi had been a life-long friend of Howard and was with him when he died (fig. 16).

The first director of the Arts Centre was Louis Fleming who, in a letter to the trustees of the Westminster, writes:

The blood, sweat, tears, pounds and pennies of thousands have been invested in this centre and in it I know lies their hopes for a new humanity ... I will with God's help and guidance endeavour to carry out the revolutionary aims and ideals of Peter Howard and of Moral Re-Armament. Twenty years ago I dedicated and committed my life to bringing Frank Buchman's revolution to the world through stage and screen and it is with tremendous satisfaction that I look forward to this next step (Fleming, 1966a, letter).

In an article for the *Westminster Theatre News*, Fleming says he envisioned the centre providing entertainment through theatre, films, concerts, lectures, photo and art exhibitions aimed at bringing about 'a revolution of moral re-armament to the world as fast as possible' (Fleming, 1967, p.1.) He adds that he wanted to provide training for writers, artists, directors, students, technicians and publicists. In a report in the MRA *Information Service* bulletin, he announces:

> We are going to challenge and prick the conscience of men and nations. The Arts Centre will be a harpoon in that part of Britain which is fat, self-indulgent and complacent and which keeps Britain endlessly and needlessly up against it, small and lacking world purpose (Fleming, 1966b, p.2)

Just as Belden was capable of making somewhat sweeping statements, so, on this occasion, was Fleming. He does not clarify what he means by 'self-indulgent and complacent', and goes on to attack contemporary theatre, claiming it has 'hoisted the flag of sadism, perversion, nihilism, in the name of experimentalism with the public's money' (Fleming, 1966b, p.2). The reference to public money could be alluding to the fact that the Arts Council was funding work at the Royal Court. This would have been anathema to MRA and considered by them to be evidence that the Government was supporting kitchen sink drama rather than the moralistic theatre that the movement was promoting. Belden appears not to have appreciated the restrictions Arts Council funding had on the Royal Court, forcing it to curb its 'kitchen sink' tendencies.

The opening of the Arts Centre gave new energy and enthusiasm to the Westminster. Activities included not only performances in the main theatre but also play readings in the foyer which doubled as a concert room. The film department, MRA Productions, supplied film versions of plays and documentaries to more than seventy countries and there were also frequent showings of films at the centre. A sound recording studio produced cassettes for worldwide distribution and for use in television and radio programmes.

Although the extensive book department operated from another building, planning for the worldwide distribution of literature was done at the centre as well as the launch of new publications and the editing of the MRA publication *New World News*. Monthly national conferences, weekly meetings, daily planning groups and evening receptions all took place in the new building. The centre included a dining room, a restaurant, which doubled as a fully equipped cinema and conference hall catering for three hundred people, and an evening snack bar. The kitchen could cater for up to one thousand people for weekend conferences, special events and wedding receptions. A report on activities at the centre states that the catering facilities provided 'an invaluable service to our force as well as being financially economic and every day there are life changing talks going on over meals,' (Report, c.1965). Outside lets included the BBC, who used it for recording television programmes, Esso, British Airports Authority and some of the major banks who used it for their own theatrical productions. Even school speech days occasionally took place at the venue. Despite such a wide variety of uses MRA's main objective was to spread its message, as the report concludes:

> All these activities spring from our central task and the centre is the scene of innumerable life-changing talks and meetings, at all hours of the day and night, so that every activity we have mentioned and many more besides are used as sources of new life in changing people (Report, c.1965).

The theatre remained an essential part of life at the centre. Howard's daughter Anne completed her father's play *Happy Deathday* which he had been working on at the time of his death. Centred on family conflicts and the conversion of a scientist to Christianity, it ran for five months at the Westminster. In that same year her own play *Blindsight* was staged and Anne followed in her father's footsteps by 'getting up early and putting in a stint of several hours before breakfast' to write the play whilst helping to run a sixteen-acre farm, support her husband Patrick, a Scottish Conservative and Unionist MP and look after her young children (*Westminster Theatre News*, 1970a, p.1.). *Happy Deathday* received favourable reviews in the *Church Times* and the *Methodist Recorder* but neither play appears to have been reviewed in the national press.

In 1971 the Westminster launched its twenty-fifth anniversary celebration with guests including British ex-servicemen ranging from a Rear Admiral and a Brigadier to privates; German and Japanese Defence attachés and King Michael and Queen Anne of Romania. The King spoke of his bitterness at his country being ruled first by the Germans and then by the Russians and said that he had overcome feelings of hatred and achieved 'peace in heart and mind ... because of Frank Buchman' (King Michael cited in *MRA Information Service*, 1971, p.1.). The Romanian royal family represented the MRA ethos – opposed to both communism and fascism but at the same time part of an élite and presumably wealthy establishment. The decision to invite military leaders and the aristocracy to the celebration would also have appealed to MRA supporters. Palmer says:

> Several studies in the early 1950s attempted to discover the basis for MRA's growth and generally hypothesised that its appeal rested in the opportunity to participate actively in a socially prestigious group which offered solutions to problems of personal guilt and social unrest while confirming basic middle class values (Palmer, 1979, p.181).

The twenty-fifth celebrations enabled MRA to review its work and to re-emphasise its aims and its successes. Belden states with his usual zeal:

It is all too easy to take the Westminster Theatre for granted. It is worth considering what the situation might be if it did not exist. The Westminster has been a rock of Gibraltar across the tides of latter-day unreason and atheism. Perhaps its greatest value is that it exists — that it stands now, as through all the past twenty-five years, for Christian truth and moral standards, not defensively, never apologetically, always militantly, forever on the attack (Belden, 1971, p.3).

In an article to mark the celebrations, Austin says 'Thousands today throughout Britain and the world look to the Westminster Theatre with gratitude and hope ... thousands feel the need for a new life concept, a new way of doing things' (Austin, 1971, p.1). While such a statement cannot possibly be verified, it concurs with Palmer's belief that 'The MRA theatre existed to make a life led by moral principles attractive to an audience and to demonstrate the way in which moral conversion could solve personal and social problems' (Palmer, 1979, p.174).

It appeared, on the surface at least, as if the success of MRA theatre in the 1960s would be repeated in the 1970s. A report on the Westminster Theatre in 1971, introduced by Air Vice-Marshall T.C. Traill, member of the Advisory Council of the Friends of the Westminster Theatre, states that in the previous ten years twenty-seven stage productions had been presented and seven had been filmed. According to the report one of the films, featuring the pantomime *Give a Dog a Bone*, was shown on British television on 1 January, 1971. The film had also been broadcast during the previous three years in twenty countries worldwide including Iraq, Lebanon, Singapore and Uganda. During the 1970s, films based on plays at the Westminster had been supplied to thirty-three countries (Traill, 1971). Plays as well as films were being staged around the world. The cast of an MRA musical *Anything to Declare* completed a 35,000 mile world tour over several years. An indication of the importance of the movement abroad is evidenced by the fact that in 1971 the Shah of Iran transported the entire cast of that musical from Europe to Iran in planes of the Imperial Iranian Airforce. Two C-130 Hercules transporters carried four and a half tons of stage equipment, stage crew, cast and luggage (*Westminster Theatre News*, 1971, p.3). Back in Britain, more than 450 industrial, medical, clergy, education and farming conferences had been held at the theatre at weekends to discuss the ideas presented in the MRA plays. Belden wrote in 1971 that the Westminster looked to the future as 'a bastion against the collapse of faith and morality' (Belden, 1971, p.3).

The future, however, turned out to be not quite as Belden envisaged. Just three years later he announced that the theatre was ending its policy, introduced in 1961, of presenting a continuous series of MRA plays. The emerging culture of the 1950s and 1960s, reflected in contemporary theatre, was fast becoming the norm. Thornhill's plays were no longer relevant to the working class and Howard's had always received their greatest acclaim from the movement's own supporters. Rising production costs, which had doubled during the 1960s, forced the Westminster's Board of Trustees to let the theatre out to other companies for part of the year. Ever the optimist, Belden was determined to put a positive spin on what must have been a detrimental move for the theatre by stating:

> Letting it out from time to time to others gives us time to reconsider what we are doing and how to do it better ... Without a doubt the greatest days of the Westminster are ahead ... supporting plays that come to the theatre when it is let to others also sustains the aims of the Westminster as a whole, by helping to build up its resources for launching the plays we expect to see there more and more in the years ahead, plays which will be of unique service to our country and the world (Belden, 1974, p.2).

Belden appears to imply that by increasing the income of the theatre through outside lets, MRA would eventually be able to revert to its policy of staging its own plays exclusively. At the same time as announcing the change in strategy, Belden claimed that the plays presented at the Westminster had been 'so varied and original that it made its mark unforgettably ... and its influence is felt far and wide across the continents' (Belden, 1974, p.1.). That influence however was not enough to enable the theatre to survive without help from outside sources.

The movement was adamant that it was not going to compromise its absolute standards but realised that, in order to appeal once again to the masses, it had to find more contemporary ways of putting across its message both on stage and on screen. Although the continuous run of MRA plays came to an end, new playwrights began to emerge, including Steadman Williams and Nancy Ruthven. They were creating plays which, whilst still promoting the MRA ideology, tackled current and controversial issues. Nevertheless, the death of such a prolific writer as Howard left a gap that could not be entirely filled. Steadman Williams explains: 'If you are to have plays with the experience of a change in human nature then we shall have to have more writers and directors with that experience too. That is the only sure way to a true renaissance' (Steadman Williams, 1969a, p.2). Henry Cass also saw that a new approach was needed. In a confidential memo, dated 18 December, 1970, Belden writes that Cass had been considering 'how to produce a new kind of presentation of our message using ... perhaps as few as half a dozen people and using songs, sketches, dramatised songs and so on in varied form. He [Cass] has been particularly influenced in this by watching pop singer Cliff Richard and the Seekers on Sunday evenings. He says

they are simple and direct but highly professional and he feels very effective'
(Belden, 1970a). MRA launched its new approach in 1972 with the production *Cross Road,* based on the life of Frank Buchman. MRA supporter Terence Blair describes the show as 'a pioneering adventure in multi-media ...
It is probably the first time stage, screen, music and recorded sound have
been used together in a West End theatre to tell the story of a man's life
and his effect on the world around him' (Blair, 1972, p.1.). He quotes from
a report in *The Stage* stating, 'Those responsible ... achieved something quite
remarkably excellent' (*The Stage* cited in Blair, 1972, p.1).

However, it appears that, from the 1970s onwards, the critics began to
ignore the Westminster and this lack of interest frustrated Belden:

> Our plays ought to be constantly referred to and reproduced on tel-
> evision and on radio. They are not, nor do they receive their due in
> the press. There are people who are as keen to destroy or frustrate
> the faith and values that the Westminster stands for as the Friends
> of the Westminster are to sustain them ... As regards our plans ahead,
> we hope to run the present plays as long as we can (Belden, 1970b,
> p.2).

While Gaskill at the Royal Court threatened to stop issuing tickets to
critics because of their negative reviews, MRA considered that getting no
mention at all was an even worse prospect. The newspapers were no longer
taking up the offer of free tickets to review the plays and Michael Henderson
began to research why. In a report on the coverage of MRA plays between
1967 and 1972, presented to Belden and other senior members of the movement, he states that there had been no reviews in *The Times* for the previous
three years and only fourteen reviews in total. He writes 'Several critics have
mentioned that, though personally favourable to us, they would not write
pieces because they claimed their management was against us' (Henderson,
1972). Henderson recommended approaching national newspaper editors

and says 'regardless of the silence, we must act in a way that gives a chance of the door being opened at least a little and does not encourage the door not only to be kept shut but locked as well' (Henderson, 1972). He adds that he initially considered taking positive action in time for the premiere of *Cross Road*, but, because one of the arguments used against the Westminster was that it was propagandist, recommended a delay until the opening of the highly popular annual Peter Howard pantomime *Give a Dog a Bone*. It was agreed that Henderson should write to the newspapers asking them to reconsider their attitude towards MRA productions. In his letter to the editors of all the national dailies, Henderson emphasised that nearly three hundred professional actors and actresses had performed at the theatre and quotes one senior Equity official as saying the Westminster was the first London theatre to 'give coloured actors a break'. The way in which the theatre was purchased and its aims and objectives are outlined and the letter continues:

> We do not want special consideration, nor do we demand favourable criticism. We would only suggest that the present silence about our plays is not objective in the best tradition of British journalism and not in the best interests of the country ... It has been suggested over the years that we are not running a professional theatre, that our plays carry a message, that there would not be a general interest in them, that these are not well staged etc and that for these or other reasons they should not be reviewed. May we first of all say that all the Westminster productions are written for the general public and not, as some would suggest, for a special audience. The plays carry a message but then most plays put on in the West End, particularly in recent years, carry a message of some kind (Henderson, 1972).

The response from the newspapers is illuminating and shows the negative attitude that they had towards MRA. Harold Evans, editor of *The Sunday Times*, writes 'We cannot guarantee a regular review because some of the productions have to be seen more as putting over a message rather than a contribution to the arts' (Evans, 1972). C.J. Lear, editor of the *News of the World*, says 'I would have supposed your plays are primarily propagandist' (Lear, 1972). B.R. Roberts, editor of the *Sunday Telegraph*, is rather more blunt: 'The simple answer is that we do not notice the plays to which you refer because they are not part of "The Theatre" in any genuine sense, but an arm of Moral Re-Armament propaganda. You must be well aware that this is the case' (Roberts, 1972). John Leese, executive editor of the *Evening News*, which had reviewed MRA plays in the 1960s, replies: 'I think you will have to agree that your productions are not theatre in the normal sense and that we could hardly ask our theatre critic to regard them as he would any other West End play' (Leese, 1972). MRA was quite open about the fact that its plays were message-driven but believed, nevertheless, that they were entertaining as pieces of theatre. While Palmer attests that 'The raison d'être for the MRA plays is the conversion of audience members to the principles of MRA' (Palmer, 1979, p.173), the desire to impart a message should not be considered either an unusual or an undesirable aim for a playwright. Nathan Saviour says:

> Since propaganda has such pervasive influence on people, it would be difficult to single out a playwright, whatever may be his inclinations, who does not begin his work with some preconceived notions about his audience and what he expects would be the effect of his work on them. It would be difficult, therefore to think of a play, be it secular or sacred, that is wholly art and free from every shade or degree of propaganda (Saviour, 2009, p.124).

Leese's assertion that MRA plays 'are not theatre in the normal sense' needs clarification. Presumably he is referring to the propagandist element of the plays, but it would be interesting to know just what he means by 'normal'. MRA staged plays that were traditional in structure and were performed on a stage, in a theatre. Theatre encompasses many movements including futurism, expressionism, Theatre of the Absurd and Happenings. All have elements of 'propaganda' about them and many, such as Antonin Artaud's Theatre of Cruelty, would not be termed 'normal' by many theatregoers. Richard Schechner lists what he regards as seven functions of performance and these include 'to entertain' and 'to teach, persuade or convince' (Schechner, 2006, p.46). Schechner suggests that Augusto Boal's Theatre of the Oppressed empowered spectators to 'enact, analyse and change their situations' (Schechner, 2006, p.46) which is exactly what MRA wished to do. Bertolt Brecht was renowned as a message-driven writer but it is unlikely that Leese would have refused to review *Mother Courage*. The replies from many newspapers seem at best defensive and at worst somewhat bigoted. Only one publication shows some creative spirit and that, not surprisingly, is the satirical magazine *Punch*. Jonathan Sale writes: 'There is no conspiracy of silence about the Westminster Theatre; we don't have an "attitude" as far as I know. Our theatre critic is interested only in theatrical standards. However, your letter has spurred him on to make sure that he visits a forthcoming production' (Sale, 1972). Despite the mainly negative response, MRA was not prepared to let the matter rest. Cass recommended that actors performing at the Westminster should write letters to *The Times* and *The Stage* stating that MRA theatre was not alone in putting across a message. Referring to the Royal Court, Cass told Henderson in a phone call, 'the point should be made that such theatres exist to put a point of view across and that we too are interested in putting a message across' (Cass cited in Henderson, 1972).

It is difficult to assess whether or not the correspondence was successful, but the next major production at the Westminster did attract reviews in the national newspapers. In 1973 MRA presented what it described as 'a topical musical revue, *GB*'. The title stands for Great Britain and launched a new venture for the movement. *GB* consists of a series of satirical sketches written by Thornhill, Henderson and Steadman Williams. Following the advent in the 1960s of television shows such as *That Was the Week that Was*, satire was becoming increasingly popular. Steadman Williams says: 'We felt that they were satirising virtue and we thought, why not satirise vice' (Steadman Williams, appendix 24, p.360). Thornhill claims that the aim of *GB* was to be 'something entirely different from anything attempted before; topical, satirical ... and yet hopeful and faith-giving for the future' (Thornhill, 1973, p.1). MRA supporter Kathleen Johnson, a music teacher who composed and directed the music for several of the movement's musicals, composed twenty-five songs for the revue, covering hypocrisy in family life, the Northern Ireland conflict, the illegal drugs scene, irresponsible bankers, working to rule, women's liberation, inflation, contemporary theatre and 'going into Europe' (promotional leaflet, 1973). One sketch, particularly poignant in twenty-first century Britain, features home-grown terrorism and involves two guerrillas. In a burst of gunfire they kill first the capitalists, then the politicians whom they regard as irrelevant, followed by Trade Union leaders 'traitors to their class' and finally themselves (promotional leaflet, 1973). The production attracted funding and commitment from the cast that no other London production could ever have envisaged achieving. A budget of £15,000 was drawn up for production and promotion costs and a retired businesswoman from Manchester started fund raising with a gift of £1,000. Some of the cast took a minimum salary and mime artist Michel Orphelin from France travelled to Britain especially to take part.

This was a production that was not ignored by the critics. Harold Hobson, whose editor had criticised the Westminster for being message-driven, writes that in an atmosphere in which 'anything can now be said on the stage and almost anything done, it should be possible to express sentiments of traditional kindness and affection without being jeered at. Even such statements as "God is love" do not seem to me, since we all fervently believe in civil liberty, to outrage public decency' (Hobson, 1973). He continues that while some sketches were 'unacceptably naïve' others, particularly a satire on drama critics, were well developed, effective and amusing. Arthur Thirkell of the *Daily Mirror* comments:

> Even the most cynical theatre critic could find himself thawing ... In the past, while not quarrelling with the sincerely-held views, I have thought MRA's entertainment value pretty awful and dreadfully naïve. I am glad to report that GB is a colourful review, a gentle backlash against permissive society. Quite funny at times too (Thirkell, 1973).

Not all theatre critics thawed however, and a review by Roger Baker, highlights MRA's inability to fully understand the society in which it existed. He says the notion that all differences would disappear if management and workers got to know each other 'strikes me as a bit naïve'. He describes as 'dishonest' a sketch in which a group of builders spend their evenings 'singing perfect plainsong' for relaxation adding, 'They were more likely to sing the bawdy medieval lyrics one finds in Carmina Burana — which, of course wouldn't do in an MRA context' (Baker, 1973). While he describes some sketches as of 'almost childish idiocy' Baker is not entirely detrimental, advising: 'A little more bite, an abrasive quality, even straightforward shock now and then would raise it from the pleasant to the memorable' (Baker, 1973). MRA believed that the range of reviews marked a change in attitude from the critics. An article in the *Westminster Theatre News* states 'Perhaps the most significant thing about the press reviews of GB is that they show a growing recognition by some critics of the role of the Westminster Theatre and the place of Moral Re-Armament' (*Westminster Theatre News*, 1973a, p.1.) The article goes on to quote from a review of GB by leading theatre critic Milton Shulman of the *Evening Standard*: 'Who can resent a show that ridicules greed, mocks the power structure, derides acquisitiveness, giggles at contemporary social values?' (Shulman cited in *Westminster Theatre News*, 1973a, p.1).

As the 1970s progressed, MRA redoubled its efforts to be relevant. In 1974 it staged a Theatre Study Weekend entitled 'Out into Battle' attended by actors, writers, producers, musicians, painters and designers. Steadman Williams says the title was taken from Alexander Solzhenitsyn's Nobel Prize acceptance speech: 'We must not seek excuses on the grounds that we lack weapons, we must not give ourselves over to a carefree life, and we must go into battle' (Solzhenitsyn cited in Steadman Williams, 1974, p.1.) Key speakers at the event included Professor Loren Winship, head of drama at the University of Texas and Shaun MacLoughlin, BBC radio producer and editor of *Saturday Night Theatre*. The battle to diversify and survive continued with the Westminster forming links with Methodist theatre company Aldersgate Productions. The organisation was formed in 1975, following a production of *Ride Ride* by Alan Thornhill, a musical based on the life of John Wesley, founder of Methodism. In 1977 Aldersgate hired the Westminster to stage a season of three plays one of which, *Fire*, was written by Steadman Williams about a media man wrestling with Christianity. Milton Shulman of the *Evening Standard* describes it as 'An avowedly Christian play and since the stage has its fair share of avowedly permissive Marxist and anti-establishment plays there is nothing wrong in that' (Shulman cited in *Westminster and Pimlico News*, 1977b). The involvement of Aldersgate suggests that the Westminster was continuing to develop more as a centre of Christian drama than of MRA philosophy. Mary Lean, whose father Garth was instrumental in introducing Howard to MRA ideology, says that in the early days of the Westminster the Sunday morning meetings at the theatre took precedence over church attendance. In later years, however, as the leases on the large houses ended and supporters moved into small family groups, the church became more important as a way not only of worshipping but of becoming involved in the local community. Mary Lean highlights the difficulties: 'As a teenager and young person I was aware of a tension between being part of MRA and being accepted as a Christian – not being Christian enough for the Christians and not being secular enough for the non-Christians' (Lean, 2015).

Just before the decade ended, MRA staged a play which tackled a controversial issue and which led to a degree of media attention that must have delighted Belden. Alan Thornhill teamed up with journalist, author and satirist Malcolm Muggeridge[12] to write *Sentenced to Life*, dealing with the plight of a paralysed woman who asks her husband to kill her. The play, which argues against euthanasia, was staged at the Westminster by Aldersgate and produced by Ronald Mann. The timing of the production was deliberate and aimed at counter-acting a pro-euthanasia play *Whose Life is it Anyway* at the Mermaid Theatre in London's West End. *New World News*

---

[12] Malcolm Muggeridge (1903–1990), former editor of *Punch* magazine, was once an admirer of the Soviet Union, but later became one of its harshest critics. He converted to Christianity in his sixties and to Roman Catholicism in his eighties.

quotes a comment from the *Financial Times*: 'They are fighting out the controversy of euthanasia at two theatres, one at each end of London' (*Financial Times* cited in *New World News*, 1978, p.1.). BBC One's *Tonight* programme featured clips from *Sentenced to Life* during a discussion between Muggeridge and Derek Humphry, whose book *Jean's Way* describes how he helped his terminally ill wife to commit suicide. Ned Chaillet in *The Times* writes 'It is good to see that the theatre can still play a role in great moral controversies. It seems to have missed a few in the past, perhaps thanks to the custom of censorship' (Chaillet, 1978). While the critics valued the subject matter, some were critical of the writing of Muggeridge and Thornhill. Michael Billington comments, 'In place of the dialectical debate on the subject of euthanasia which I had been anticipating, one gets a curiously evasive melodrama in which most of the interesting moral issues are ducked and in which rational argument is replaced by cloudy mysticism' (Billington, 1978). Jack Tinker of the *Daily Mail* was even less impressed: 'They succeed only in making the exit signs seem like stars pointing the way to heaven' (Tinker, 1978). Nevertheless the play achieved what MRA was hoping for – it encouraged debate on a sensitive subject and attracted the attention of the media.

It seemed that at last the Westminster was becoming relevant again but as the 1980s dawned the movement faced a bigger battle from within its own ranks. In 1979 Belden produced a confidential report to the trustees on the financing of the theatre. In it he states that a gap between income and expenditure of £88,000 had to be bridged annually. Bridging that gap meant the continuous running of the theatre which, Belden claimed, was difficult to maintain:

Plays are not always obtainable, or are not suitable for our theatre, making some dark periods unavoidable. At other times we need to keep the theatre available for an essential production like *Sentenced to Life* and this may incur some dark weeks before or afterwards ... The theatre, therefore, while often a main source of income, tends to be unpredictable ... In recent weeks the Trust has again reached the limit of its over-draft possibilities. In the past few months the Trust has had to use £13,000 out of its small invested capital to keep solvent (Belden, 1979a).

Belden highlighted the fact that many people involved in staging MRA plays were touring with productions abroad. He advised that new sources of income needed to be found and suggested encouraging people to make deeds of covenant, to remember the theatre in their wills, and to increase donations from overseas. What he did not envisage was the closure of the theatre altogether. However, as will be discussed later in this book, a growing contingent within MRA wanted the theatre sold, believing that the message could be better communicated through forums and conferences than through plays. Drama off-stage began to rival that on the stage itself, but one initiative, on which all were united and which attracted praise from a wide ranging non-MRA audience and the critics alike, was the Day of London Theatre. The following chapter investigates how this initiative became so popular with thousands of schoolchildren and why it proved to be a lasting legacy for the Westminster.

5

MRA Theatre for Children

The Westminster Theatre changed the whole pantomime scene in London. It meant you could take children to the theatre. 'Give a Dog a Bone' was good fun. It did make a lot of difference to people and it had packed audiences (audience member, 1960s).

MRA theatre's greatest success during its fifty-year history at the Westminster was in its innovative work with children, which received consistent praise from the media, schools, education authorities and the young people themselves. The move to write and present shows for children was driven by MRA's belief that, in the 1960s in particular, there were no suitable plays for children being shown in the West End. This is not entirely true because, as Steve Nicholson points out, musicals such as *Half a Sixpence*, *My Fair Lady* and *Oliver* were all popular family favourites during that decade (Nicholson, 2012, p.56). The Westminster's first and most successful production for children was Peter Howard's *Give a Dog a Bone*, which opened at Christmas 1964 and ran for eleven seasons until 1975. An MRA leaflet issued for a revival concert version in 1997 claims:

It [*Give a Dog a Bone*] started a new trend in children's entertainment at Christmas. By the mid-1960s the traditional pantomimes, which previously had catered for all the family, had largely degenerated into adult variety shows, replete with blue jokes and very little in them for children to enjoy. After the success of *Give a Dog a Bone*, plays and musicals for children during the Christmas holidays sprang up, not only in London but all over the country (leaflet, 1997).

Whether or not the traditional pantomime had in fact degenerated into 'adult variety' is open to interpretation. However, in the mid-sixties, while the stars were invariably fairly innocuous pop singers, the supporting acts were often best known for their roles in the *Carry On* films, infamous for their sexual innuendoes. MRA would no doubt have considered Cliff Richard a suitable candidate to play Buttons in *Cinderella* at the London Palladium in 1966–67, but he was accompanied by Ugly Sisters, Hugh Lloyd and Terry Scott, who might well have been considered somewhat risqué for the period. Kenneth Connor and Sid James, who played the robbers in *Babes in the Wood* at the Palladium in 1965, were associated more with bawdy humour than with children's entertainment. Singers Tommy Steele and Mary Hopkins would have met with MRA approval, as stars in *Dick Whittington* in 1969, but their co-star Arthur Askey was associated with a somewhat suggestive 'naughtiness' which the movement would not have considered suitable for children.

Give a Dog a Bone specifically targeted under-privileged children and as such presented a special attraction, not replicated in the West End at the time, which no doubt contributed to its success (figs. 17, 18, 19). A fund-raising campaign, which included house-to-house collections, bring and buy sales, collections in shops and donation tins in pubs all around the Westminster area, ensured that year after year thousands of children living in poverty and those in care were given free tickets to the pantomime (*Westminster Theatre News*, 1970a, p.1.). A report by Belden states that it cost between fifteen shillings and one pound to provide a needy child with a seat, an ice-cream and transport. The report adds that in the first seven years around £15,000 had been raised to pay for nearly thirty thousand children to see the show. In that time more than four hundred voluntary societies, youth organisations and foster parents had been invited to submit names for free tickets (Belden, 1970b, p.2). The production, which launched the career of the West End musical star Elaine Page as Miss Sheep, was also filmed in colour and shown on television in sixteen countries around the world including Ethiopia, Iraq, Uganda, the United States and Lebanon. A report by MRA, thought to have been written in 1971, states that in August 1969 the City of Lagos education office arranged for the film version of *Give a Dog a Bone* to be shown to seven thousand children from fifty-five schools

Figure 17: It cost between 15 shillings and one pound to give these children a treat to remember at *Give a Dog a Bone*

(report, c1971, p.2). The show was the only Westminster Productions film to be broadcast on British television and was televised by Westward Television on 1 January, 1971. The stage and film sets were designed by MRA worker Bill Cameron-Johnson, who designed the sets for MRA's first professional production in 1961 of Peter Howard's *The Hurricane*. He was also responsible for the associated publicity connected with both stage and screen versions of *Give a Dog a Bone*. These included a colouring book, a song book with eleven songs arranged for piano and guitar, two EP records containing fourteen songs from the show and a shortened play script for use in schools.

Give a Dog a Bone was the most popular of all Howard's works. Howard is quoted in a promotional leaflet on the play: 'It is based on the belief that part of the heart of a child that is born within us never dies' (leaflet, 1997) and it did appear to appeal to adults and children alike. The show features a selection of wholesome, happy songs, with music by George Fraser, who co-wrote several musicals with Howard. The hero, a 'Beatle-cropped hound' (*Westminster Theatre News*, 1964, p.1) called Ringo may well have been named after drummer Ringo Starr of The Beatles pop group. This may have been an attempt by Howard to attract younger audiences by associating with the current music culture. Ringo meets a spaceman who has come to earth to help people. Mr Space asks, 'What's the matter with everybody down here?' giving Ringo the opportunity to start delivering the MRA message: 'People have never learnt to behave like decent dogs. They're never satisfied with what they've got' (Proctor, 1968, p.4). Ringo and Mr Space team up with a young boy, Mickey Merry, who is hoping to escape his erstwhile no-good parents and make his fortune in London. On the journey to the big city the trio meet evil King Rat who has magical powers which enable him to turn humans into animals if they say 'I couldn't care less'. Fortunately they only have to utter 'please', 'thank you' and 'sorry' for the spell to be reversed. The message for children about the importance of good manners and taking responsibility is simple and straightforward. However, Howard has a slightly more complex, but no less obvious message, for the adults. King Rat stands on a soap box in Hyde Park with a banner reading 'The Me First Party'. He claims that his followers will have fun and calls for 'Fun Palaces for everyone ... Down with America, Down with Russia. And Down with decency' (Proctor, 1968, p.25). Howard could be alluding here to the Fun Palaces of Joan Littlewood. In 1961 Littlewood and architect Cedric Price, who were introduced to each other by Tom Driberg, conceived the Fun Palace as 'a utopian agent for change for the individual, community and environment' (Holdsworth, 2011, p.211). Like Howard, they wanted to change the individual and ultimately society but, unlike Howard, they were left-wing and anti-authoritarian. Their vision was to create spaces 'dedicated to pleasure, entertainment, communication and learning' using the latest technological advances (Holdsworth, 2011, p.206) but King Rat's cry of 'Fun Palaces for everyone ... down with decency', appears to indicate that Howard was no supporter of Littlewood's concept of a new society. He may not have appreciated that Fun Palaces were about making the arts accessible to all and not about immorality or indecency. Whereas the Marxist Little-wood and 'evil' King Rat appear to want a change that is non-conformist and anti-establishment, Howard and the 'good guys', Mr Space and Ringo, advocate a change that involves adopting MRA's absolute standards. How-ard, as usual, is careful to imply that he is against both capitalism and com-munism with his condemnation of both Russia and America. King Rat goes on to shout 'down with aristocracy' to a large pig sporting a coronet and a pink velvet suit. Choosing a pig, traditionally associated with greed, to portray the aristocracy is Howard's attempt at showing he is no supporter of the foppish, extravagant members of the upper echelons of society. In London, King Rat manages to turn the majority of people into animals because none of them can say 'please', 'thank-you' and 'sorry' and most of them at

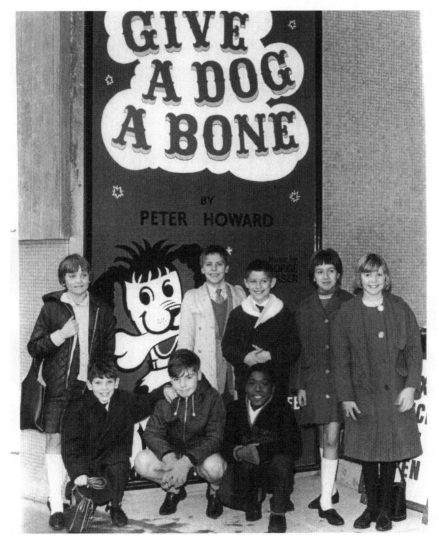

Figure 18: Poster for Give a Dog a Bone

some point manage to announce 'I couldn't care less'. Eventually however, thanks to Mr Space and Ringo, everyone manages to adopt 'good manners', is turned back to a human and the show concludes with a song 'Wonderful, wonderful world', including the words:

> Come on then, live in the sun.
> Every man working as one,
> Build a new tomorrow in our
> Wonderful, wonderful world (Proctor, 1968, p.43).

The message might seem somewhat outdated for twenty-first century children but it is not too far removed from that of Walt Disney's popular West End musical *The Lion King* in which lion cub Simba discovers the drastic consequences of not obeying his father. Both *The Lion King* and *Give a Dog a Bone* highlight the importance of playing by the rules and both end happily in a chorus of utopian positivity.

MRA believed that the success of *Give a Dog a Bone* inspired other West End producers to follow suit. A report in the *Westminster Theatre News* states that in its first eight years more than a quarter of a million people had seen the show:

> *Give Dog a Bone* has proved time and again at the Box Office – the place that counts for West End managements – that people will pay to see a clean show where right comes out on top, especially when it holds up a mirror to the way we live. The commercial success of *Give a Dog a Bone* is one reason why it will have several competitors in the West End this Christmas (*Westminster Theatre News*, 1972, p.1.).

Give a Dog a Bone was the first of many plays for children presented at the Westminster and led to the development of MRA's most innovative programme, The Day of London Theatre for schools (fig. 20). It was one of the most extensive and longest running independently operated theatre programmes for schools in the country, lasting for twenty-two years. Launched in 1967, and led by the movement's education officer Joy Weeks, it aimed to give children an insight into the workings of the theatre and every aspect of production, from stage design and lighting to costume and rehearsal techniques. MRA full-time worker Mary Lean writes that, at its height, the Day of London Theatre ran three programmes a year – for 16 to 18-year-olds in the autumn, for primary school children in December and January and for

Figure 19: Audience participation at *Give a Dog a Bone*, Westminster Theatre.

12 to 15-year-olds in the spring and catered in total for more than 200,000 pupils and teachers (Lean, 1998, p.6). While the initiative concentrated on the staging of a play, MRA did not miss the opportunity to deliver its message. An article in the *Westminster Theatre News* states that the day usually began with the children visiting the restaurant to view a mosaic with the inscription: 'Miracles of science have been the wonder of the age but they have not brought peace and happiness to the nations. A miracle of spirit is what we need' (*Westminster Theatre News*, 1979, p.2). Pupils would then meet the stage doorman, visit the actors' Green Room and the film department and be given a detailed account of how a professional show was developed. The programme also included a 'History of Theatre', with slides presented by the theatre's resident designer Cameron-Johnson, a tour of the costume department with wardrobe mistress Jill Hazell and the chance to see a performance on stage, followed by a discussion with some of the cast. Hazell began helping at the theatre in 1967, whilst working as a nanny in London, and the way in which she obtained her position as head of the wardrobe highlights MRA's policy of prioritising enthusiasm and dedication to its ideology over experience. Training was in-house and if a supporter showed an interest in a specific role, they were given the chance to take it on, as evidenced by Hazell:

> I used to come and sell books and records during *Give a Dog a Bone* and used to change in the usherette's room in the basement, which used to be the crypt of a church. One day I walked into the wardrobe instead of the usherette's room by mistake and saw an empty dog suit hanging there drying out. I had never given a thought to what went on behind the scenes. Judy Pearson was the wardrobe mistress in those days and she invited me to have a coffee. I ended up ironing a whole load of peasants' shirts! ... Suddenly a job came up. MRA was making a film on location of the play *Happy Deathday* and I was asked

to be dresser and wardrobe assistant. I later became wardrobe mistress at the Westminster and loved it' (Hazell, 2014, appendix 11, p.313).

In addition to getting an understanding of the work behind the scenes, students were also given the transcript of a play and encouraged to look at the various ways in which it could be interpreted. Notes on one workshop, featuring the Lord Goring proposal scene in Oscar Wilde's *Ideal Husband,* discuss the historical and moral context and how it could be performed in the present day. Questions for the students include 'If you discovered your boy/girlfriend had done something really terrible, would you still marry them? Would you forgive them if you were already married to them? What would you do, what would you say?' (Day of London Theatre, n.d.). Choosing a play that was set in Victorian times added another dimension for the students who were encouraged to explore the language of the period, the morality of the Victorians compared with the present day and the use of costumes and staging both currently and in the past. A report by Joy Weeks states that the students were shown the difference between the sound and lighting of Oscar Wilde's time and that of the 1980s: 'The audience is transported from a Victorian drama when off-stage sounds were made by coconut shells and rain machines on to the realistic sound tracks now available on tape' (Weeks, 1989, p.5).

The Day of London Theatre gained favourable publicity from education authorities and the educational press. An article in the *Times Educational Supplement* in 1967 describes how 'girls and boys from secondary schools in and around London have been attending a weekly series of day courses in stage production' (*Times Educational Supplement,* 1967). It reports that activities included talks on stage production by professionals such as

179

Len Maley of the Corona Stage School in Hammersmith, plus introductions to stage management, costume design, make-up, lighting and sound by the heads of the departments at the theatre. The *Westminster and Pimlico News* highlights the contribution made to the Day of London Theatre by French mime artiste Michel Orphelin who coached ten thousand children from one hundred and eighty-six schools over a two month period. The report states that a total of sixty-five thousand schoolchildren had spent a day at the Westminster during the previous ten years (*Westminster and Pimlico News*, 1977a). The aim of the programme was not merely to educate children in the workings of the theatre but to introduce them to MRA ethics. The newspaper report quotes Robert 'Ken' Rundell, education director of the Westminster: 'The theatre has at least as much effect in moulding children's attitudes as the school curriculum. The aim of our programme is to teach children to derive the maximum from the theatre and drama in terms of understanding human nature and the interaction of human beings on each other in society' (*Westminster and Pimlico News*, 1977a). Rundell's son Peter says his father was inspired to work with children because 'he wanted to reach an audience that might not yet be formed in the cynicism and self-indulgence he perceived in contemporary culture' (Rundell, appendix 21, p.347). Looking back on the Day of London Theatre, Peter Rundell writes:

> The programme was the first in what has become relatively routine today; outreach by theatres to potential future audiences. While elements of the day were perhaps amateur by today's standards (the sections on diction and movement would hardly pass muster with a media-savvy class accustomed to *Strictly Come Dancing* and reality TV), I still recall other elements like the lighting and costume sections as admirably suited to an audience whose next experience of theatre might be a school play or community drama group. It retained throughout a didactic thrust which might no longer work, together with a set of strong messages from MRA which were delivered in a

more direct form than would be effective today (Rundell, appendix 21, p.347).

One of the highlights of the day-long event, for MRA at least, was the discussion that took place after the matinée performance between the audience members and the cast. Here was a chance for the movement to emphasise its ideology. An example of this is in a report in the *Westminster Theatre News* referring to the play *Jonas*, by Father Daniel Pearce, about a 12-year-old whose parents had decided to divorce. During the morning the director, Alby James, and the cast improvised scenes, exploring family relationships, with students aged sixteen to eighteen years. At the end of the afternoon performance the audience members were asked about the characters in the play and the way in which they communicated with each other. This is reminiscent of the work of Brazilian performance practitioner Augusto Boal and his Forum Theatre, in which scenes of conflict are played out and then solutions discussed with the audience. The MRA report says conclusions reached included families being honest with each other, acknowledging thoughts and feelings, facing reality, being a friend to others in difficulties and learning to forgive (*Westminster Theatre News*, 1981b).

A special issue of *Westminster Theatre News* in 1980, featuring the Day of London Theatre, emphasises not only the enormous success of this project but also the struggle to finance it without statutory grants. MRA playwright and director Nancy Ruthven reports that the costs of the work 'are terrifying' adding that, despite promoting the Government's policy on the arts, MRA had received no grants from the Arts Council or civic authorities but relied on funds from bodies such as the Phyllis Konstam Memorial Fund (Ruthven, 1980, p.1). Ruthven quotes the Minster for the Arts, Norman St John-Stevas, as stating; 'Man is boldly, mind and spirit. Health and

Education are vital but the arts feed people's spirit. In fact many people nowadays find their spiritual values through the arts. Art is essential in maintaining the best values of civilisation' (St John-Stevas cited in Ruthven, 1980, p.1). MRA believed its aims were the same as those of the Government and found it difficult to understand the lack of financial support:

> The plays we produce for the schools are always about the human dilemma. We have given plays about family life and the generation gap, about great Saints and great humans and their impact on civilisation, about the drug problem and how to find a real purpose in life. We have drawn our subjects from history, from the press, from the Bible, from the classics and from the classroom. The common denominator has been the element of God's spiritual dynamic that can change lives and give new direction to men and nations ... Those of us responsible for the Educational Programme draw our inspiration from a sense of God's calling. We believe it is important to the children of this country. We also believe it has a bearing on the values that emerge through the cultural voice of the nation (Ruthven, 1980, pp1–2).

St John-Stevas, who was Minster for the Arts in 1979 under Margaret Thatcher's first Conservative administration, appears to have had an enlightened attitude where the arts were concerned. He not only believed in their value but actually maintained, during his brief time in the position, government funding to the arts, despite a recession. It is quite understandable that MRA should consider that it spoke with the same 'cultural voice' as the government, promoting the same spiritual values, and should therefore receive funding. Thatcher was 'the last British prime minister openly and emphatically to acknowledge the influence of Christianity on her thinking, in particular terms not fuzzy ones' (*The Economist*, 2013, online) and St John-Stevas, educated at both Oxford and Cambridge, was a member of the establishment and also a Catholic. However, the second Thatcher administration drastically cut arts funding and the Arts Council, as will be shown in the final chapter, did not share the movement's 'cultural voice' until it was too late.

Although MRA's children's programme did not get statutory funding, other initiatives did. The first Theatre in Education project took place at Coventry's Belgrade Theatre in 1965 — just two years before the launch of the venture at the Westminster. In many ways it was similar to the MRA project in that it aimed to give young people not only a greater knowledge of the mechanics of producing a play but also 'an enjoyable and thought-provoking experience' (Belgrade Theatre, 2010, online). Where it differed from MRA was that it was teacher-led and local authority funded. Initially set up by Gordon Vallins, a former teacher, it was concerned as much with the role of Drama teachers as it was with students and one of its aims was to get Drama established as part of the curriculum. Vallins' initial proposal for Theatre in Education involved training actors as teachers who would visit schools to deliver a programme as well as presenting it at the Belgrade. His plan was to provide a free service to every state school in Coventry, and the city council agreed to put an extra halfpenny on the rates and contribute £15,000 for a trial period of twelve months. The scheme proved successful and in 1966 a permanent company was established which was granted £12,000 of ring-fenced funding on an annual basis (Belgrade Theatre, 2010, online). From the late 1960s onwards Theatre in Education became an established force throughout the country. Until 1966 theatre for young people had been explicitly excluded from Arts Council support but the Belgrade project inspired a new way of thinking. In 1965 the Arts Council set up a committee to 'enquire into the present provision of theatre for children and young people in the widest terms, to make recommendations for future development and in particular to advise on the participation of the Arts Council in such work' (Jackson, 1980, p.17). An Arts Council report in 1966, entitled 'Theatre for Young People', led to the allocation of new funds but the Day of London Theatre did not receive any of that money. When Ruthven was writing in 1980, the attitude of the Conservative government towards the Arts Council was hardly positive. Ashley Dawson comments, 'By the 1980s the very concept of state patronage of the arts was under attack with critics such as Norman Tebbit, charging that the Arts Council was politically biased' (Dawson, 2013, p.12). Presumably what Tebbit, a senior cabinet minister in the Thatcher government, was alluding to was that the arts had traditionally been thought of as liberal and leaning towards the left; certainly, the Arts Council at the time was not favourably disposed towards a moralistic, seemingly right-wing movement such as MRA. However the council had not always supported the left. Although in the mid-1950s it awarded grants to the left-wing experimental Royal Court Theatre, it refused to back Marxist Joan Littlewood's Theatre Workshop until the early 1970s when, according to Nadine Holdsworth, a 'new generation of Arts Council employees such as Philip Hedley, who eventually took over as artistic director of the Theatre Royal in 1979, recognised Littlewood's contribution to British theatre' (Holdsworth, 2006, p.41). As the 1980s progressed into the 1990s, moves were made to privatise a substantial amount of the council's revenue and encourage personal fund-raising. This could have led to a change of focus and been the reason why, in the 1990s, the Arts Council offered to contribute five and a half million of the eight million required to transform the Westminster into a Christian Arts Centre, described in the following chapter.

While there is no evidence to suggest that MRA's educational programme was trying to convert young minds to any particular religion, it is clear that its inspiration was a spiritual one and its aim was to show those participating in the programme the benefits of living by the moral standards of the movement. This gave the Day of London Theatre initiative an added dimension that other schools programmes did not have. Although the actors were professionally trained and paid, most of the other people connected with the theatre learned their craft through working at the Westminster and were volunteers united in a common aim — to encourage everyone to adopt MRA principles. Unlike Theatre in Education at the Belgrade, MRA volunteers were not trained teachers. Nevertheless, the numerous letters from schools and education authorities praising the initiative indicate that it was well run with a professional approach to performance techniques. A letter to Joy Weeks from Jill Davies, the Inner London Education Authority (ILEA) adviser on personal relationships and moral education, and George Oliver, the ILEA inspector for religious education, praises the way in which audience and actors discussed possible endings to a play about relationships and responsibilities. The letter adds that the way in which the project analysed plays and encouraged debate offered young people 'the chance to look at and even become involved in serious issues without feeling pressured. In terms of our own work in religious and moral education we value very highly the creation of this kind of open yet challenging situation' (Davies and Oliver, 1982). Geraint Lloyd-Evans, general adviser for English and Drama with the London Borough of Enfield, writes, 'I commend the Westminster Theatre for acknowledging a comprehensive understanding of what is meant by educational support as well as offering professional performances in their own right' (Lloyd-Evans, 1982). A letter from Michael Bell, inspector with the London Borough of Croydon education department, states, 'I have no hesitation in recommending schools to participate in day visits and feel pupils have much to gain in both educational and social terms' (Bell, 1982). The ILEA obviously had a high regard for the project because it devoted an entire page of a 1987 issue of *ILEA News* to a feature on the Day of London Theatre. Reporter Bernadette Tod joined pupils at the Westminster and writes 'It's not often you get the chance to tread the boards of a West End stage. But on Wednesdays and Thursdays the Westminster Theatre in Victoria make it possible with their Day of London Theatre' (Tod, 1987, p.3). Feedback forms filled in by schools include the following comments: 'It is nice to hear experts discussing the important role they play and the planning needed for a performance', 'history of theatre and a costume demonstration excellent' (feedback reports, 1988). There are some criticisms however and these indicate the inability of MRA to entirely appreciate the culture of the time, particularly in relation to the roles of women and ethnic minorities, in the catchment areas of the schools it attracted. The head of drama at Hornsey School for Girls, reflecting on a workshop attended in 1988, begins with positive comments including 'A good introduction to the whole theatrical experience — lighting, costume, sets etc.' She adds however that the programme was:

> Very ethnocentric. Our group, like most London schools, is very multi-racial. No sign that this has been acknowledged. Perhaps the girls could have talked to one of the black actresses about how they became actresses. This would include the black girls far more. Also we felt it could have been stated that stage managers, designers, lighting designers and directors are frequently women, even though this is not the case at the Westminster (feedback reports, 1988).

Whilst running the Day of London Theatre, MRA was also staging new productions for children. In 1981 Westminster Productions teamed up with Aldersgate Productions to stage a new Christmas musical, *Gavin and the Monster*, written by Steadman Williams. In an article in the *Westminster Theatre News*, Dick Channer describes the 'boldness and daring' of the new venture (Channer, 1981). As usual, the movement launched a fund-raising campaign and in six months had raised £36,000 of the £51,000 needed. This included £16,000 from Trust Funds, £75 from a group of Belfast pensioners, £100 from a London couple's house warming party, £250 from Berkshire farmers, £500 from a retired schoolmaster and many smaller donations. MRA had not lost the entrepreneurial spirit that it had shown

Figure 20: Secondary school pupils at the Day of London Theatre showing somewhat less enthusiasm for the project than their younger colleagues in Figure 17

when it raised money to buy the Westminster Theatre and to build the arts centre. Supporters cleared their attics and cupboards to sell items and Ronald Mann donated £1,000 from the sale of his water colour paintings. Channer writes that there had been 'an extraordinary response in terms of sacrifice, as scores of people up and down the country have dug deep into their pockets'. He adds that *Gavin and the Monster* was 'a bold bid to deal with the Monsters of hate, fear and greed in our midst and give God's truth a chance to reign in our land' (Channer, 1981).

In 1988 MRA took an educational theatre project on a tour of Indian public schools in order to 'discuss and illuminate through the media of theatre, important issues such as family life, addictions, the use and abuse of power, corruption and communalism. To leave behind the germ of the idea that life can be lived to a higher purpose' (Report, 1988). Over a two month period a 'Theatre in Education' tour, led by Ruthven, delivered workshops and performances to fifteen schools in Delhi, Panchgani, Dehra Dun, Ootacamund, Sanawar and Gwalior. G. Ramchandani, headmaster of the Doon School in Dehra Dun, wrote 'These young people were drawn out of their shell and started responding to the guidance with increasing self-confidence. They received encouragement at each step and we could see that the students were becoming more creative' (Ramchandani, 1988). MRA had maintained an association with India since Buchman visited the country in 1915. Edward Peters, vice president of the international council of IofC, says that Christians worked in partnership with Hindus, Sikhs, Jews, Muslims and Buddhists 'who found in MRA a common ground' (Peters, 2015, online). Rajmohan Gandhi, grandson of Mahatma, has been a key figure in the movement since the mid-1950s and was president of IofC International in 2009 and 2010. IofC has operated a centre in Panchgani, near Mumbai, since 1967 where it currently runs a series of training courses, many supported by the government, on conflict resolution and IofC principles, for a variety of professions including army officers, teachers and road sweepers.

An undated report by Westminster Productions gives details of a proposal to take a small group of actors to schools and colleges in the Soviet Union in 1990 (Report, c.1989). The report recommends approaching the British Council and other UK grant making bodies to underwrite production costs and return fares. Plays that were being considered for performance in the Soviet Union included, *Mr Wilberforce MP*, by Thornhill; *Clashpoint*, by Ruthven and Betty Gray and *A Christmas Carol* by Charles Dickens, but the proposal did not come to fruition. Steadman Williams believes the plan was instigated by Ruthven: 'She had already taken a similar tour to India. But sadly she was killed in a car crash and it was never pursued any further' (Steadman Williams, appendix 24, p.360).

Although the Day of London Theatre was criticised for being 'ethnocentric', MRA was not entirely unaware of the problems facing young people in the 1970s and 1980s. Two plays in particular addressed contemporary issues: *Clashpoint*, dealing with racial conflict and *Return Trip*, about drug abuse. The subject matter of the plays demonstrates an increasing desire by MRA to tackle controversial and problematic issues, whilst putting across its message to young people in a way that was relevant to them. An analysis of the plays shows MRA was trying not only to relate to the culture of the times but to stage its plays in a more contemporary manner. In the case of *Clashpoint*, this involved introducing popular music and breaking the theatrical 'fourth wall', by having actors appearing in the audience. However, whilst one of the writers of *Clashpoint* was actively engaged in projects involving young people in deprived areas, beyond the realms of MRA, *Return Trip* was created by two full-time, long-term supporters of the movement and the difference in approach is clear on closer investigation.

Return Trip was written in the early 1970s by Thornhill and Steadman Williams, with the Christian message superseding MRA ideology. It was not the first time the two had collaborated but this was somewhat different because the play was based on a true story. Steadman Williams recalls:

> Alan Thornhill told me about Frank Wilson, an ordained minister who had thought to open a centre for drug addicts. It had more than sixty percent success rate because he gave them a living faith in Jesus Christ. He introduced us to one young man who had come back for a second time. This man said he had found the faith to come off drugs but when he went home his parents, both academics and atheists, argued him out of it so he went back to drugs (Steadman Williams, 2015, appendix 24, p.360).

Thornhill and Steadman Williams wrote the play in just four weeks, whilst staying at the MRA conference centre in Panchgani. The premiere took place during the World Assembly of Moral Re-Armament at the Swiss conference centre in Caux on 14 July, 1974 and was translated simultaneously by volunteers into French, German, Swedish and Dutch. A report on the performance says the audience included a large number of university students as well as delegates from industry, politics and the diplomatic corps:

> A cabinet minister commented after the performance, "It showed me how easy it is to put public life ahead of family responsibilities. The first thing I have to do when I return to my country is to give time to my son who I was too busy to see before I left". A doctor commented "Totally authentic, it shows we all have addictions to something or other and what's needed to break them" (Report, 1974).

In a talk at an education conference at the Westminster Theatre Stead-man Williams highlights the problems he encountered, whilst writing *Return Trip*, in trying to portray change in human nature: 'It takes time to change but in a play you don't have much time — two hours, or if it is radio or television maybe only one hour or less' (Steadman Williams, 1975, p.2). He adds that a sudden modification in a character could lead to a loss of credibility but was advised by a television producer that this depended on what the writer did with the character after the change:

> If as a result of accepting change, life became incredibly more diffi-cult for the character, with opposition, persecution, mistakes, back-sliding, people betraying him, ruining him, destroying him then the audience accept it as much more believable. They nearly always side with the character who is battling against heavy odds ... It's what Alan Thornhill and I have tried to do with our play *Return Trip* in which we show the return of the drug addict, having been through a cure, to a hostile home environment (Steadman Williams, 1975, p.2).

But despite Steadman Williams' attempts to do otherwise, the change from newly drug-free converted Christian back to drug addict atheist does not appear realistic, as will be seen in the following analysis of the play.

Return Trip begins in the living room of the home of Ernest and Madge Barrow, a middle-class family living in a small town in the north of England and operating a bookshop on their premises. Madge is a social climber, very conscious of her position in society, and as the curtain rises she is rehearsing a speech thanking the local Member of Parliament for visiting to open a new community centre. While she is resplendent in large flowered hat, her husband is 'a scholarly, whimsical but disillusioned man who has long since given up the fight for life and sought refuge in books' (Steadman Williams and Thornhill, 1974, p.5). Their elder son Geoffrey is an ambitious young local newspaper reporter, doted on by his mother, whilst their younger son

Paul, is about to return from a drug rehabilitation centre. Madge is hoping that Geoffrey will develop a relationship with Cynthia, daughter of the newspaper proprietor, but it becomes obvious when Paul returns home that she prefers the younger brother. Act One concludes with Paul coming face to face with Elaine, the assistant in the bookshop who, unbeknown to his parents, is an addict whom Paul introduced to drugs. Paul tells his parents that the people at the rehabilitation centre introduced him to God and he proceeds to write an article for the newspaper describing his fight with addiction. Madge, who is aiming to become a magistrate, demands that he withdraw the article and Geoffrey tells him 'I wish you'd go back to the drop-outs and the addicts and the scum of the earth' (Steadman Williams and Thornhill, 1974, p.40). Paul replies, 'Let me tell you those scum, as you call them, have got more understanding and care and … Christianity in their little finger than you have in your whole body. You're like the Pharisees who've persecuted Christ all down the ages' (Steadman Williams and Thornhill, 1974, p.40). Eventually, however, Paul returns to drugs, with a little persuasion from Elaine. Steadman Williams falls into the trap he was trying to avoid — creating a change of heart that is all too quick and convenient. The following conversation appears to indicate a young man with strongly held religious beliefs:

> Elaine: You got me started, Paul. But after that I was always stronger than you wasn't I?
> Paul: You're not stronger than Christ.
> Elaine: We'll have to see about that won't we? Didn't He say 'My God, my God, why hast Thou forsaken me?'
> Paul: He rose again. Rose from the dead.
> Elaine: Did he? Look around the world. Look around this town. It's hard to be sure.
> Paul: I'm sure
> (Thornhill and Steadman Williams, 1974, p.42).

The scene ends with Elaine trying to tempt him into taking drugs again and Paul vowing he will never deny Christ: 'I won't. I won't. Never' (Thornhill and Steadman Williams, 1974, p.42). In the next scene, just three weeks later, Paul is taking drugs again and has turned his back on religion. Cynthia, however, has been so impressed by Paul's initial conversion to Christianity that, while he backtracks to atheism, she does the opposite. Both 'conversions' are too slick to be believable because Steadman Williams has not provided any build up in the text to account for their changes of heart. Just as MRA ideology is 'absolute' with no room for compromise, so the characters in *Return Trip* are either atheists or believers, drug addicts or drug free with no room for anything in between. The action continues with Paul having one drug fix too many and being taken to hospital. Ernest accompanies him and is met by Mr Carter from the drug rehabilitation centre who, according to Ernest, 'pulled a Bible out of his pocket and read the bit where Peter denied his master three times ... I tell you in that bare, ugly room, I knew Christ's presence" (Thornhill and Steadman Williams, 1974, pp 60-61). The final act is neatly, but somewhat unrealistically, concluded. All the characters have a rather dramatic, sudden change in character. Paul returns to the centre with Mr Carter; the 'perfect' son Geoffrey admits he has stolen money from his parents; the dominated unworldly husband Ernest suddenly gives 'a terrible roar such as he has never used before' and says 'Madge! You're going to learn to listen and do what you're told' (Steadman and Thornhill, 1974, p.62) and egocentric Madge becomes the devoted mother. After admitting 'I'm a lot of froth on the beer and no body to it' – an unlikely phrase for Madge to use – she announces that instead of judging others she is 'going to the hospital to see my son. After all we've got a lot in common' (Steadman Williams and Thornhill, 1974, p.63) and the curtain promptly closes. It is interesting to note that Steadman Williams and Thornhill wrote the play in just four weeks, because it is reminiscent of Howard's plots — sudden conversions which seem unbelievable not only because of the speed at which they occur but because the characters have not been drawn in any depth. Theatre critic Roger Gellert deplored the sudden conversions in *The Diplomats*, describing them as 'beatific crassness' (Gellert, 1964) and W.A. Darlington claimed Howard was not sufficiently competent as a writer to make a 'sudden change of heart believable; his characters are like puppets' (Darlington, 1964). As with Howard's plays, the characters in *Return Trip* appear one-dimensional and the language is, at times, unrealistic. It is highly unlikely, for example, that a young British man of the 1970s would have quoted the Bible quite so frequently and in such detail as Paul, and the Christian message is as unsubtle as the MRA one is in *The Diplomats*. It appears that Steadman Williams and Thornhill had fallen into the trap of attempting to tackle a controversial and highly topical subject like drug addiction, using a style and a language that failed to represent the culture of the time. By emphasising a Christian message, rather than an MRA one, the play was unlikely to have appealed to a multi-ethnic audience. By the mid-1970s, parts of London and other cities in the UK had taken on a multi-racial, multi-religious character and the overtly Christian message of *Return Trip* would have alienated whole sections of those communities. MRA reports favourable comments but there are no independent reviews available of the play to make an objective judgement. A note in the programme of *Return Trip* states 'Dealing specifically with the question of drug addiction, this play takes a searching look at family life and the reactions of a younger generation who feel the world has let them down' (programme notes, 1975). It is difficult to assess whether or not the play had an effect on young people but Mary Lean cites one teacher as commenting, after a visit to the Day of London Theatre and a performance of *Return Trip*, 'You've done more for my pupils today than I have in two years' (Lean, 1998, p.6).

Whilst it is debatable whether or not this play totally reflected the views of the young people that Steadman Williams was hoping to engage, another Day of London Theatre play, *Clashpoint*, had clearly comprehended the political situation of the time. This play, published in 1983, about conflict between Asians, blacks and whites at an inner-city comprehensive school in the North of England, was written specifically in response to the race riots two years earlier in Brixton, Southall, Toxteth, Moss Side and Handsworth. Two years later in 1985, while the play was still being performed at a variety of venues, violence erupted on the Broadwater Farm Estate, Tottenham. Sally Tomlinson describes the 1980s as 'a decade in which immigration assumed less importance as a politically exploitable issue but conflicts surrounding the acceptance of black Britons into a multiracial, multicultural society and their equal participation as citizens became the major contested issue' (Tomlinson, 2008, p.70). Tomlinson quotes the Scarman Report of 1982 as stating that the 1980s riots were the result of unemployment, poor education, discriminatory housing policies in areas where 'unemployment is high and hopes are low' and poor police methods (Scarman cited in Tomlinson, 2008, p.77). Police discounted a racial motive when thirteen young black people died in a fire at a house in New Cross, London, in January 1981. Fifteen thousand black people then marched from New Cross to Westminster demanding an end to racial murders and cabinet minister Michael Heseltine recommended a major coordinated attempt to combat racial disadvantage. Benjamin Bowling highlights the failure of the police to deal with racism during the riots. He writes:

The apparent failure to deal effectively with violent racism was only one issue among many for which the police were criticised. In particular ethnic minority communities were expressing considerable concern about policing in general, Moreover, the whole question of how the police should be held accountable to the community gained prominence (Bowling, 1998, p.17).

Clashpoint, written by Nancy Ruthven and Betty Gray, toured some of the main trouble spots of the UK including Toxteth, Brixton, St Pauls in Bristol and Chapel Town in Leeds. Gray was a member of the Newcastle Community Relations Council and the Tyneside Committee for Racial Harmony and therefore had first-hand experience of the subject matter. She had also been a teacher and says:

In writing *Clashpoint* I wanted to offer an idea that could heal the bitterness of the divisions of class and race which so affect the life of our country. The plot is based on my own experience of such an idea ... Moral Re-Armament, with its guidelines of absolute honest, purity, unselfishness and love, and its emphasis on the truth that God will show us what to do if we listen to Him, shows people the way to experience that kind of change and to relate it to the needs around them (Gray and Ruthven, 1983).

It is relevant that the authors chose not to situate their play in London – the obvious place for racial conflict. Huge changes were taking place during the 1970s and 1980s, where immigration was concerned. Colin Holmes states that in 1945 'vast areas of Britain had never engaged in any direct contact with immigrants and refugees... This situation changed within a short space of time ... Whereas in 1945 blacks and Asians had been located in London, a number of ports and as students in several university centres, by the 1970s these groups could be found in all the major conurbations in Britain' (Holmes, 1991, pp 216-217). By setting their play in the North of England, Gray and Ruthven highlight the changing and developing locations of immigrants.

Clashpoint investigates the resentment between blacks and Asians, the perception amongst whites that they are about to be overrun, the imperialist attitude of some whites that they understand and can resolve the problems of the ethnic minorities, the relevance of Christianity, trade unions, Marxist philosophy and of course the importance of MRA ideology. While it attempts to tackle too many issues at once and therefore lacks a certain depth, it is obvious that the authors have a clear understanding of the attitudes of the different groups they portray, something which is lacking in *Return Trip*. The authors' descriptions of the cast at the beginning of the script reveal a degree of stereotyping that reflects the period in which it was written. Head of the school is Mrs Clarke Jones, a white middle-aged 'Cambridge-type educator' and the deputy is Mr Mohan Varna, an Indian with a 'quiet and wise authority about him' who represents the MRA ideology (Gray and Ruthven, 1983, p.1). He tells head boy Suresh Pathak, who is 'Indian, brainy and mature for his age' to listen to the inner voice, seeking the 'absolute truth, the way Mahatma Gandhi taught us' (Gray and Ruthven, 1983, p.11). Suresh's father is conscious of class divisions, the importance of education and his position in society. He has a shop but hopes that if his son becomes a doctor or a lawyer 'they'll all respect us' (Gray and Ruthven, 1983, p.10). Deputy head boy is Cornelius Browne, 'West Indian, big, explosive and extrovert' whose mother Hazel is 'a staunch member of the church'. Other characters include pupil Pat Jennings; her mother Rose, 'deep in every sort of political activity', and president of SWOP, the Society for World Oppressed People; Pat's father Tom, who is branch secretary of his firm's union and Pat's unemployed brother, John (Gray and Ruthven, 1983, p.1).

The first act begins with an investigation by the Headmistress into a fight that has broken out in the playground following the distribution of leaflets from the British League containing the words: 'The Battle's lost if we're too feeble, East Moor School for our own white people' (Gray and Ruthven, 1983, p.6). In the 1980s there were a number of relatively minor fascist groups operating in Britain. The most effective was the British National Party developed, the year before *Clashpoint* was published, by John Tyndall from his New National Front Party. In the 1940s, when MRA purchased the Westminster, one of the main fascist groups was the British League of Ex-Servicemen and Women, formed in 1937 as a former soldiers' welfare group but which became absorbed into Oswald Mosley's Union Movement in 1948. It is possible that Ruthven and Gray based their 'British League' on an amalgamation of these two groups.

The issues between blacks and Asians are explored through the relationship between Suresh and Cornelius. Suresh complains of Cornelius, 'He talks big all the time as though his lot were the only ones who get discrimination ... my mum — she can't speak English and these kids come and shove her off the pavement and she won't go out of the house alone now' (Gray and Ruthven, 1983, pp 9-10). Cornelius tells Suresh: 'All we hear is how brilliant you are — scholarship to University, a credit to East Moor School. I tell you man, it makes me sick' (Gray and Ruthven, 1983, p.19). Suresh says that respecting his parents is part of his culture adding 'you haven't any culture of your own, that's why you don't like ours', to which Cornelius replies 'We got culture — three hundred years of British culture' (Gray and Ruthven, 1983, p.19). His resentment is obvious when he says to Suresh 'There'll be a job waiting for you. Making up prescriptions in daddy's shop' (Gray and Ruthven, 1983, p.20). Suresh has the close, traditional family background associated with the Asian community whilst Cornelius is from a one-parent family. His mother, Mrs Browne, urges him to be friends with Suresh, quoting from the Bible and telling him 'I walked without shoes to get my education ... if you had a daddy now you'd get a good beating for your lazy ways' (Gray and Ruthven, 1983, p.21). Although Mrs Browne quotes frequently from the Bible it is easier to tolerate than the preaching tone of *Return Trip*, possibly because in the 1980s the black community was associated with the charismatic Pentecostal church and was one step removed from the white, Church of England, version of Christianity. It was stereotypical, but nonetheless more culturally acceptable, for a black woman to spout Bible verses than for a white former drug addict son of an academic bookshop owner to do so.

The next scene begins with Cornelius singing a song reflecting the hopelessness of ethnic minority groups in the 1980s, which is still relevant in the twenty-first century:

> Feel like the whole world's stacked against me.
> Ain't got nobody to be my friend.
> There don't seem no way out of this prison
> When will it end, I'm asking, when will it end
> (Gray and Ruthven, 1983, p.23).

Feelings of isolation and economic deprivation, such as those expressed by Cornelius, were experienced by many of the ethnic minorities in Britain in the 1980s, and led to the riots mentioned earlier. Colin Holmes claims immigrants continued to suffer from discrimination throughout the second half of the twentieth-century:

In considering the history of post-war immigration and its consequences, it is difficult to detect any automatic, inexorable cycle of development as a result of which immigrants and refugees have moved from an initial encounter with hostility, through a later stage of toleration, towards the nirvana of acceptance ... In considering the post-war history of immigration some positive changes can be detected. However, there is no shortage of evidence to indicate that since 1945 immigrants and refugees in Britain have encountered persistent antipathy and relative disadvantage (Holmes, 1991, p.229).

In *Clashpoint* Cornelius feels victimised not only by the white community but by other ethnic minorities and by the authority that is charged with protecting him, namely the police.

Having identified some of the issues surrounding racism, the authors go on to investigate the divisions within families, the role of women and the attitude of the white community towards immigration. Rose Jennings is planning a march on behalf of SWOP but her family resents her involvement in politics and daughter Pat claims: 'You can't move without falling over banners and leaflets. We live half the time out of the freezer and the other half fending for ourselves on what's left over' (Gray and Ruthven, 1983, p.26). Mr Jennings, the trade unionist, observes that his wife has neglected to water his prize leeks: 'You didn't water them did you, Rose? You didn't bloody water them! Here give me a cup of tea' (Gray and Ruthven, 1983, p.27). Meanwhile their unemployed son John announces he has become a political activist: 'I'm not going to be cheap labour fodder for some firm' (Gray and Ruthven, 1983, p.28), to which his father replies, 'Get off your backside, John, and get yourself a job — any job' (Gray and Ruthven, 1983, p.28). Although Mrs Jennings believes she is championing the rights of the 'oppressed', Mrs Browne is concerned at the aggressive way in which SWOP, clearly consisting mainly of white people, is campaigning on behalf of ethnic minorities. 'There must be another way to get justice for our people' she says and begins quoting from the Bible: 'All they that take the sword shall perish with the sword' (Gray and Ruthven, 1983, p.32). Mrs Jennings tells her that Christianity is a drug 'What's it done for your people? Christian men kept them as slaves and helped themselves to your women, after reading the Bible every day, of course' (Gray and Ruthven, 1983, p.32). The two women learn that the British League is going to hold a march at the same time as SWOP and Mrs Browne warns that marching past the school could result in violence and children getting hurt. When Mrs Browne decides to resign from SWOP, Mrs Jennings reveals her own prejudices by crying out, 'You can't resign, you're the only West Indian we've got on the committee ... This march is for your people' (Gray and Ruthven, 1983, p.33). Mrs Browne replies 'You don't give a damn about my people ... You have all these laws about race discrimination and social workers running around the place ... And who controls it all? ... whites like you. You don't really care about us or listen to what we say' (Gray and Ruthven, 1983, pp. 33–34). It seems that even with the best of intentions the white British population could not resist its imperialist roots and continued trying to control the ethnic minorities.

Suresh and Cornelius finally find a way to work together, through a mutual love of cricket and meet in a cafe run by an Irishman, Paddy. This gives the authors the chance to refer to the Irish conflict with Paddy announcing 'Everyone in my country joins one thing, marches for another – and they're none of them any bloody good' (Gray and Ruthven, 1983, p.38). Suresh, Cornelius and Pat decide to form SFPWA, the Society For Putting the World Aright, and it is no coincidence that the ethnic minority, in the shape of Mrs Browne, delivers the MRA message to them: 'If you want to put the world right, you've got to start with yourself' (Gray and Ruthven, 1983, p.40). Pat urges Mrs Browne to make peace with Mrs Jennings and the two women agree to meet. During that meeting Mrs Jennings explains that she is a Marxist, as 'it's the only possible route to economic justice' (Gray and Ruthven, 1983, p.45) and reveals her resentment at being turned down as a governor of the school because of her political beliefs. She then admits that this is the real reason she is staging the march past the school, at the same time as the fascists. At this point Mr Jennings appears, furious that his son has been handing out SWOP leaflets and undermining his work with the union. He tells his wife 'I've had enough ... you don't give a damn about me Rose, you don't give a damn about my meals, my men ... did you water those leeks? ... Every black in the country comes before me ... Indians, Chinese? ... women's libbers? ... nuclear crackpots ... they all come before me' (Gray and Ruthven, 1983, p.50). No doubt Mr Jennings' comments about 'nuclear crackpots and women's libbers' refer to the Greenham Common Women's Peace Camps which began in 1981 and were protesting at the Government's decision to allow United States cruise missiles to be based in the area. At the time the play was written, women were becoming increasingly professionally and financially independent and beginning to encroach on the traditionally male-dominated world of politics. However, Mr Jennings clearly believes his wife's role is to cater for his every need, reflecting the fact that women in the 1980s were still regarded, on a number of levels, as inferior to men. Joel Krieger says, 'Until the 1986 Social Security Act, the household was treated as a single unit for the assessment of supplementary benefits and the award was payable to the man of the house rather than his married or cohabiting partner' (Krieger, 1999, p.91). Mr Jennings' outburst regarding ethnic minorities highlights the effect that Thatcher had on racism. Stephen Howe writes, 'Empire had been the incubator of British racism and an alleged atavistic revival of aggressively imperialist emotions under Thatcher ... had renewed or intensified this with the acquiescence or even active encouragement of the Prime Minister herself' (Howe, 2012, p.247). The next scene begins with John walking through the audience armed with leaflets and chanting, 'Join the anti-fascist march, protect your rights, protect your freedom ... I want a job, I want a place, I want the world to listen because I am me, I want a goal that is worth it. I want to make a difference, I want a world of justice, I want a destiny' (Gray and Ruthven, 1983, p.53). Through John the writers show their understanding of some of the underlying causes of the riots in addition to racism. Young people, regardless of race, were suffering the effects of unemployment, leading to feelings of hopelessness. In 1982 Thatcher was heckled in the House of Commons after it was revealed that unemployment had risen to more than three million for the first time since the 1930s, with one in eight people out of work (British Broadcasting Corporation, 2005 online).

The day of the demonstration dawns and, in the headmistress's study, both Mrs Clarke Jones and Mr Varma are preparing themselves for trouble. They have staff on every door as they are warned that the two opposing groups will be passing the building, with around three thousand representing the British League and five thousand SWOP. Mrs Jennings and Mrs Browne arrive at the school asking to see the head and Mrs Clark Jones initially refuses, describing Mrs Jennings as a 'rabid communist' (Gray and Ruthven, 1983, p.55). The following conversation highlights the problems faced by those in the white community when they decide to back the cause of the ethnic minorities

Mrs Clarke Jones:	I get on well with most of the other parents but I always feel waves of dislike coming my way whenever I meet her [Mrs Jennings].
Mr Varma:	She's always very friendly to me.
Mrs Clarke Jones:	Of course she is, Mohan, you're one of the immigrant community. You're persona grata with that kind of women. Me, I'm a wasp, the wicked middle-class white! It's a new type of snobbery
Mr Varma:	Does it bother you?
Mrs Clarke Jones:	It irritates me! I think it's all so mindless – this interminable preoccupation with outdated class concepts (Gray and Ruthven 1983, p.56).

When Mrs Jennings finally gets to meet Mrs Clarke Jones she urges the headmistress to use her public address system to call off the SWOP march adding that she has changed her views and has information that the British League is planning to rush the school gates and place its banner over the sixth form centre. Mrs Clark Jones refuses to act but Mrs Jennings then reveals that she lived in the same street as the headmistress as a child, only at the 'working class end' (Gray and Ruthven, 1983, p.58). Mrs Jennings describes being bullied at school for being poor and resenting Mrs Clarke Jones becoming headmistress because 'I felt you were the wrong person to take care of children who were the victims of race and class discrimination' (Gray and Ruthven, 1983, p.59). Just as Howard did in his plays, Gray and Ruthven show that conflicts between communities originate in conflicts between individuals and therefore difficulties can only be resolved 'through personal change ... public unrest is rooted in private unrest' (Boobbyer, 2005, p.211). As the women are talking, shouting can be heard from outside, with the British League chanting 'England for the English, niggers out, niggers out' and SWOP crying 'No discrimination in East Moor School. Fascists, fascists, kill, kill kill' (Gray and Ruthven, 1983. p.59). There are clashes in the school playground, shops in the city are looted, cars set on fire, petrol bombs hurled, police injured and Cornelius suffers a fractured skull. As the lights fade on the scene, an announcer is heard stating 'the coloured youth injured during fighting on the school premises is still in a critical condition' (Gray and Ruthven, 1983, p.61). The final scene takes place in the sitting room of Mrs Browne's home with everyone resolving their conflicts. Mrs Browne announces that her son will take two years to recover and may never be entirely fit again, while Mrs Jennings admits that she is praying for forgiveness from both God and Mrs Browne. Cornelius appears and begins to open a present from Mr Varma. It is a book on Martin Luther King and the play ends with Cornelius reciting from the famous 'I have a dream' speech — a fitting end to a play that promotes MRA moral standards and racial harmony. Luther King's dream of a world where 'all of God's children, black men and white men, Jews and Gentiles, Protestants and Catholics will be able to join hands and sing in the words of the old Negro spiritual "Free at last! Free at last! Thank God Almighty, we are free at last"' is consistent with the MRA vision of the future (Luther King cited in Clayton, 1968, p.118).

There are no reviews of the play in the archives but one of the original performers provides an insight into the audience response it received at the time. Christine Channer toured with the play as well as performing in it at the Westminster. She alternated between portraying Mrs Clarke Jones and Rose Jennings, and describes her experiences:

> The cast was a good mix of Carib/Brits, Indian/Brits, Coloured South African/Brits and us white/Brits, and we were touring all the trouble spots as well as the Day of London Theatre. That is where one got the most public feedback ... How one can quantify the effect one just doesn't know, but all one can say is that the audience hung about for a long time after the curtain had come down just wanting to talk and discuss. The ideological thing about it was that it was

created to answer a problem in the country (Channer, appendix 3, p.292).

Channer reveals that the 'clashpoints' were not confined to the stage:

> We were living in each other's pockets on tour, which is what usually happens, and hurt feelings, misunderstandings, etc, would get aired in the time we always had together before the show. Things needed to be sorted out before we went on stage for the play to have the special power it did have. It wasn't a great masterpiece of writing, but it was a genuine piece written for the sake of people and the country so it had to have that integrity between us to hit home (Channer, appendix 3, p.292).

Despite the apparent success of plays such as *Clashpoint* and the positive feedback on its work with schoolchildren, the Day of London Theatre finally came to an end in 1989 and it seems that there is doubt about the exact reason for its demise. Christine Channer believes one reason could have been that the chief organiser got married, moved to New Zealand and there was no-one to replace her. However, Elisabeth Tooms, a leading member of Renewal Arts, the artistic arm of IofC, who has been associated with the Westminster Theatre since the 1970s, says, in an email, 'I always understood that it came to an end because of a change in the funding that schools were able to get in order to pay for taking pupils to things like A Day of London Theatre. So it was more a victim of a change in policy' (Tooms, 2015). Tooms' view seems to be the most likely. The 1988 Education Reform Act, known as the Baker Act after Secretary of State Kenneth Baker, introduced the National Curriculum and paved the way for the abolition of the ILEA. Derek Gillard comments, 'The Act was presented as giving power to the schools. In fact, it took power away from the Local Education Authorities and the schools and gave them all to the Secretary of State' (Gillard,

2011, online). Gillard continues that the introduction of the National Curriculum prevented teachers in schools from delivering 'curriculum innovation [and] demoted them to curriculum delivery' (Gillard, 2011, online). The Belgrade project also suffered from the 1988 Act, claiming that 'the management of school budgets was devolved to individual institutions, meaning LEAs lost the power to provide city-wide schemes ... There was an ideological and organisational shift within the country's education system and the new atmosphere was not conducive to the autonomy and flexibility to which TiE [Theatre in Education] companies had become accustomed' (Belgrade Theatre, 2010, online).

Just as the Day of London Theatre was closing, the Westminster was embarking on another innovative and successful programme — First Floor Theatre. Unfortunately, however, that initiative was to last for only one year and was the forerunner to the most disastrous decade in the theatre's history. The road from success to near bankruptcy is detailed in the following chapter.

6

A Step Too Far – 'Temptation' Puts an End to a New Beginning

One crucial test of any theatre or any culture is: does it or does it not equip us to deal with the age we are living in (Kenneth Belden, 1968, p.7).

Although Belden did his best to keep the theatre operating as a viable force following the death of Howard and although the Day of London Theatre proved to be a major success, MRA was beset by disputes, which escalated as the twentieth century drew to a close. One of the first major confrontations occurred during the late 1960s and early 1970s when there was a split between the movements in Britain and America. Whilst the British contingent wanted to concentrate on promoting the four standards and listening to God, the American arm was more concerned with staging large-scale musicals, which attracted numerous young people, but, according to the British, compromised the essential core beliefs. Steadman Williams describes the difference as 'a tension between the message and the art' (Steadman Williams, appendix 23, p.263). According to him, the Americans got sponsorship for the shows from commercial outlets, but as a result the message was toned down. In addition, he claims 'The Americans sold off a lot of our assets such as the Mackinac Island conference centre and all the money went into the shows' (Steadman Williams, appendix 23, p.354). A casualty of the dispute was Louis Fleming, director of the Westminster Arts Centre, who had an American mother, Canadian father and grew up in Canada. In a tribute at his funeral in January 2015, Steadman Williams describes, Fleming's time at the Arts Centre as becoming 'increasingly unhappy':

> An unfortunate split had occurred between the work of MRA in Britain and that in America. The deeper the divide became the more an atmosphere of fear and control came to dominate the British work. Lou, because of his many associations with friends in America, was regarded with suspicion. He was increasingly side-lined and found that decisions were being taken elsewhere and that he had become largely a figurehead. To Lou, a big man with big vision and big ideas and immense capabilities, this eventually became intolerable. In 1975 he resigned and returned to Canada (Steadman Williams, appendix 24, p.360).

Fleming died on Christmas Eve 2014, aged 89. He described, in an interview for this book two years earlier, his feeling of alienation and his view of some of the British supporters:

> The British leadership in MRA saw that a lot of money was being spent on the Westminster. They were not interested in film and drama but they didn't have an alternative. In 1975 I decided to go back to Canada as the Westminster had fizzled out as far as MRA plays were concerned. I can remember taking morning walks and thinking 'What on earth are we going to do with the Westminster?' There were people in the British leadership who wanted to keep the message 'pure and simple' and the American MRA group which was very active and felt totally undermined by the leadership. Buchman would have sent those British academics out of Britain so they didn't have a chance to set up their own fiefdoms and I think that would have been right (Fleming, appendix 7, p.300).

The split between America and Britain was a taste of what was to come in the 1980s and 1990s, when there was intense disagreement over the future role of the Westminster.

Figure 21: Hugh Steadman Williams

MRA worked closely during the late 1970s and 1980s with Aldersgate Productions as well as hiring out the Westminster to banks, The Globe Players and the BBC for their own events. Christmas 1979 was celebrated with a successful run of the musical *Joseph and his Technicolour Dreamcoat*, starring pop singer Paul Jones. In the early 1980s popular professional productions included *The Jeweller's Shop*, written by Pope John Paul II and directed by Bill Kenwright, who went on to become one of the West End's leading impresarios. The play starred leading British actresses Hannah Gordon and Gwen Watford. Clive Dunn, of the television series *Dad's Army*, played the leading role in *The Gingerbread Man* and nearly two thousand under-privileged children saw Steadman Williams' play *Gavin and the Monster* (*Westminster Theatre News*, 1982). The Day of London Theatre also continued to prove popular throughout the decade. However, costs were rising; it was becoming more and more difficult to fill seats and there were not enough MRA plays being written. There were those within the movement who believed that the theatre was no longer the most effective means of promoting the message. Chris Evans, former chairman of the Board of Trustees of the Oxford Group, the governing body of MRA, and its treasurer from 1991 to 2003, says that throughout the 1980s he and others were examining which initiatives were having most effect. He believed that other targeted projects were meeting a need that the theatre was not. In his view:

> The financial and human sustainability was an issue. The sheer effort of keeping it [the theatre] going. People were getting older, people's attention was moving elsewhere. The network around the country was unable to give it the energy they had done in the past. It was getting a steeper and steeper road to follow (Evans, appendix 6, p.299).

Not surprisingly there were many with an opposing viewpoint. Steadman Williams says:

> The 1980s were a very difficult time for the Westminster as there was a constant battle about whether we should keep the theatre or not. In the mid-1980s the management introduced The Pause during which, for a couple of years, virtually no plays were staged and only video productions were made. There were big disagreements and a lot of people felt the Westminster was taking up too much of our resources and too many people. They felt it wasn't worth it but there were others like me who were passionate about it (Steadman Williams, appendix 24, p.360).

Christine Channer was against any plans to get rid of the Westminster and reveals the depth of feeling within the movement: 'I fought against the whole business of the theatre. I very often felt we were battling with knives in our backs from our best friends. It was very difficult as we were giving all of our art for "nowt" and we felt that some of our team were not behind us' (Channer, appendix 3, p.292).

In 1988 those supporting the theatre had a breakthrough when a deal was struck in which Westminster Productions, the resident production company, took over the entire running of the theatre from the Oxford Group. However, it remained a difficult time, both emotionally and financially. A year before the take-over, the play *The Miracle Worker* by William Gibson, about the life of deaf/blind author and political activist Helen Keller, closed early and, according to a report, 'through the unaccountable failure of that moving play we fell flat on our faces' (*Westminster Theatre News*, 1988, p.7). Some Friends of the Westminster Theatre believe, in hindsight, that the failure was a result of not having any well-known names in the cast to attract the general public. MRA supporters, however, proved once again that when finance was needed they were generous to a fault. A report in the *Westminster Theatre News* reveals that, following the announcement of the closure of *The Miracle Worker*, one person donated £10,000 from the sale of her house to boost funds; other Friends of the Westminster Theatre gave individual sums ranging from £3 to £1,000 and the Christian Arts Trust donated £5,000. Altogether £31,000 was raised in gifts and £10,000 in interest-free loans (*Westminster Theatre News*, 1988, p.7).

Although it had an enviable degree of patronage, the Westminster was the only Christian-based member of the Society of West End Theatres and had specific disadvantages compared with its competitors. It was small, in London terms, with around six hundred seats, and because the Oxford

Group wanted only plays staged that had a Christian or a positive theme, this would have restricted audience appeal and inevitably have affected profitability. Among those involved in taking over the running of the theatre was the assistant manager John Locke (fig. 22). Inspired by the Theatre Upstairs at the Royal Court, which was renowned for presenting ground-breaking new work, Locke and his colleagues set about transforming an upstairs room into the First Floor Theatre (FFT).

Figure 22: John Locke

Their aim was to attract Christian companies and to show cutting edge new work whilst at the same time, in the main theatre space, present plays written by people not specifically associated with the MRA ideology. The culture that was emerging in the 1980s provided MRA with the ideal environment in which to present new writing on current and controversial issues to a more traditional theatre-going public, neglected in previous decades by the Royal Court and by anti-establishment practitioners such as Joan Littlewood. FFT aimed to fulfil Belden's early dream of creating work that would 'equip us to deal with the age we are living in' (Belden, 1968b, p.7). Although MRA did not reflect the sexual revolution and cultural changes that took place in the 1960s and 1970s, as the 1980s progressed and Margaret Thatcher's Conservative government increased in popularity, the movement's absolute standards and its emphasis on the power of the individual began to take on a new relevance. John Campbell says Thatcher's aim was 'the moral reinvigoration of the nation' and quotes her as declaring, in 1981, 'Economics is the method ... the object is to change the soul' (Thatcher cited in Campbell, 2008, p.5). In her 1987 speech to the Conservative Party Conference Thatcher's views on morality echoed those of Howard and Belden: 'Civilised society doesn't just happen. It has to be sustained by standards widely accepted and upheld. And we must draw on the moral energy of society. And we must draw on the values of family life' (Thatcher, 1987, online). She claimed 'When the broadcasters flout their own standards on violent television programmes, they risk a brutalising effect on the morally unstable ... local councils, teachers, broadcasters, politicians: all of us have a responsibility to uphold the civilised values which underpin the law' (Thatcher, 1987, online). Howard, like Thatcher, believed the media was a powerful tool for both good and evil and that, if exposed to immoral or violent ideas, an audience could go out into the streets 'more animal like than when they went in' (Howard cited in Boobbyer, 2005, p.210). One MRA supporter recalls that many within the movement were pro-Thatcher when it came to upholding traditional family values, morals and making a stand against the unions. Stanley Kiaer, administrator of the Westminster Theatre and founder of the Institute of Business Ethics, maintains that, whilst MRA did much in its early years to resolve conflicts within the mining industry, by the 1980s the National Union of Mineworkers under Arthur Scargill[13] had become 'too strong' (Kiaer, 2015, conversation). He also highlights the collapse of the British shipbuilding industry in the 1980s commenting, 'Places like Korea were building them cheaper. Not everything was Mrs Thatcher's fault' (Kiaer, 2015, conversation).

Locke believed that FFT was the 'chance of a lifetime' for MRA theatre to become relevant again, adding 'We knew a substantial number of Christian-based theatre companies that were touring but did not have a base in London. We felt we could use the room upstairs as a show case and invite these groups to London. The Westminster Theatre could become a home of Christian positive theatre in the country' (Locke, appendix 16, p.329). In the February 1989 issue of *Westminster Theatre News*, Westminster Productions published its aims. These included providing entertaining, relevant work of artistic excellence exploring 'hope, in a world of fear, cynicism and defeatism; compassion, in an age of violence, hatred and indifference; faith,

---

[13] Arthur Scargill was president of the National Union of Mineworkers (NUM) from 1981–2002 and the figurehead of the March 1984 strike in response to pit closures. A year later the NUM voted to return to work, resulting in a huge defeat for Scargill and the union and a political victory for Thatcher.

in a climate of materialism, scepticism and meaninglessness' (*Westminster Theatre News*, 1989, p.7). The article continues, in the same rhetorical tone familiar to MRA supporters:

> Under our management we will aim to stir up at the Westminster Theatre a challenging ferment of creativity, appealing to a spirit of daring and adventure in artist and audience alike. It will be no place for the timid, the faint-hearted, the compromiser (*Westminster Theatre News*, 1989a, p.7).

In April 1989, a memo to leading members of Westminster Productions from Ronald Mann, who founded Aldersgate Productions, gave details of the way in which FFT was to be financed through trusts, business sponsorship and an endowment fund. The proposal was to underwrite the venture for at least the first two years; to create a list of ten thousand supporters by the end of 1990 and from that list to make a bid to create an endowment fund (Mann, 1989). In May 1989, a report in the *Westminster Theatre News* explained how the upstairs theatre would be a dual use area, operating as a dining room during the day and a one hundred and eight-seat theatre space at night. There were to be two seasons a year, of ten weeks each, consisting of both in-house MRA shows and visiting productions (*Westminster Theatre News*, 1989b, p.3). An article by Nancy Ruthven states that FFT would provide a platform for new writers and encourage debate after the shows. While the main auditorium would present established works and be self-financing, FFT would stage new plays on controversial subjects and provide a London venue for a number of touring companies sympathetic to the MRA ethos: 'These productions could run for two to three weeks each ... draw a vital young audience and not cost the earth to mount' (Ruthven, 1989, p.3). Ruthven refers to the ethos of the Royal

Court's Theatre Upstairs, and its aim in the 1960s to encourage new writing, adding 'The Westminster Theatre wants to provide a venue where new young writers can try out their work and sharpen their skills and ideas' (Ruthven, 1989, p.4). Claiming that there was 'a crying need' for plays about faith and moral and spiritual dilemmas, she states that FFT should encourage people to 'think ... to ask themselves the right questions ... there is a chemistry about a small venue which is sometimes missing in a bigger auditorium. The stage and audience become one. People go away with new ideas for life' (Ruthven, 1989, p.4).

The Royal Court was continuing to work with new writers at the time FFT was established and although ideologically very different to the Westminster, suffered similar divisions within its ranks which threatened its future. In the 1980s, under the artistic directorship of Max Stafford-Clark, the Royal Court faced both financial disaster, in the shape of Ian Dury's play *Apples* and success with Timberlake Wertenbaker's *Our Country's Good*. Philip Roberts says that 1985 in particular was 'a difficult and depressing year ... The ability of the Court to sustain writers had become sharply diminished' (Roberts, 1999, p.192). Stafford-Clark had a rocky relationship with both the hierarchy at the Court and the Arts Council and for nine months in 1989, a short while before the launch of FFT, Theatre Upstairs had its own 'Pause' and stopped presenting plays altogether. However, there was a political shift taking place in Europe and Dominic Shellard writes, 'As the eighties drew to an end with the collapse of communist regimes throughout Europe and the fall of the Berlin Wall, Stafford-Clark reaffirmed the Royal Court's commitment to political writing and new drama' (Shellard, 2000, p.222). FFT differed from Theatre Upstairs in that its priority was to create a space for discussion about its own ideology. While it wanted to encourage new writing, it was essential that the MRA message was delivered by the final curtain. As a result, FFT offered an experience that was not being presented elsewhere on the London stage – plays in which current and controversial issues were contextualised within the ideology of the movement.

John Locke, who began his theatrical career with the National Youth Theatre productions of *Zigger Zagger*, *Macbeth* and *Twelfth Night* and later joined Joan Littlewood's Theatre Workshop company, was appointed manager of FFT. He had appeared in a number of London productions and his credits included film and television work. At one time, he was the youngest member of Equity ever to be elected to the governing body. FFT's artistic director was Carol Henderson, who had less experience in the theatre than Locke but a background that would have appealed to MRA. Announcing her appointment, the *Westminster Theatre News* states that she was educated at top independent girls' school Roedean and came from a 'distinguished family with strong Christian roots' (*Westminster Theatre News*, 1989b, p.4). Her grandfather, Sir William Dobbie, was Governor of Malta during World War Two, and her father Colonel Orde Dobbie was the original chairman of the Christian Nationwide Festival of Light, which was supported by Malcolm Muggeridge, Cliff Richard and that guardian of the public morals, clean-up TV campaigner Mary Whitehouse. Henderson had been a nurse but had given up her career because of a back injury and went on to work on features and documentaries for Dutch television. Described in the *Westminster Theatre News* as an 'avid theatre goer' she was married to Liverpool poet Stewart Henderson. The disparity in the theatrical experience of Locke and Henderson, with Locke having a far greater hands-on knowledge of the industry, could have been a reason for their difference of opinion regarding the way in which the venture was to be financed. An appeal for FFT raised £100,000 but Locke did not think this was a substantial enough sum to enter into contractual agreements with paying artists and companies. He was also concerned about the Westminster Theatre's reputation amongst the public at large:

> Companies needed to take responsibility for filling the place as much as the Westminster. I wanted to operate on a box office split from the very beginning as this would establish the nature of the venue and its relationship with incoming companies. Carol wanted an initial impact, to hit the ground running. She felt it would take too long to promote the theatre as a venue, that our position would not necessarily be trusted because of historical reticence about the Westminster Theatre and that we needed to approach existing groups and build a programme that would be attractive to Christian audiences (Locke, appendix 16, p.329).

Locke adds that the cost of equipping the theatre was a modest £20,000. Between £500 and £1,000 was paid a week to in-coming shows, apart from special performances which could cost as much as £1,000 a night. The budget was £30,000 a season but by the end of the second season a total of £80,000 of the £100,000 bank balance had been spent. Locke claims:

> Even if we filled it every night we could not cover the costs of the season … Carol's seasons were of outstandingly high quality but managing them on a theatre basis, whilst operating the Westminster Theatre, also presented a number of logistical problems in terms of audience management. There were also certain frictions between those in the building who were not happy at the loss of the space as a staff restaurant (Locke, appendix 16, p.329).

He claims however that these difficulties were relatively minor compared with the problem of persuading incoming companies to promote their shows when the fact that there was no box office split left them with no real incentive to do so. During the second season Locke managed to persuade Westminster City Council to provide its first ever grant to a West End theatre company, on the basis that FFT was providing a studio theatre for local young people. 'They gave £1,000. This was a phenomenal breakthrough but I was concerned that at the end of the second season there was insufficient money for the next season. As it turned out the issue was sterile because there was insufficient money to continue running the main house' (Locke, appendix 16, p.329).

Despite financial problems, FFT had what Locke describes as 'two absolutely scintillating, glorious, exciting seasons that were spectacularly successful ... The first season had seventy to seventy-eight per cent capacity and the second over eighty per cent capacity. We took full page ads in Christian newspapers and magazines. It was a wonderful conception – theatre with a positive approach that attracted audiences of all persuasions and not only Christian audiences' (Locke, appendix 16, p.329). One of the early plays to be performed at FFT, in November 1989, was Ruthven's *The Widening Gyre* about Britain's relationship with Northern Ireland. Ruthven, who was associate director of the Westminster Theatre, was killed in a car accident, at the age of sixty-two, whilst on her way to the Edinburgh Fringe Festival just a month before FFT opened. A review of her play by William Cook, written for *City Limits*, and published in the *Westminster Theatre News*, provides an insight into why FFT attracted such good audiences. Cook claims that *The Widening Gyre* involved 'conservative audiences in a debate from which less cuddly drama excludes them and in its own small way re-affirms what a bloody mess we're all in over "England's Ireland"' (Cook cited in *Westminster Theatre News*, 1990a, p.4). As Cook observes, MRA was catering for a section of the public that did not feel comfortable with the left-wing exper-

imental theatre that existed in places like the Royal Court or Joan Littlewood's Theatre Royal, Stratford. The FFT audiences wanted to watch theatre that dealt with controversial issues but was delivered to them in a con-
ventional manner, rather than in the style of Harold Pinter, Edward Bond
or Joe Orton, for example. The movement was providing the kind of theatre
that those who supported the ideology and the moral standards of MRA
could identify with and which was becoming increasingly popular again in
the culture of the 1980s. Stanley Baran and Dennis Davis quote philosopher John Dewey as believing that 'communities, not isolated individuals,
use communication (and the media of communication) to create and maintain the culture that binds and sustains them' (Dewey cited in Baran and
Davis, 2015, p.52). Nicholas Cull, David Culbert and David Welch claim
that 'propagandists assess the context and the audience and use whatever
methods and means they consider most appropriate and effective' (Cull,
Culbert and Welch, 2003, p. xx). FFT appeared to have successfully assessed
its audience and the critics were far more positive than in previous decades,
indicating that its 'methods' were proving to be effective. Cook writes 'Terence Rattigan — eat your heart out' and describes *The Widening Gyre* as 'long
on soliloquy, short on interplay' but adds 'meticulous characterisation from
playwright and players alike renders this contrived drama nonetheless com-
pulsive' (Cook cited in *Westminster Theatre News*, 1990a, p.4). Paul Chand
in *The Stage* claims 'characters tend to spout politics, but it's a stimulating
well-made play' (Chand cited in *Westminster Theatre News*, 1990a, p.4). James
Kingston in *The Times* claims the play is 'not, strictly speaking, an MRA job,
though she [Ruthven] appears to have been a member and her play shares
the general style of simplifying problems. At least she does not insult us by
advancing a simple solution' (Kingston, 1989). Other plays staged at FFT in

its first season included *The Letter* by Ann Clifford about marriage break-up, a lesbian relationship and child abuse and *Adult Child/Dead Child* by Claire Dowie, about a child denied love and affection. In its first year FFT attracted 2,400 members, presented eighteen shows in eighteen weeks, eleven of them new works, staged ninety performances and had a total audience of 4,500 (Locke, 1990, p.4). However, FFT was proving to be expensive and an unforeseen disaster was lurking in the wings.

Although FFT began operating in September 1989 it did not have its official opening until 19 April, 1990, when pop singer Cliff Richard was the star guest at a gala attended by two hundred people. Richard unveiled a plaque listing the names of the founder members who had each donated £400 to launch the project. He is quoted in a report on the opening: 'A new showcase for performers and another option for punters have to be good news for London's theatre world' (Richard cited in *Westminster Theatre News*, 1990b, p.5). Also in attendance was Luke Rittner, general secretary of the Arts Council, who announced 'First Floor Theatre, as challenging as it can be rewarding, is particularly welcome as it can satisfy a whole variety of needs right across the arts spectrum' (Rittner cited in *Westminster Theatre News*, 1990b, p.5). The support of the Arts Council is indicative of the way in which this organisation altered its funding policy in the late 1980s. Shellard writes: 'The gradual withdrawing of funding from politically provocative companies such as Joint Stock and the Scottish 7:84 company had signalled the Arts Council's disapproval of drama that interrogated the administration of power' (Shellard, 2000, p.199). MRA theatre, even at its most controversial, was not likely to undermine authority and it is therefore not surprising that Rittner should publicly support it. John Bull says that by the beginning of the 1990s the Arts Council had 'moved away from an emphasis on direct funding, to one on personal fund-raising and in particular to a reliance on corporate partnerships' (Bull, 1994, p.26). MRA had always been extremely successful in its private fund-raising initiatives which was very much in keeping with the Arts Council ethos at that time and another reason for the government to publicly approve of its efforts. The optimism with which FFT was greeted at the gala however was extremely short-lived. Ironically, the report of the launch featured in the same August 1990 issue of the *Westminster Theatre News*, as the announcement of the closure of the theatre. An Editor's Note states 'It might seem odd to combine the account of the spectacular Gala Opening of FFT with the shattering news of its suspension in one issue but I felt that it is important to be reminded in these darker times of what can and has been achieved' (*Westminster Theatre News*, 1990b, p.5). The darker times began barely a year after the launch of FFT. Steadman Williams says that the venture was only financially viable if it could be supported by the main theatre box office and in 1990 Westminster Productions decided to bring to the main stage a southern folk-style musical from America, *Cotton Patch Gospel*. Whilst MRA put up some of the money it also had another financial backer, but during rehearsals in New York that backer pulled out, preferring instead to help finance the musical *Chess*. Steadman Williams recalls: 'We had to pay the cast for three weeks rehearsal and then we had an empty theatre for a month. We were already in a weak position by the time we decided to stage *Temptation*' (Steadman Williams, appendix 23, p.354).

It is easy to understand why the play *Temptation* and its author Václav Havel, the Czech political dissident who went on to become president, should appeal to MRA. In 1990, Czechoslovakia had just emerged from a communist dictatorship led by Gustáv Husák and Havel had risen from political prisoner to president. He had spent five of the previous twenty years in prison on political charges and during the communist regime his plays were banned. Shortly before the opening night of *Temptation* at the Westminster, on 6 June 1990, Havel was invited by Thatcher to a dinner in his honour at 10, Downing Street. She told him:

> During the darkest years of Stalinist oppression, you were an inspiration to your people. In your plays, you exposed and opposed the deceits and injustices of totalitarian rule, You stayed true to your principles through long periods of imprisonment and illness ... Today we pay warm and genuine tribute to you and your colleagues in 'Charter 77'[14] who pointed the way to freedom and brought Czechoslovakia to its rightful place as one of the free and democratic nations of Europe (Thatcher, 1990, online).

A man prepared to go to prison in the fight against communism and who was also admired by Thatcher would no doubt have appealed to MRA as a fitting playwright to promote at the Westminster. Havel conceived the idea for *Temptation* whilst in prison and wrote it in just ten days, in 1985, two years after serving his sentence. He was incarcerated again when the play had its American premiere in April 1989 in New York. Havel, like Howard, Steadman Williams and Ruthven, wrote plays in response to specific situations. In an interview with the *New York Times* Havel states 'Theatre is in a particular way tied to its social, intellectual and cultural home. It is written out of a particular situation and for a particular situation, for a particular audience' (Havel cited in Mestrovic, online, 1989). Steadman Williams, producer of *Temptation*, says 'We looked at what he had written.

---

[14] Charter 77 was a petition drawn up by Czechoslovakian writers and intellectuals demanding that the communist government recognise some basic human rights.

We read several of his other plays but we liked this one' (Steadman Williams, appendix 23, p.354).

Temptation is borne out of an experience Havel had whilst a prisoner. Innocent comments he made were twisted and used to discredit him and at the same time Goethe's Faust and Thomas Mann's Dr Faustus arrived in his cell. As a result, Havel based Temptation on the Faust legend of a man who sells his soul to the devil. He told the New York Times: 'I had strange dreams and strange ideas. I felt I was being – quite physically – tempted by the devil; that I was in his clutches' (Havel cited in Mestrovic, online, 1989). Havel chose to set Temptation in a scientific institute in the Soviet Union of the Cold War era and investigate the relationships of the people working there. The play ends dramatically and, as will be seen later, somewhat prophetically for MRA, with Dr Foustka's cape catching fire followed by an explosion symbolising a world about to go up in flames. Thick clouds of smoke engulf the stage and the curtain falls, ending the play. The script contains much that is in line with MRA's spiritual ethos. Its themes, involving politics and morality, corruption, the battle between good and evil, altruism and personal benefit, appear ideally suited to the MRA ideology and give no hint of the disaster that was to come. In Temptation Dr Foustka announces, in what could easily be the voice of Kenneth Belden:

> When a person casts God from his heart he opens a door to the devil. When you think about the increasingly stupid wilfulness of the powerful and the increasingly stupid submission of the powerless and the awful destruction committed in today's world in the name of science, isn't that all truly the work of the devil? (Havel, 1989, p.37).

A couple of years earlier the play had been successfully performed by the Royal Shakespeare Company (Banham, 2000, p.476) and Steadman Williams could therefore be excused for believing that it would not only be a play appropriate for MRA but also a box office success. Steadman Williams managed to get £25,000 in sponsorship from APV, a big food processing company with a large interest in Czechoslovakia

and £25,000 from a Japanese electronics company. A letter from Sir Peter Cazalet of APV to Steadman Williams states, 'With the tremendous political change that is taking place and with my company's substantial involvement in Eastern Europe, we are naturally keen to be able to contribute to the new democratic movement' (Cazalet, 1990). A total of £200,000 was raised towards the over-all cost of £250,000 and the remaining £50,000 was borrowed from the bank.

Westminster Productions decided that James Roose-Evans would be the most suitable person to direct *Temptation*. He had dramatised and directed *84 Charing Cross Road* by Helene Hanff on both Broadway and the West End and had won awards on both sides of the Atlantic for best director and best play. He founded the Hampstead Theatre Club and was the first British theatre director to be ordained a non-stipendiary priest. However, Steadman Williams admits, in hindsight, that his fatal mistake was to spend so much time raising money for the production and organising publicity that he did not see the play until the dress rehearsal. When he saw what Roose-Evans had done with the script, Steadman Williams was mortified. This was definitely not a production that reflected MRA ideology:

> We kept to standards of absolute purity and there were scenes simulating the sex act, a scene of copulation, very sexy scenes with Rula Lenska [the leading actress]. We had spent a lot of money and could not consider putting a halt to it but it wasn't the production we hoped it would be (Steadman Williams, appendix 23, p.354).

The original version of *Temptation* did not contain any overtly sexual scenes and Steadman Williams believes the decision to add them was a personal one: 'I know Roose-Evans had experience of MRA in the 1940s and it was not a happy experience. Maybe he felt he had to put the knife in' [15] (Steadman Williams, 2013, appendix 23, p.354). Westminster Productions organised a meeting with the director and tackled him about the sex scenes. Roose-Evans told Steadman Williams that, as a non-stipendiary Church of England clergyman, he would not do anything to undermine Christian values but Steadman Williams remained concerned:

> I told him I would lose the audience and he said 'yes, but I will get you a whole new audience'. But it was not a success. We did not get good reviews. We didn't get the audiences. I got him to modify some things by use of lighting but it still upset the MRA family terribly. There was a huge outcry. My name was mud (Steadman Williams, appendix 23, p.354).

Roose-Evans chose to transpose the setting for *Temptation* from a scientific institute in what appears to be a communist country to a contemporary English setting, drawing a parallel between Thatcher and Husák. In his opening notes to the cast, Roose-Evans states that staging the play in its original context would have made it less relevant to an audience which no longer regarded communism as a threat. He believed, however, that the struggle for power continued and 'wherever state bureaucracy, indeed any bureaucracy, encroaches upon the rights and conscience of the individual,

---

[15] Roose-Evans has not replied to emails regarding this book and so it has not been possible to obtain his response to this allegation.

then one has to resist. It happened in America under McCarthy[16] and there are signs of it happening here' (Roose-Evans, 1990, p.2 and p.8). Roose-Evans said his production would be 'a Beckettian comedy about life; all that remains of the Faust story is the theme of temptation' (Roose-Evans, 1990, p.2). He defended his interpretation in the press, telling freelance arts journalist Nick Smurthwaite 'I will not have the play morally censored. You're bound to get erotic images in this play. It's seething with sexuality. Under the Communists in Czechoslovakia sex was the cheapest, easiest and most enjoyable hobby for most ordinary people — that's why there is so much sex in it' (Roose-Evans cited in Smurthwaite, 1990). Roose-Evans goes on to claim 'I don't think the Westminster knew what they were taking on with this play. They were hooked on the ideological content, on Havel's message that you must dare to speak up for what you think, to have the courage of your convictions, even if it means going to prison' (Roose-Evans cited in Smurthwaite, 1990). It would seem quite understandable, however, that MRA should look at the ideological content of *Temptation* and, rather than not knowing what they were taking on with the play, it was more a case of not knowing what they had taken on with the director.

Ironically *Temptation*, the one play that MRA would rather have forgotten about, generated more publicity than any other production at the Westminster. The reports began the night before the opening with a prophetic warning from Smurthwaite: 'Audiences at the Westminster Theatre,

---

[16] Joseph McCarthy was a US Republican Senator from 1947 until his death in 1957 and conducted a witch-hunt against communists and homosexuals which became known as McCarthyism.

which aims to "advance the Christian religion" and provide spiritual enlightenment are in for the devil of a surprise' (Smurthwaite, 1990). Many critics did not think much of Roose-Evans's interpretation. Milton Shulman in the *Evening Standard* writes that moving the setting to England and suggesting that the communist regime of Eastern Europe was similar to that of Thatcher's Britain was a 'clumsy analogy' that distanced the audience from Havel's work rather than bringing it closer (fig. 23). The characters 'lost their ironic native qualities without acquiring anything remotely English to replace them' (Shulman, 1990, p.36). He does add however that this was 'not a fatal flaw because Havel's parable has enough profundity and wit to withstand such misguided tinkering' (Shulman, 1990, p.36). Nicholas de Jongh of *The Guardian* claims 'Mrs Thatcher's Britain, however much you abhor it, is not the repressive state that Czechoslovakia was' (de Jongh, 1990, p.37).

Figure 23: Rula Lenska in 'tempting' pose. Credit: Evening Standard

The irony of staging the play at the Westminster was not lost on de Jongh: 'James Roose-Evans's sexy production is well-placed in the Westminster. For here is a theatre which bans alcohol and whose fortress-like exterior catches the spirit of the play, if not its owners the Moral Re-Armament movement' (de Jongh, 1990, p.37). He concludes that, while he did not like the style of the play, 'there is no missing its force and vigour' (de Jongh, 1990, p.37). Petronius, writing in *The European*, highlights the political controversy that Roose-Evans's interpretation caused, observing that Havel 'is a great admirer of Prime Minister Margaret Thatcher and he may not like the notion of his play, written in prison about the horrors of Gustáv Husák's communist police state, being translated into Mrs Thatcher's Britain ... One right-wing British MP has called for Havel to disown the production' (Petronius, 1990, p.13). A later edition of the paper features a photograph on

Figure 24: Rula's 'naked truth' according to Lee-Potter. Credit: Daily Mail

the front page of Havel dancing at a wedding reception with the headline 'More fun than kissing babies: Havel courts votes at home but his play hits trouble in London' (*European*, 1990, p.1). Maureen Paton of *The Daily Express* claims the 'elegant RSC production of the play two years ago was far superior' (Paton, 1990, p.13). Paul Taylor of *The Independent*, who persists in calling Roose-Evans 'Ruth Evans', says there is 'little to light up the stage … This temptation is, I'm afraid, rather easy to resist' (Taylor, 1990, p.12). Benedict Nightingale writes in *The Times* that Havel's text does not need to 'italicize the grotesque or gild the silly. Yet this is what Roose-Evans has done' (Nightingale, 1990, p.20). Charles Osborne of *The Daily Telegraph* also criticises Roose-Evans's interpretation claiming, 'he has succumbed to a weird temptation of his own and has tried to transform Havel's cry of impotent rage against an all-too-real Communist society into one of those diatribes against that most unreal of countries to be seen in the theatre since Franz Lehar's Pontevedro. You've guessed it — Thatcher's Britain' (Osborne, 1990, p.16).

Although the theatre critics were not, on the whole, inspired by Roose-Evans's interpretation, the play received the level of coverage that in the past Belden and MRA could only have dreamt of. However on this occasion the publicity, highlighting the fact that the scantily clad Rula Lenska was appearing on stage at a theatre known for its moralistic stand, was an embarrassment to the movement. It is easy, from the reports, to understand why Westminster Productions was horrified by what Roose-Evans had done with a seemingly innocuous script. Benedict Nightingale writes 'The action occurs on and round a pink hospital bed guarded by a leather-overcoated girl with roses and a Heavy in dark glasses' (Nightingale, 1990, p.20). Maureen Paton's review is accompanied by a picture of Rula Lenska, kneeling bare legged on a bed with the caption 'agony and ecstasy'. Paton claims: 'The sight of Rula Lenska's endless legs wrapped round the neck of a young man on the stage of London's only Christian theatre is calculated to unnerve Old Nick himself ... Even more bizarre is the back projection showing mercifully blurred soft porn images in black and white' (Paton, 1990, p.13). The reviewer refers to Roose-Evans's religious affiliations stating, 'As a churchman, he cannot resist showing us he's an expert on sin. Thus audiences will be forced to see Ms Lenska strip to a semi-diaphanous nightie, whether they like it or not' (Paton, 1990, p.13). Almost every review is accompanied by provocative photos of Lenska: on all fours on a bed; holding an apple to the mouth of a man wearing only the briefest of underpants; showing her stocking tops. *The Daily Mail* went one step further with a double page centrespread headlined 'Naked truth about Rula' (fig. 24). Journalist Lynda Lee-Potter quotes the actress as saying she refused to tone down the performance for her father — 'it's part of the play. It's called *Temptation* and I'm the temptress. But the simulated eroticism has certainly offended some people' (Lenska cited in Lee-Potter, 1990, pp 28-29).

Not all the criticism was negative. Jack Tinker of *The Daily Mail* disagrees with Paton over her comparison with the RSC presentation: 'His [Roose-Evans] beautifully orchestrated production is indeed a far sexier and more seductive affair than the version we first saw and acclaimed a couple of years ago at the RSC ... It is good to welcome it back in this joyously celebratory production' (Tinker, 1990, p.3). There is at least one report which fails to mention Rula Lenska and Roose-Evans's interpretation in its review and that, not surprisingly, is *The War Cry* — the newspaper of the Christian Salvation Army. Instead it discusses Havel and his views of God and Christianity, urging the playwright, 'When you first went to prison, Mr

President, you decided to study the Bible in detail. Please take another look at the teaching of Jesus ... And all the best, Mr Playwright, for your show here in London' (*War Cry*, 1990, p.2). Havel was in London at the time of *Temptation* and, according to *The Times*, 'seems certain to come under pressure from the right in Britain to disown the production' (*Times*, 1990). He did not attend and Steadman Williams suspects, 'He may have been warned off it by the cultural attaché of the Czech Embassy in London who had seen the play and said he did not think it would be to Havel's taste. He explained that although in his private life Havel was quite a ladies' man, he did not like overt sexuality on the stage' (Steadman Williams, appendix 23, p.354).

Having tried desperately to get Roose-Evans to tone down his production, with little success, it appears that Steadman Williams put on a brave face for the public. He is quoted in *The Daily Express Diary*: 'It's certainly a new dramatic departure for the Westminster. There was a bit of a hoo-ha at the start, but it was just over a few small artistic points and now we're delighted' (Steadman Williams cited in *Daily Express*, 1990). Whether or not this was accurate reporting on behalf of *The Daily Express*, there is no doubt that the uproar over *Temptation* resulted in far more than just 'a bit of a hoo-ha' and there was not much 'delight' amongst the ranks of MRA supporters. Mary Lean reports, in the MRA magazine *For a Change*, 'Many of MRA's supporters had been deeply offended by the play's staging; some felt that Westminster Productions had betrayed their trust. There were accusations of everything from bad judgement to infamy and strident demands for repentance and apology' (Lean, 1998, pp 4-9). Looking back on that turbulent time, more than twenty years later Steadman Williams says:

A lot of young people in MRA were very supportive but the old guard sat in the foyer night after night trying to persuade people not to go in. I very much regret that I didn't get to rehearsals sooner. We could have modified it and changed direction. There had been an earlier production of it by the RSC in their studio theatre which was not as explicit. I don't think James [Roose-Evans] pulled it off artistically. I think he got carried away by his own agenda. The wife of the translator saw it and walked out saying "it is a travesty" (Steadman Williams, appendix 23, p.354).

It must have been deeply distressing for Steadman Williams to witness his MRA colleagues, many of whom had not even seen the play, urging audiences not to go into the theatre and therefore risking financial disaster. Their actions were not in accordance with the absolute standards of honesty and unselfishness, but it appears that no-one within the movement was prepared to challenge such behaviour. MRA was somewhat naïve in thinking that because it had selected a director who was a non-stipendiary priest, that he would interpret the play within the movement's own strict moral guidelines. Steadman Williams was correct in admitting that he should have watched rehearsals but the responsibility was not his alone – it appears that everyone on the board of Westminster Productions was content to leave Roose-Evans to his own devices, despite some at least being aware that he might not have subscribed to all aspects of MRA ideology. Added to that, alarm bells should surely have been ringing when it was known that Rula Lenska was to take a leading role; Lenska was renowned for her sexuality on stage. This is another example of MRA wanting to change society through theatre without being fully aware of what was happening outside the confines of the Westminster.

Not everyone within the MRA fold was against the production. Monsignor George Leonard, a member of the board of Westminster Productions and head of public affairs for the Catholic Diocese of Westminster, told

Steadman Williams there was not much to be concerned about and a United Reformed Church clergyman said that 'it just fell short of redemption but highlighted an important part of the Bible message and underlined a neglected doctrine about hell' (Steadman Williams, appendix 23, p.354). MRA supporter Tony Sursham reviewing the play for the *Westminster Theatre News*, writes 'I thoroughly enjoyed the whole show' adding that he intended to invite his MP and other acquaintances to see it (Sursham, 1990). David Locke, who was involved in the marketing of the theatre, recalls 'This wasn't quite MRA but at the same time it was artistic. I didn't personally make a great deal of fuss but others felt vehemently that it was absolutely atrocious. Without MRA support it was doomed' (Locke, appendix 15, p.324). Stanley Kiaer, secretary of Westminster Productions at the time, believes the fatal mistake was in commissioning Roose-Evans without retaining directorial rights: 'This should have been a great success. We had outside backing for it. *Temptation* lost us our reputation and some of our support. People were divided in their opinions. Friends of mine came and thought it was fine. I felt this play could go on at any other theatre and it would be terrific but not at the Westminster where we had to have a certain standard we could not go beyond' (Kiaer, appendix 14, p.321). In a letter dated 19 June, 1990, to senior MRA supporter Dick Channer, Michael Henderson urges caution over the movement's public response to the play. At the time Henderson was living in Portland, Oregon, but he had been sent newspaper cuttings about *Temptation* from Channer. In the letter he says he had been part of a decision by MRA in the United States to give five thousand dollars to the production. He writes:

> It seems to me to be a very good investment. I fear that in all the controversy about the manner of its staging we are losing sight of the importance of the play and our association with it. In terms of the

public image of MRA I can see little harm in the press coverage or the production itself. It is probably not a bad thing in this day and age that people should know that we are involved in controversial matters and even that we are not of one mind on them (Henderson, 1990).

Henderson goes on to add that MRA had to accept a degree of risk if it chose to hire someone from 'outside our ranks'. He tells Channer 'I think we do have the temptation in our work to get too uptight on issues like this ... I think the world, and probably some of our younger people, may be watching how maturely we can handle all this' (Henderson, 1990).

Those MRA supporters who urged people not to attend the play were successful. It closed on 14 July, 1990, after a six-week run, instead of the expected six months, and Westminster Productions was faced with repaying a £50,000 bank loan and the very real possibility of bankruptcy. The Oxford Group offered a bail-out on condition that the theatre was closed. Steadman Williams was devastated by the news: 'They had been angling for this throughout the 1980s and we had to do it. I had to give notice to twenty-five people. It was terrible' (Steadman Williams, appendix 23, p.354). In an article in the *Westminster Theatre News* a month after the closure of *Temptation*, he wrote 'How difficult it is to fully understand a play in which the author and director are breaking new ground. So often the presuppositions we bring with us to a play determine what we come away with at the end' (Steadman Williams, 1990, p.7). This was, of course, exactly what Steadman Williams, Howard and Belden had been doing when they condemned the kitchen sink theatre of the 1960s, thirty years earlier. Just as they had not understood the experimental new theatre of Pinter, Orton and Littlewood, and had interpreted it in the light of their own personal knowledge and 'presuppositions', now many of their colleagues were doing the same with work being performed in their own theatre. While John Locke, Steadman Williams and other theatre enthusiasts wanted the Westminster to provide theatre that represented the culture of the 1980s and 1990s, they were overruled by a faction within MRA which no longer felt the theatre had a place within the movement.

Kiaer made an announcement in the *Westminster Theatre News* explaining that not only had the main theatre closed but FFT and the education programmes had also been suspended (Kiaer, 1990, p.2). Steadman Williams says Westminster Productions managed to sell the modern lighting equipment in FFT to the Swiss Caux Foundation, for £25,000, and tried in vain to carry on: 'We tried to persuade the trustees of the Oxford Group to let us do Christmas shows but they wouldn't even allow that' (Steadman Williams, appendix 23, p.354). The way in which the theatre was forced to close devastated John Locke who believed that *Temptation* had offered the Westminster 'a way out of the rut associated with internal MRA playwriting which, although good in its time, now lacked the popular appeal' (Locke, appendix 16, p.329). He adds that the controversy surrounding the play 'brought to a head the feeling within MRA that the theatre was an expense they could ill afford and its day was past' (Locke, appendix 16, p.329). In the *Westminster Theatre News* of August 1990 Locke maintains a positive stance and writes:

> First Floor was a triumph for those who gave their money to see it brought from an embryonic idea to a glorious blooming. I would like to think that, like the best of the flowers, it is only the frosts of autumn which have killed the bloom. But there is the promise of a glorious spring, as yet unseen, in the future. I know not how, but First Floor Theatre will be back (Locke, 1990, p.4)

237

Privately, however, Locke was absolutely furious that FFT should have had such a brief life: 'I was so distressed at the closure and the way I had seen my good friends Hugh [Steadman Williams] and Stanley [Kiaer] treated that I felt I did not want to stay in the theatre' (Locke, appendix 16, p.329). True to his word, he left the profession in 1990, got a job as a housing services support officer for a local council and did not return to the theatre for more than twenty years. Looking back on his time at the Westminster he says, 'I believe passionately in using drama as a means of spreading uplifting, inspirational messages. I am proud to have been part of the Westminster and the inspirational work of Hugh [Steadman Williams], Stanley [Kiaer], Ron Mann, Nancy Ruthven and others. Working at the Westminster Theatre was, for me, a pinnacle of my professional life' (Locke, appendix 16, p.329).

In the August 1990 issue of *Westminster Theatre News* Neville Cooper, chairman of the Friends of the theatre, announced a meeting to discuss the future declaring, 'Like all of you, I was dismayed to be informed of the decision by Westminster Productions to cease running the theatre and shocked by its suddenness' (Cooper, 1990, p.3). One hundred and eighty-six supporters of MRA attended that meeting at the movement's Cheshire centre, Tirley Garth. Following an in-depth discussion on the future of the theatre, a letter was sent to senior supporters stating, 'The theatre experiment came to an end in a way that none of us would have chosen ... It is clear that we cannot continue professional Christian theatre in the Westminster Theatre' (Evans, Hore-Ruthven, Lester and Morshead, 1990). It continues that there was agreement that theatre, in some form, should continue and that there was a need for a central London venue. Six options were considered: continuing to use the building but using the auditorium only when needed; continuing to use the building but letting out the auditorium; selling the building and moving to more suitable premises; selling the building with planning permission for redevelopment by the new owner; redeveloping the building in partnership with a developer whilst retaining one floor and finally, what the letter describes as 'the unknown option', believing that God would point the way forward. No-one voted for the first two options and most opted for selling the building and moving elsewhere. The letter states 'Our unanimous recommendation is that, subject to some further professional advice, we should pursue option three and place the building as it is on the market with a view to moving to a different and more suitable building' (Evans, Hore-Ruthven, Lester and Morshead, 1990).

The theatre went up for sale in 1991, at a volatile time in the property market. Neither Kiaer, who was overseeing the sale, nor the estate agents handling it, Debenham, Tewson and Chinnock, could come up with a price. Brian Attwood in a report in *The Stage* in May 1991, quotes John Earl, director of the Theatre Trusts, as claiming that the commercial property market had been depressed since 1989 and a comparison with neighbouring theatres was almost impossible: 'It's very rare at the best of times that any of them are sold and then they are rarely comparable with one another' (Earl cited in Attwood, 1991). Kiaer reports in the *Westminster Theatre News* of December 1991, 'It is easier to decide to put a building on the market than to effect a sale, particularly with the fall in the property market' (Kiaer, 1991, p.1). He adds that, because local authorities needed to be consulted about possible planning issues, it was likely to be at least eighteen months before a sale could be concluded. In the meantime the theatre would be closed to outside lettings and put on a care and maintenance basis, although in-house activities would continue.

While the trustees of the Oxford Group were making plans to sell the theatre, the Friends of Westminster Theatre were determined to continue staging small scale events. In October 1990 more than one hundred people packed into FFT to discuss the future of Westminster Productions. Neville Cooper reports in the *Westminster Theatre News* 'For the moment the theatre may be dark. The vision continues. It is our privilege to keep it alive' (Cooper, 1990, p.3). An article on the front page of *Westminster Theatre News* in February 1991 announced that Westminster Productions had cleared all its debts, repaid all its loans and was involved in a venture with the Catholic Stage Guild to present a new play *The Rack* by Anglican minister and member of Westminster Productions, Daniel Pearce, at The Notre Dame de France parish hall just off Leicester Square in the West End (*Westminster Theatre News*, 1991, p.1). In July 1991 the Friends of Westminster Theatre decided that, from January of the following year, its name should change to the Friends of Westminster Productions and the newsletter be altered from *Westminster Theatre News* to *Friends News*. Announcing the change of title Cooper said that, during the twenty-seven years of its existence, much work had been done by the Friends 'outside the confines of the theatre' (Cooper, 1991b, p.1). He revealed that future plans included small-scale theatre projects encouraging new writers and joint theatrical ventures in the belief that the purpose of the Friends was 'primarily related to sound theatrical activity and the battle for a healthy artistic culture rather than to bricks and mortar in themselves' (Cooper, 1991b, p.1). The following year the Friends demonstrated their determination to continue the FFT policy of promoting relevant new works by presenting a studio theatre production with Straight Talk

Theatre Company of *Joshua's Coat*, a play by Ann Clifford about 'AIDS, death and eternity' (*Friends News*, 1992, p.1). In 1993, with no prospect of a sale in sight, Cooper decided that the Friends should become more pro-active concerning the future of the Westminster Theatre. In the *Friends News* he writes, 'We are told that alternative premises would cost less — but how can we judge the merit of that if we do not know what the alternative would consist of? ... Would new facilities have adequate theatre accommodation?' (Cooper, 1993, p.2). Adding that it was 'deplorable' that the theatre was so little used, Cooper reports that the Oxford Group had agreed to discuss the current financial situation with members of the Friends' committee.

Meanwhile, Steadman Williams and others were working on ambi-tious plans to create a Christian Arts Centre in Central London, or at the Westminster Theatre, if finance could be found to purchase it. A steering committee was formed in October 1991, comprising representatives from several arts groups, including Westminster Productions and Aldersgate, as well as experts on arts centre development and finance plus five clergy and the press officers of the Diocese of London and the Catholic Bishops Con-ference. In an article in the *Friends News* of 1994 Steadman Williams, who was executive secretary of the Christian Arts Trust and secretary of the steer-ing committee, describes the brief for the new centre which would include two performance spaces, an exhibition area, film and video viewing, work-shops, offices and a catering facility open to the public (Steadman Williams, 1994, p.4). The Christian Arts Trust committed more than a third of its capital to commissioning two feasibility studies, one of the whole project and a second on the refurbishment of the Westminster Theatre building. The steering committee set about raising funds to purchase the freehold of the Westminster and carry out major restructuring of the building at a projected cost of £10 million. A charitable trust made the first pledge of £500,000 and well-known figures from the world of entertainment were invited to be patrons. They included comedy duo Tommy Cannon and Bobby Ball, television presenter Jill Dando, singer Cliff Richard and John Witney, a director of Andrew Lloyd Webber's *Really Useful Group*. The Oxford Group offered to sell the Westminster to the Christian Arts Trust for £2.5 million and the committee was confident that the building could reopen as an arts centre in the autumn of 1997 (Steadman Williams, 1994, p.4). Unfortunately, however, the optimism was short-lived. Steadman Williams recalls:

> The Christian Arts Trust made a grant of £50,000 for a feasibility study which was carried out by Theatre Projects Consultants. They came up with a brilliant design. To realise that together with the purchase price and some endowment would require £8.5 million. We approached the National Lottery Arts Fund who were very encouraging and indicated that if we could find twenty per-cent of the total they would fund the remainder. This is where we hit the buffers. We approached several wealthy Christian business people but they just did not rate the arts as highly as we did and we got nowhere. So we just had to give up our scheme (Steadman Williams, appendix 24, p.360).

To the surprise of most people in the movement, the theatre took seven years to sell. In 1995 the Oxford Group decided that, with no prospect of a sale in the foreseeable future and with the Christian Arts Trust being unsuccessful in raising the necessary funds, steps should be taken to make more use of the building again. The Oxford Group's trustees announced in a letter to their supporters that the theatre would remain on the market but would not be sold for less than £2.5 million. In the meantime some improvements would be undertaken to make the building more accessible and steps taken to encourage short lets of the auditorium. It is clear from the letter, however, that divisions remained within the movement over the future of the theatre:

> The past years and months have been testing ones for us as a Council because we have reflected among ourselves the differences of a perception about God's will for the building which exist within the MRA fellowship as a whole. While not being dismayed that individuals equally committed to God may sometimes disagree, it has not always been easy to know how to move forward unitedly. However we have been shown at each stage a united next step' (Craig A., et al, 1995)

This statement is remarkably restrained for a movement more used to delivering dramatic rhetoric, and does not reflect the strong emotions that some MRA theatre enthusiasts were experiencing. Christine Channer, for example, says, 'That was a truly horrible period of conflict and grief, especially for those of us who had sweated our guts out there' (Channer, appendix 3, p.292). There was a brief resurgence of hope when Cooper announced, in the March 1996 edition of *Friends News*, the change of plan by the Oxford Group:

> There is good news on the theatre. The landlords, The Oxford Group, will not immediately sell it for development but will refurbish and use the premises, at least pending satisfactory planning consent for any proper redevelopment ... So we continue to have the opportunity, limited only by people's creativity, imagination and commitment, to use this place to impact the thinking and culture of the nation (Cooper, 1996a, p.2)

In the same issue, Kiaer writes 'We can now go ahead with our first-rate programme for 1996 and beyond' (Kiaer, 1996, p.6). Both men clearly hoped that the Westminster could resume the impact it was beginning to have with FFT and have a major influence on British culture.

The Oxford Group proposals for refurbishment were possibly influenced by the fact that the fiftieth anniversary of the purchase of the Westminster was to take place in 1996. At an anniversary lunch in May of that year, Cooper delivered a speech with a clear message to the Oxford Group stating that, if the creative will existed, then the required finance could be found. He also drew attention to the fact that those attending the anniversary celebrations included servicemen and women who had been on stage at the Westminster to mark Armistice Sunday in November 1946:

> Despite controversies over the theatre's future (almost like those over Europe!) the fact is that it is here now and will be here for many years to come. I wish therefore that there was the vision and commitment from a much wider group to use it for the regeneration of the nation. I do not believe that our creative action is limited by finance – but that finance is limited by lack of creative action (Cooper, 1996b, p.5).

The celebrations were marked by two performances on the main stage – the first with members of the Saltmine Theatre Company performing *The Screwtape Letters* by C.S. Lewis and the second a programme of opera highlights by singer Grant Dickson. Once again, the theatre became a venue for a variety of MRA productions and the theatre enthusiasts became optimistic that the Westminster had a future. However, Cooper's earlier optimism that the theatre would continue 'for many years to come' turned out to be misplaced because just two years later the announcement came that many had been dreading. In the November issue of *Friends News* Cooper reveals: 'At the time I am writing the situation is that the theatre may be sold within weeks – but it may not – and there is no timescale on the basis of which we can plan' (Cooper, 1997, p.1). In January 1998, Cooper led an open discussion entitled 'The Future of the Friends' at the annual general meeting when those attending were asked 'What difference would the possible sale

244

of the Westminster Theatre make? Should the Friends continue? If so, what should be our role and activities?' (Friends of the Westminster Theatre, 1998). The overwhelming and unanimous response was that the Friends should continue. Cooper told the meeting:

> If we are to continue to bring people hope and to promote the values on which personal, family and national life depend, it must happen through the media and the arts – for apart from one-to-one conversation, that is the only way to communicate with the nation at large (Cooper, 1998a, p.2).

Cooper was right to be cautious about whether or not the theatre would be sold 'within weeks' because there were several setbacks. Kiaer reports in the *Friends News* of March 1998, 'It is fair to say that in the theatre the drama is not solely confined to the stage' (Kiaer, 1998, p.1.). It had been thought that a consortium would buy the theatre and develop it into an international arts centre but at the last moment the backers refused to provide a banker's guarantee. Pinecrest Properties, loosely connected to the consortium, then made a bid which was accepted by the Oxford Group. There was, however, the problem of where MRA should move to. The movement had spent many months searching for a replacement centre but none of the properties viewed were suitable. Kiaer writes that, as the contract with Pinecrest was about to be signed, a freehold building, just ten minutes' walk from the theatre, came on the market. There was space for a dining room, conference centre, offices and overnight accommodation and the movement agreed to snap it up. Kiaer adds 'We are due to take possession of the new centre in June and vacate the Westminster Theatre by the end of October. This just about gives enough time to do the necessary refurbishment' (Kiaer, 1998, p.1). A letter from the Oxford Group to MRA supporters, dated 16 March, 1998, reads 'We acknowledge that there are some who feel pain that this move has been felt right and necessary but our overriding sense is one of gratitude for the outcome of such a long and at times difficult process' (Craig, Evans, Kiacr and Lean, 1998). The letter states that the council of management had kept to its original promise not to accept less than £2.5 million for the building and it was eventually sold for £2.7 million. The cost of buying the new freehold premises was £2.25 million and it was expected that the money needed for adapting and refurbishing it would use up the difference. The new building was intended as the base for a number of MRA initiatives not connected with the theatre such as Hope in the Cities, dealing with race, reconciliation and responsibility; the International Communications Forum, promoting an ethical press; Foundations for Freedom, working with young people from former communist countries; and Agenda for Reconciliation, focussing on conferences for young people from areas of conflict.

The final major public event, a 'Recital of Songs', with Sylvie Soderlund, soprano and John Burrows on piano, took place in October 1998. Cooper, addressing the audience, recalled the early days of the Westminster in the immediate post-war years when there were packed houses for *The Forgotten Factor*, followed by the 1960s with the 'brilliant and life-changing plays by Peter Howard which spoke to the conscience of the nation and, in more recent times, by Hugh Williams and others' (Cooper, 1998b, p.1-2). During its fifty year reign at the Westminster, MRA had been vilified by some and praised by others, regarded as both a centre for preaching, moralistic propaganda and a place where people found new meaning in their lives. Cooper told those at the final event:

> One thing is clear — the fundamental contribution of this place lies
> in the people throughout this land and far beyond who have found
> a new victory and purpose and direction in their lives and have begun
> to put right what is wrong around them. All else follows from that
> (Cooper, 1998b, p.2).

What Cooper could not have envisaged when he made his farewell speech at the Westminster was how long it would take to move to the new premises. The front page of the March 1999 issue of *Friends News* states that MRA expected to move to the new premises at 24, Greencoat Place, Victoria, in late April or early May of that year (*Friends News*, 1999, p.1). However, because of delays with building work, it was to be another year before MRA had a new and permanent home.

The millennium finally brought resolution after twenty years of conflict over the role of the theatre within the movement, a role that even Peter Howard might eventually have been prepared to relinquish. Wolrige Gordon says 'Theatre is no longer the top means of communication in our age and my father would have moved on, probably to television' (Wolrige Gordon, appendix 27, p.368). Mary Lean maintains that the delay in the sale was costly both financially and in terms of time and emotional energy but adds 'with hindsight, it seems that it may have been necessary to allow for healing and for the right new centre to emerge' (Lean, 1998, p.9). Kiaer, who fought until the bitter end to prevent the sale of the Westminster, now believes, 'Running a theatre is very expensive, especially now. It was a thing of its time — it fulfilled a post-war need to rebuild' (Kiaer, appendix 14, p.321). And while he recognises that the Westminster did not achieve its aim of changing the culture of Britain, he maintains a positive outlook on the work that took place there: 'We didn't win the battle,' he says, 'but we certainly affected national life' (Kiaer, appendix 13, p.316). The conclusion to this book debates the reasons for the failure of MRA's propagandist theatre, despite a fifty-year battle for the hearts and minds of the people of Britain.

Conclusion

How can anyone doubt that inspired art can melt barriers in human hearts, barriers unaffected by exhortation, analysis and persuasion? My gratitude, admiration and love to the men and women who will take the Westminster Theatre and its Arts Centre to the twenty-first century (Rajmohan Gandhi cited in New World News, 1986).

Rajmohan Gandhi's confidence that the Westminster Theatre would continue into the twenty-first century was unfortunately misplaced. The reasons for the demise of the theatre were many and various and whilst *Temptation* was the catalyst for the closure it was certainly not the cause. Other factors played a major part and included the movement's difficulty in understanding the changing culture, a lack of effective propaganda plays, increasing costs and a desire amongst senior supporters to look at different ways of promoting MRA ideology.

One of MRA's greatest setbacks at the Westminster was the demise of Peter Howard and a lack of talented writers able to produce suitable propagandist material. Steadman Williams observed, five years after the death of the movement's most prolific playwright, that in order to present plays that could create a change in man and society, 'We shall need the writers who can write them and the producers who can produce them' (Steadman Williams, 1969a, p.10). Belden also highlighted the problem: 'We particularly want new writers. It is easier to raise a hundred thousand pounds than find a play worth putting on' (Belden, 1968b, p.10). No-one could write plays at the speed and in the quantity that was accomplished by Howard. David Locke maintains that while there were financial reasons for selling the theatre — for example, seats had become more expensive following the introduction of VAT — the main difficulty was a lack of suitable material to stage:

> Because Peter Howard had died we did not have the plays to put on. His plays continued to be performed for some years but there were no new ones from him. Alan Thornhill, Nancy Ruthven and Hugh Steadman Williams provided some material but this was not enough. We then moved to putting on Christian type plays but, as Leone Exton [who ran the catering services at the Westminster] said, they did not have the last act, by which she meant that of real change in people which was the essence of the MRA message (Locke, appendix 15, p.324).

Leone Exton is correct in observing that there was a fundamental shift in playwriting following Howard's death. Whilst Howard's plays, and the earlier ones of Thornhill, emphasised the MRA ideology of the absolute standards and listening to God daily in silence, later works preached Christianity, often at the expense of MRA beliefs. Buchman had always emphasised that there should be respect for other religions, with the MRA message as the common denominator, but it is clear that, in the 1970s and 1980s for example, works such as *Return Trip* by Steadman Williams, were going much further than embracing Christian values; they were, in fact, clearly promoting the Christian gospel. John Locke believes that its emphasis on Christianity was actually the Westminster's strength. He explains, 'As the only theatre in the country to base its ethics on Christian values and themes without necessarily proselytising the Christian faith, it set a unique and courageous path in the face of bigotry, opposition and professional dissent' (Locke, appendix 17, p.336). However, crucially, he perceives that many of the plays that had been staged had failed to attract a wider audience 'beyond MRA supporters and fellow travellers' (Locke, appendix 17, p.336). Monsignor Leonard acknowledges that part of the failure of the theatre was its inability to relate to those who did not agree with MRA ideology, or to gain sufficient support from those who did. He explains, in the *Westminster Theatre News*:

> One of the functions of Christian theatre is to pose questions to the people of our time ... That means ours has to be, in a positive sense, a subversive theatre, which of course causes controversy. Naturally any avowedly Christian theatre is fiercely resented by those who feel threatened by its convictions. It would be naïve to expect critical acclaim from today's liberal and permissive establishment. Unfortunately we also failed to convince committed Christians of the crucial importance of imagination and creativity in the service of truth. We had neither the space nor resources to carry out the necessary campaign of persuasion (Leonard, 1990, p.3).

For a theatre to exist purely to promote an ideology is a brave, yet herculean task. If Peter Howard had not died in 1965, if more MRA playwrights could have been recruited, if the number of supporters able to work voluntarily had not dwindled, it is still unlikely that the Westminster could have survived. Richard Palmer maintains that, measured in financial terms, 'the success of the MRA theatre eclipsed any comparable producing organisation in the left wing theatre' (Palmer, 1979, p.172). He highlights the fact that MRA was able to attract huge donations and 'function on a truly grand scale' in a way that its ideological opposite could not (Palmer, 1979, p.179). Palmer quotes the *Reader's Digest* of May 1967 as claiming that MRA had raised $2.5 million to keep full time casts of its American production *Sing Out* on the road (Palmer, 1979, p.179), no doubt as a result of Buchman's campaign to attract the rich and famous. But the aim of MRA theatre was to promote its beliefs and, according to Palmer, this is where it failed. He claims, 'As is often the case with propagandistic theatre, the effectiveness of MRA plays in gaining converts was limited by the simplistic treatment of plot, character and theme' (Palmer, 1979, p.185). He attributes the demise of the theatre to what he regards as naïve MRA philosophy, plus the 'narrowness of assumptions as to what constitutes effective propaganda' and 'the limited talent of the writers' (Palmer, 1979, p.185). The reasons for the closure of the theatre however are not as straightforward as Palmer would have it. For example, it was no longer possible to rent, at reasonable rates, the substantial houses in the area surrounding the Westminster and therefore the large group of supporters became fragmented. The costs of running any theatre — even the successful commercial enterprises in the West End of London — had become astronomical. In 1973 MRA's budget for producing and promoting its musical GB, was just £15,000 whereas in 1990 the cost of staging Temptation was £250,000. Perhaps most important of all is that many of those influential within the movement believed the theatre was no longer the most effective way in which to promote propaganda. Those wanting the theatre sold and replaced by targeted initiatives were supported by the argument that the costs of running the theatre outweighed the benefits. The Westminster's nemesis, the Royal Court, had become the respectable face of contemporary theatre; it had the backing of both the artistic community and the government. In 1995, at a time when the Christian Arts Trust was trying unsuccessfully to raise funds to purchase the Westminster, the Royal Court was awarded a £16 million grant from the National Lottery.

While it is possible for someone unconnected with the movement to analyse the reasons for the successes and failures of the Westminster objectively, it is important to consider how some of its key workers view the strengths and weaknesses of the theatre from a twenty-first century stand-point. Stanley Kiaer believes that the theatre was successful because it stood up for 'faith and the battle between good and evil in a secular age' but claims its downfall was due to 'massive increase in costs and the deaths of Peter Howard and Alan Thornhill as playwrights' (Kiaer, appendix 14, p.321). David Locke recalls the positive aspects of being involved in MRA theatre both as an audience member and behind the scenes:

> In the 1960s it [the Westminster] provided a focus for the MRA team. Something we could all do together to take the message to the country and it was an enjoyable way of doing it. After all, churchgoing was declining rapidly — many people hesitated to go into a church, but a theatre was a neutral space. As a result thousands came to the theatre over many years. Some came and enjoyed the entertainment. Others came and were influenced. However, some people came and their lives were changed (Locke, appendix 15, p.324).

According to FFT manager John Locke, the Westminster's greatest achievement was 'quite simply that it survived for so long and flourished in a hostile atmosphere that became deeply suspicious of its purposes and intentions' (Locke, appendix 17, p.336). He claims that the theatre was sold because Westminster Productions could not raise the money to purchase it and MRA, due to diminishing resources, could no longer afford to run it. He adds:

> MRA decided, collectively, that there were too many other areas of interest in which they were becoming involved and that theatre should no longer hold the supremacy it once did as part of their mission. From this perspective the Westminster Theatre simply did to give value for money (Locke, appendix 17, p.336).

It is certainly an achievement that the Westminster managed to continue to stage its propagandist plays for more than forty years and John

Locke is correct in observing that MRA had always had to cope with hostility. Nevertheless, any movement which claims to have the answer to the world's problems and advocates a way of living at odds with the culture of its time is bound to create enemies. Boobbyer suggests that the fact that Howard's plays were 'in a sense counter cultural: their strong moral and spiritual message was at odds with prevailing intellectual currents' may have contributed to the opposition (Boobbyer, 2005, p.218). MRA maintained a strict moral and ethical outlook which conflicted with twentieth-century culture but its mantra of absolute honesty, unselfishness, purity and love and listening daily in silence to either God or the inner voice could hardly be considered offensive. The movement did try to adjust to the cultural changes taking place. Its stance on homosexuality, for example, altered as the movement acknowledged the change in outlook of the majority. The launch of First Floor Theatre, with its aim of staging plays tackling current controversial issues, demonstrated a will to adapt.

Kenneth Belden describes those who set up the memorial fund to purchase the theatre in 1946 as having 'an unusual and far-sighted idea of seeking to purchase a West End theatre to provide not only entertainment but a constructive drama of ideas, relevant to the post-war world and based on Christian faith and moral values' (Belden, 1965b, p.23). There is no doubt that the Westminster did provide such drama, particularly in the immediate post-war years when its theatre was an effective means of gaining recruits. As Jane Plastow and Solomon Tseyahe state, 'Propaganda theatre has been utilised by any number of liberation and political movements and it has often been a popular and effective means of winning hearts and minds'

(Plastow and Tsehaye, 1998, p.51). Vladimir Maximov[17] highlighted the importance of literature and its influence on the individual when he spoke at a 'Freedom and the Media' MRA forum in the Westminster in 1978:

> The greatest mistake made by the Soviet leaders was not to destroy the Russian classics. From them the children get homilies in ortho-dox, boy-scout morality. At school the authorities teach the children they should lie when it suits the Party and should spy on their parents. Then they come home and read in Pushkin and Tolstoy that they should always tell the truth and should love their parents. And these things are so very much better expressed. The Chinese Communist leaders were wiser: they destroyed the classics (Maximov cited in McKay, 1978).

In its early years MRA theatre was successful because, like *The Forgotten Factor*, it reflected the dominant culture, whilst also acknowledging that a new era was beginning. John Bull says that from the end of the First World War to the mid-1950s, British drama was 'both class and geographically based. Its central concern was with questioning the details of a settled moral order – with the ruling classes of England securely at its centre – and not with subjecting the very foundations of this moral order to examination' (Bull, 1994, p.40). The analysis in this book of *The Diplomats*, a play origi-nally written in the mid-1950s, indicates that MRA drama was exactly as Bull described. The movement, which had the ruling class at its core, had noble aims: to bring about world peace, but for MRA the 'revolution' had to begin with a change in the hearts and minds of individuals, through ad-herence to the four absolute moral standards and ideology of the move-ment, not with the overthrow of a state or a political party. The four stand-ards were not a threat to the politics or the culture of the immediate post-

---

[17] Maximov was editor-in-chief of the literary journal he founded with Solzhenitsyn, *Konti-nent*, published in Berlin in four languages.

war era in Britain. Buchman stated in 1956 that those planning to build bonds between East and West needed the power of a strong belief system to support them: 'Do not think of changing the motives of men; or changing the purposes for which men and nations live. It takes an ideology to do that' (Buchman cited in *New World News*, 1956b, p.35). That ideology, however, has to be entirely relevant to the people it is trying to change and MRA could not, or would not, adapt to the changing times. Belden said in 1964 that the movement aimed to provide relevant theatre that was aware of current problems, but approached them 'from a wholly different standpoint ... Our purpose at the Westminster Theatre is to build up and extend this theatre of the relevant' (Belden 1965a, p.5). Belden's 'different standpoint' was the MRA ideology that the plays promoted, which resulted in the Westminster providing a form of entertainment not found elsewhere. However, the fact that MRA theatre was unique did not mean that it represented the emerging political and cultural landscape of Britain.

When referring to 'theatre of the relevant' Belden was no doubt alluding to the fact that Howard's plays, in particular, addressed political and moral concerns. Howard, as a former Fleet Street journalist, was acutely aware of the political situation at home and abroad. The subject matter of his work was relevant in the 1950s and the theatre-going public of that era was far more attuned to his style of writing than that of Samuel Beckett and his contemporaries. The fact that plays at the Westminster were delivered in a traditional, naturalistic format must have come as a relief to those initially mystified by genres such as Theatre of the Absurd. Theatre critics may have abhorred MRA theatre but audiences at the Westminster expected, and got, traditional well-made plays that reflected current issues through the lens of the movement's belief system. However, MRA did not have the monopoly on relevance; the Westminster's left-wing arch rivals — the Royal Court and Joan Littlewood's Theatre Workshop — were also addressing contemporary issues and doing so in a way that was reflecting the emerging culture of the 1960s. MRA realised that the Christian values and absolute moral standards it was promoting at the theatre were gradually being superseded by standards of a different kind. The movement wanted to provide an alternative to the increasingly popular avant-garde theatrical entertainment but did not really appreciate what it was trying to overcome. Belden writes: 'Modern drama fails in its social purpose. There is a vast area of reality which such plays never touch and which twentieth century theatre must learn to portray. The world today needs a theatre which shows people how to act constructively. People not only enjoy entertainment at the Westminster; they go out and do things afterwards' (Belden, 1965b, p.35). He describes contemporary theatre as 'a theatre of diagnosis. It is a theatre which goes on probing endlessly in ever greater detail and so-called frankness, the problems that everyone knows already but offers no glimmer of hope of how to deal with them' (Belden, 1968a, p.6). Belden was not alone in believing that the experimental theatre emerging in Britain was incomprehensible. For those used to the structure of the well-made play, as Belden clearly was, works by playwrights such as Samuel Beckett, Edward Bond and Harold Pinter would have appeared impenetrable. Martin Esslin says the works of Beckett and others of a similar genre initially 'puzzled and outraged most critics as well as audiences. And no wonder. These plays flout all the standards by which drama has been judged for many centuries; they must therefore appear as a provocation to people who have come into the theatre expecting to find what they would recognise as a well-made play' (Esslin,

1967, p.7). Belden claimed, for example, that Samuel Beckett's *Play* was not only 'trivial ... it will not help our modern youth' (Belden, 1965a, p.7), but positively dangerous. *Play* features three characters, trapped in identical funeral urns, reciting fragments of sentences which at times appear unintelligible. Andrew Kennedy writes that 'the immobile and breathless speakers recreate a minimal retrospective plot – of farcical/melodramatic adultery and inevitable suffering' (Kennedy, 1991, p.92). Belden's view is more extreme:

> It paralyses action. It makes you feel that here is nothing to be done about a world in which selfishness, greed, hatred, violence and lust will inevitably reign supreme. The very emotions it arouses increase your frustration because it is so plain that nothing can be done (Belden, 1965a, p.5).

Steadman Williams agreed with Belden's sentiments and, whilst recognising that playwrights had a 'serious and benevolent purpose in mind', writes: 'This does not mean that we have to abandon our judgement and criticism ... Genuine some of these people may be, but they are nevertheless guilty of a profound misreading of human nature' (Steadman Williams, 1969b, p.3). However, whenever the term 'human nature' is used it invariably refers to the viewpoint of whoever is making the statement. MRA was just as guilty of 'misreading human nature' as those it was accusing. Steadman Williams maintained that plays at the Westminster examined 'the vast reaches and ranges of life that so many other plays ignore' adding that the 'obsession with violence and sex' of the theatre in general, could only lead to a 'dead end', whereas exploring man's capability for evolution and greatness led to an 'endless journey of discovery' (Steadman Williams, 1969b, pp.7–8). It is clear that what concerned MRA was not only sex and violence but the lack of a religious message, particularly a Christian one. However

Belden, Steadman Williams, and others within MRA were not looking beyond the obvious; they had not grasped that contemporary theatre was not merely about violence and sex. Esslin describes the underlying themes of the genre that so disturbed MRA:

> It is true that basically Theatre of the Absurd attacks the comfortable certainties of religious or political orthodoxy. It aims to shock its audience out of complacency, to bring it face to face with the harsh facts of the human situation as these writers see it. But the challenge behind this message is anything but one of despair. It is a challenge to accept the human condition as it is, in all its mystery and absurdity, and to bear it with dignity, nobly, responsibly; precisely because there are no easy solutions to the mysteries of existence, because ultimately man is alone in a meaningless world. The shedding of easy solutions, of comforting illusions may be painful, but it leaves behind it a sense of freedom and relief ... the Theatre of Absurd does not provoke tears of despair but the laughter of liberation (Esslin, 1967, p.23).

In addition to being concerned about the avant-garde and what it regarded as the negative messages being promoted by contemporary theatre, MRA was aware of the emergence of a different class of playwright. In 1969 Steadman Williams observed that theatre was attracting a 'new breed' of writers such as Arnold Wesker, from an East End Jewish family: 'It is no longer just the province of a social set or intellectual elite, but it is gradually emerging as the arena of the ordinary man' (Steadman Williams, 1969b, p.2). He writes that the Westminster had taken a lead in this by actively encouraging large parties to come to the theatre from the shipyards, mines and factories. There were no miners or factory workers amongst its playwrights however and, on the whole, MRA's works seem to have preached to the converted. John McGrath highlights the importance of understanding the audience if one wishes to reach them:

To create a kind of theatre that tells the story from a different perspective, in a language that a different group of people understand
i.e. to create a working-class form of theatre appropriate to the late
twentieth century we have to look at the language of working-class
entertainment, at least to see what kind of language it is (McGrath,
1984, p.22).

MRA's origins, in the hallowed halls of Oxford University, ensured
that it remained very much the province of the middle-class intelligentsia
and on the whole its plays reflect that, rather than the world of the working-
class. McGrath maintains:

It is the job of anybody who wishes to continue to write, particularly
for the theatre, to extend their experience, not only to observe but
essentially to live through as great a variety of experience as they can
lay claim to, to explore this experience in depth as well as in breadth
and to find out, if possible at first hand, what is going on in the world
at large, and how their society operates in particular (McGrath, 1984,
p.92).

This is something that many MRA playwrights, particularly Howard,
found difficult to accomplish. It would have been problematic to have explored at first hand, or in depth, what it was like to be working class, for
instance, whilst remaining within the confines of the movement. The movement's greatest strength in the 1940s and 1950s, of living and working together to promote the Westminster Theatre, became a weakness as the twentieth century progressed. As the changes in culture and society that took
place during the 1960s gradually became accepted as mainstream in the latter half of the twentieth century, the MRA plays began to appear less relevant. Other playwrights were presenting their own messages in very different
ways and audiences were beginning to adapt and respond. Directors such as
Peter Brook and writers such as Pinter, who had been chastised in 1958 but
was largely accepted by 1964, were intent on experimenting with new theat-

rical styles, while the Westminster remained firmly entrenched in traditional, naturalistic theatre. Richard Palmer claims that naturalism attracted not only MRA but also those using the theatre to promote communism. He explains, 'Both were trying to persuade audiences to accept their respective world views; so the accessibility and believability of the plays to the audience were of paramount importance' (Palmer, 1979, p.184). Neither ideology was prepared to trust the audience to understand the message unless it was 're-peatedly spelled out' and the result, therefore, was 'stereotypical, flat, semi-allegorical characters' (Palmer, 1979, p.184). Dialogue was dominated by 'rhetorical rather than dramatic concerns. Aphorisms and harangues abound, often at the expense of consistency in characterisation and the progression of plot' (Palmer, 1979, p.184). Howard emphasised that the main reason for the Westminster's existence was not a theatrical one but to spread the MRA message: 'I write to preach. I write for the sake of propaganda. I write with a message and for no other reason' (Howard, 1964a, p.15). As has been seen throughout this book, the Westminster Theatre was denigrated for the preaching, bombastic tone of many of its plays and Howard's statement, that there was 'no other reason' for writing his plays than to pronounce a message, presents a serious flaw in the movement's method of propaganda and in its understanding of theatre as a means of communication.

Just five years after Howard's death, Steadman Williams claimed that MRA plays had moved beyond just providing a message and that theatre was in danger of becoming too didactic: 'I think we at the Westminster have gone far beyond telling people, or teaching or preaching. What we have to communicate is not simply a message. It is an experience' (Steadman Williams, 1969b, p.7). Steadman Williams also expressed concern over the lifting of theatre censorship — not because he believed theatre would become more violent, but rather the opposite. He maintained that, once the first effects of the abolition of the Lord Chamberlain's censorship had worn off, playwrights would no longer feel the need to experiment because the challenge of breaking the rules and pushing the boundaries would have disappeared. As a result, theatre would resort to feeding its audience on 'a diet of superficiality and seemingly harmless but sentimental unreality. Let us not fool ourselves. People with commercial interests are waiting for the swing to do just that ... They may make money out of violence today; they will want to make it out of sugar tomorrow' (Steadman Williams, 1969b, p.10). His prediction proved to be an accurate one. Nearly twenty years later, in the *Westminster Theatre News*, he argued that, for financial reasons, the theatre industry had 'fallen back on playing safe, with lavish musicals, frothy farces and comedies and ingenious thrillers that break no new ground either theatrically or in terms of ideas' (Steadman Williams, 1986, p.8). He warned that, in the longer term, the world would become more violent and less stable and that, in this environment, a theatre tackling serious, relevant issues, would increase in popularity:

> Anyone who has sat among far less affluent and much more long-suffering audiences in East European theatres will have experienced their almost tangible expectancy, the hope stretched taut like an archer's bow, that some new idea will emerge from the stage that evening that will feed their minds and spirits with the hope of change (Steadman Williams, 1986, p.8)

There is no way of knowing exactly how many people converted to MRA ideology after visiting the Westminster. Although many of the theatre critics clearly disliked the plays, their reviews cannot be said to necessarily represent those of the audience. Helen Freshwater says the problem with many reviews is that they 'often blithely ignore the possibility of a range of audience response' (Freshwater, 2009, p.8). She adds that they project the subjective responses of the critic on to the rest of the audience, 'discursively producing the audience the critic would like to imagine rather than accurately reflecting the complexity and potential diversity of collective and individual response' (Freshwater, 2009, pp 8-9). Many critics of MRA plays assumed that they were reflecting the views of an entire audience. For instance, David Pryce-Jones, in *The Spectator*, describes *The Diplomats* as 'intellectually non-existent. Like the freak that it is, the play is tied up in its own cage at the MRA theatre, the Westminster, although properly it should go crack-potting back to Hyde Park Corner' (Pryce-Jones, 1964). However, the play attracted good houses, the MRA supporters appear to have enjoyed it and fifty years later, in 2013, it was regarded as entertaining and relevant by many in the audience with no previous knowledge of the movement. Eric Bentley stresses the difficulties involved in attempting to measure the effectiveness of propaganda in the theatre:

> You are made to feel strongly about a certain thing and if the dose is repeated often enough, your feelings will perhaps harden into a habit. One believes this; yet one cannot measure any of the factors involved. For example the theatre might help to inculcate patriotism but if a theatregoer is a patriot, how can you tell how much of his patriotism actually came from the theatre? (Bentley, 1987, p.151).

Bentley also observes that the theatre, more than the other arts, 'depends for its existence on groups or societies of individuals' (Bentley, 1987, p.153). MRA had always attracted the rich and famous and the Westminster Theatre was backed by a committee and advisory council consisting of several Air Vice Marshals, plus a number of 'Sirs' and 'Ladies'. Palmer claims the appeal of MRA rested in the opportunity 'to participate actively in a socially prestigious group' (Palmer, 1979, p.181) and, as already stated, the emphasis on living and working together as a group was one of the movement's greatest strengths in its early years.

Nearly twenty years after the sale of the Westminster, MRA, now known as Initiatives of Change (IofC), still exists but has evolved with the changing times. While Stanley Kiaer, David Locke, Chris Evans, Philip Boobbyer and others continue to work on a voluntary basis, many of its leading officers are now paid and recruited from outside of the movement. Its theatre arm, Renewal Arts, links artists from around the world on a variety of projects but there has been a change of emphasis and there are now no large-scale theatrical events. Instead, IofC has taken on a more corporate identity. It organises forums and targeted projects world-wide and its platform no longer relies on the stage but includes social media and websites. It is a respected Non-Governmental Organisation, working with representatives of the United Nations and the international community on a variety of projects dealing with issues such as religious conflicts in Nigeria, the rights of women in the Sudan, corruption in India and the Western banking crisis. Its annual Caux conferences attract a range of high-level international speakers. In July 2013 Kofi Annan, former United Nations secretary general, delivered the concluding address at a 'Trust and Integrity in the Global Economy' conference at Caux. Other speakers have included Joe Garner, deputy chief executive of HSBC Bank in the UK.

It should not be forgotten however that the roots of MRA were developed in the theatre. Its plays may have been unpopular with many theatre critics and ignored by theatre historians, but MRA played a valuable and unique role in giving people a choice, giving them an opportunity to experience a different kind of theatre in an era dominated by the left-leaning and the avant-gardes. No other theatre in London in the latter half of the twentieth century was offering the propagandist moralistic theatre associated with MRA; no other theatre existed, first and foremost, to promote its own ideology; no other single play, before or since, has had quite the effect on British industry that *The Forgotten Factor* had in 1946. It is difficult to sum up the place of MRA theatre within the wider field of literature. It was propagandist but in a sense this term could be applied to all theatre because at some level all plays promote a message. It wanted to change society but it did not want to overthrow political systems in the way that Brecht and Joan Littlewood hoped to do. In its later years it could be described as delivering Christian theatre, but this would not be an accurate description of MRA theatre as a whole which, under Buchman and Howard, aimed to attract all religions. Playwright Arthur Miller sums up the value of theatre as a tool for change and could almost be speaking for MRA when he writes:

> Embarrassing as it may be to remind ourselves, the theatre does reflect the spirit of a people, and when it lives up to its potential it may even carry them closer to their aspirations. It is the most vulgar of the arts but it is the simplest too ... All you need is a human and a board to stand on and something fascinating for him to say and do. With a few right words, sometimes, he can clarify the minds of thousands, still the whirling compass needle of their souls and point it once more towards the stars ... Theatre is not going to die, it is as immortal as our dreaming (Miller, 1994, p.xix-xx)

MRA had the 'board' and it had the 'human'. Initially, it had the right words that 'clarified the minds' of many of those who attended the performances of plays such as *The Forgotten Factor*. And throughout its reign at the Westminster, the movement managed to influence people and turn the souls of many of its audience 'towards the stars'. John Locke says 'The achievements of the Theatre, far greater than its eventual fate, will, in the course of time, hopefully be recognised' (Locke, appendix 17, p.336). Nearly seventy years after MRA purchased the Westminster, its work has at last been documented and can now hopefully take its rightful place in the history of British theatre.

Bibliography

Adams, M., 1994. *The Best War Ever: America and World War II*. Maryland: John Hopkins University Press

Attwood, B., 1991. Westminster Up For Sale. *The Stage*, May 16. Worcester: MRA/IofC archives, files UK 26.6 – 26.8

Austin, H.W. and P. Konstam, 1969. *A Mixed Double*. London: Chatto and Windus

Austin, H.W., 1971. The Westminster Theatre and its Outreach. *The Westminster Theatre News*, No.40, February. Worcester: MRA/IofC archives, file UK 26.0

Baker, R. 1973. *Limelight*. MRA/IofC archives. Worcester: MRA/IofC archives, file Westminster Theatre Press Cuttings

Banham, C., 2000. *The Cambridge Guide to Theatre* (1995). Cambridge: Cambridge University Press.

Baran, S. And D. Davis, 2015. *Mass Communication Theory: Foundations, Ferment and Future*, S.E., 2009. Stamford, Connecticut: Cengage Learning

Belden, K., 1963. Theatre of Tomorrow [article]. *Westminster Theatre Brochure*. Worcester: MRA/IofC archives, file UK 26.5

————1964a. Drama's Purpose. *The Daily Telegraph*, July 2. Worcester: MRA/IofC archives, file Westminster Theatre Press Cuttings

————1965a. *Theatre and the Future* (1964) [pamphlet]. London: MRA/IofC archives

————1965b. *The story of the Westminster Theatre*. London: Westminster Productions

————1967. *Theatre and the War Against God*, [report]. Worcester: MRA/IofC Archives, file UK 26.5

————1968a. *Theatre in the Modern World* (1965) [pamphlet]. London: MRA/IofC archives

————1968b. *Theatre and the Task of the Century* (1967) [pamphlet]. London: MRA/IofC archives

————1970a. *Memo regarding Henry Cass* [memo]. Worcester: MRA/IofC archives, file 6.0121

————1970b. Salute to the Friends of the Theatre [article]. *Westminster Theatre News*, No.38. October. Worcester: MRA/IofC archives, file UK 26.2 26.3

————1971. Bridgehead into the Thinking of Nations' [article]. *MRA Information Service*. Worcester: MRA/IofC archives, file UK 26.0

————1972. *Where There's Change There's Hope* [pamphlet]. London: Friends of the Westminster Theatre.

————1974. It's a Great Thing to Know Who Your Friends Are. *Westminster Theatre News*, No. 57. Worcester: MRA/IofC archives, files UK 26.2 - 26.3

————1979a. *Confidential Report*. [report]. Worcester: MRA/IofC archives, file UK 26.5

————1979b. *Meeting Moral Re-Armament*. London: Grosvenor Books

————1992. *The Hour of the Helicopter*. Somerset: Linden Hall

Belden, K. and R. Wilson, 1965. *The Importance of the Westminster Theatre* [letter] (personal communication to the Friends of Westminster Theatre, 2 March). London: Belden archive

Belden, S., 1964b. *Report*. Worcester: MRA/IofC archives, file UK.26.1

Belgrade Theatre Company, 2010. *A History of Theatre in Education at the Belgrade Theatre Company*. [online] Available at www.belgrade.co.uk/files/downloads/192/TIE+education+pack.pd [accessed 24 February, 2015]

Bell, M., 1982. *Response to Day of London Theatre* [letter] (personal communication to Joy Weeks, Westminster Theatre, 8 February). Worcester: MRA/IofC archives, files UK 26.2 - 26.3

Bentley, E., 1981. *The Brecht Commentaries, 1943–1980*. London: Eyre Methuen

————1987. *Thinking about the Playwright: Comments from Four Decades* (1952). Illinois: North Western University Press

Berger, R., and Choi, C.J., 2010. Ethics of Celebrities and Their Increased Influence in 21st century Society. In *Journal of Business Ethics*. pp. 313-318. [online]. Available at: https://www.idc.ac.il/publications/files/530.pdf. [accessed 19 March, 2016].

Billington, M., 1978. *Sentenced to Life* [review]. *The Guardian*. Worcester: MRA/IofC archives, file 12.046

————2008. Fighting Talk [article]. *The Guardian*, 3 May. Available at: http://www.theguardian.com/books/2008/may/03/theatre.stage. [accessed 21 March, 2016]

————2015. Look Back in Anger: How John Osborne Liberated Theatrical Language [article]. *The Guardian*, 30 March. Available at: http://www.theguardian.com/stage/2015/march/30. [accessed 16 June, 2015]

Birmingham Post, 1963. Theatre Walk-out by Head Praised [article]. *Birmingham Post*. Worcester: MRA/IofC archives, file UK 26.0

Blair, T., 1972. Irish Launch New Era [article]. *Westminster Theatre News*, No.48. Worcester: MRA/IofC archives, file UK 26.4

Bollington, M., 2013. *Statistical First Release* [report]. London: Department for Business, Innovation and Skills.

Boobbyer, P., 2003. Moral Re-Armament in Africa in the Era of Decolonization. In *Missions, Nationalism and the End of Empire*. Ed. B. Stanley. Michigan: William B. Eerdmans

——————2005. The Cold War in the Plays of Peter Howard. *Contemporary British History*, Vol.19. No.2. pp. 205-222

——————2013. *The Spiritual Vision of Frank Buchman*. Pennsylvania: The Pennsylvania State University Press

Boorne, B., 1964. Dare You Take Your Daughter to the Theatre? [article]. *The Evening News*, 2 July. Worcester: MRA/IofC archives, file UK 26.1

Bowling, B., 1998. *Violent Racism: Victimization, Policies and Social Context*. Oxford: Oxford University Press

Brannigan, J., 1998. *New Historicism and Cultural Materialism*. London: Macmillan.

Brecht, B., 1964. *Brecht on Theatre: The Development of an Aesthetic*. Ed. And translation J. Willett. London: Methuen

——————1972. *Collected Plays: Bertolt Brecht*. Vol. 5 (1970). Eds. R. Manheim and J. Willett. New York: Vintage

——————1977. *The Measures Taken and other Lehrstücke* (1955). London: Methuen

Brien, A., 1966. Own Golden Centre 42 [report]. *Sunday Telegraph*, 22 May. Essex: Pamela Jenner personal theatre archive

British Broadcasting Corporation, 2005. UK Unemployment Tops Three Million. *On this Day 1982*. [online]. Available at: http://news.bbc.co.uk/onthisday/hi/dates/stories/january/26.newsid_2506000/2506335.stm [accessed 04 February, 2015]

Brown, C., 2001. *The Death of Christian Britain*. London and New York: Routledge

Buchman, F., 1947. *Remaking the World*. London: Blandford Press

Bucks Free Press, 1965. Influence of Modern Theatre [article] 4 May. *The Bucks Free Press*. Worcester: MRA/ IofC archives, file UK. 26.0

Bull, J., 1994. *Stage Right*. Hampshire: Macmillan

Burton. T., L. Nicklin, H. Quince, M. Webster, A. Wilson, 1946. Letter to the Editor [letter]. *Yorkshire Evening News*, 3 July, 1946. Worcester: MRA-IofC archives, file UK 26.1.1

Cahn, V., 1994. *Gender and Power in the Plays of Harold Pinter*. Basingstoke: Palgrave Macmillan

Cairncross, A., 1991. The United Kingdom. In: A. Graham with A. Seldon (1990). *Government and Economics in the Post War World: Economic Policies and Comparative Performance 1945-85*. London and New York: Routledge

Campbell, J., 2008. *Margaret Thatcher. Volume Two: The Iron Lady* (2003). London: Random House

Cass, H., 1964. Henry Cass Addresses First Forum Session [article].*Westminster Theatre News*, No.2. September 1964. Worcester: MRA/IofC archives, file UK.26.4

Cazalet, P., 1990. *Letter to Steadman Williams on behalf of APV* [letter]. 20 February. Sussex: Hugh Steadman Williams personal archive

Chaillet, N., 1978. *Sentenced to Life* [article]. *The Times*, 18 May. Worcester: MRA/IofC archives, file 12.046

Chambers, C., Ed., 2002. *The Continuum Companion to Twentieth Century Theatre*. London and New York: Continuum

Chand, P., 1990. *The Widening Gyre* [review]. *Westminster Theatre News*, January. Worcester: MRA/IofC archives, file UK 26.4

Channer, D., 1981. Cash for 'Gavin' Production [article]. *Westminster Theatre News*, No. 98. December. Worcester: MRA/IofC archives, file UK 26.4

Clark, W.H., 1985. *The Oxford Group: Its History and Significance*. New York: Bookman Associates

Claxton, E., 1968. A Moral Dunkirk [article]. *Westminster and Pimlico News*. Worcester: MRA/IofC Archives, file UK.26.0

Clayton, Ed., 1986. *Martin Luther King: The Peaceful Warrior* (1964). New York: Simon and Schuster

Commemorative Brochure, 1946. A Theatre is Commissioned. [article]. *Commemorative Brochure*. Worcester: MRA/IofC archives, file UK 26.1.1

Cook, W., 1990. *The Widening Gyre* [review]. Reprinted in *Westminster Theatre News*, January. Worcester: MRA/IofC archives, file UK 26.4

Cooper, N., 1990. Message to all Friends [article]. *Westminster Theatre News*, August. Worcester: MRA/IofC archives, file UK 26.4

————1991a. A Meeting of Friends [article]. *Westminster Theatre News*, February. Worcester: MRA/IofC archives, file UK 26.4

————1991b. The Friends … And the Future [article]. *Westminster Theatre News*, July. Worcester: MRA/IofC archives, file UK 26.4

————1993. Chairman's Challenge [article]. *Friends News*, April. Worcester: MRA/IofC archives, file UK 26.4

————1996a. An Exceptionally Wide-Ranging Programme [article]. *Friends News*, March. Worcester: MRA/IofC archives, file UK 26.4

————1996b. Salute to the Pioneers [article]. *Friends News*, March. Worcester: MRA/IofC archives, file UK 26.4

————1997. The Future of the Westminster Theatre and the Future of the Friends [article]. *Friends News*, November. Worcester: MRA/IofC archives, file UK 26.4

————1998a. Friends still have a Vital Role to Play [article] *Friends News*, March. Worcester: MRA/IofC archives, file UK 26.4

————1998b. Remembrance, Gratitude, Re-dedication [article]. *Friends News*, November. Worcester: MRA/IofC archives, file UK 26.4

Copsey, N., 2009. Opposition to the New Party: An Incipient Anti-Fascism or Defence against 'Mosleyitis'? [article]. *Contemporary British History*, 23:44, pp 461–475.

Craig, A., G. Craig, C. Evans, J. Hore-Ruthven, J. Htet Khin, S. Kiaer, M. Lean, J Lester, C. Montrose, E. Peters, P. Ridell, M. Spooner, and G. Wise, 1995. *Letter to Friends* [letter], 11 December. Worcester: MRA/IofC archives, file UK 1.3

Craig, G., C. Evans, S. Kiaer, M. Lean, 1998. *Letter to Friends* [letter], 16 March. Worcester: MRA/IofC archives, file UK 1.3

Croydon Advertiser, 1964. Triteness is All [article]. *Croydon Advertiser*, 17 January. Worcester: MRA/IofC archives, file 12.054

Cull, N., D. Culbert and D. Welch, 2003. *Propaganda and Mass Persuasion: An Historical Encyclopaedia, 1500 to the Present*. California: ABC-CLIO

Daily Express, 1990. After all the hoo-ha, La Lenska Rules [review]. *The Daily Express Diary*, 8 June. Surrey: Hugh Steadman Williams archives

Daily Mirror, 1946. Theatre sold to group is "lost to us", Actors say' [article]. *The Daily Mirror*, 27 April. Worcester: MRA/IofC archives, file UK. 26.1.1

Daily Worker, 1946. Oxford Group takes over London Theatre [article]. *The Daily Worker*, 27 April. Worcester: MRA/IofC archives, file UK 26.1.1

Darlington, W. A., 1964a. Theatre No Place for Propaganda [article]. *The Daily Telegraph and Morning Post*. July. Worcester: MRA/IofC archives, file 12.054

————1964b. When the Message Kills the Play [article]. *The Daily Telegraph and Morning Post*, Monday 29 July. Worcester: MRA/IofC archives, file 12.054

————1964c. Peace Theme for Wishful Thinkers [article]. *The Daily Telegraph and Morning Post*. 1 July, 1964. Worcester: MRA/IofC archives, file 12.054

————1967. What Will the Puritans do Now? [article]. *The Daily Telegraph*. 3 July. Worcester: MRA/IofC archives, file UK 26.0

Davies, A. and P. Saunders., 1983. Literature, Politics and Society. In *Society and Literature 1945–1970*, Ed. A. Sinfield. New York: Holmes and Meier

Davies, J. and G. Oliver, 1982. *Westminster Theatre's Educational Work*. [Letter to Joy Weeks, Westminster Theatre]. Worcester: MRA/IofC archives, file UK 26.2/26.3

Dawson, A., 2013. *The Routledge Concise History of Twentieth Century British Literature*. Oxon: Routledge

Day of London Theatre, n.d. *Transcript of First Ideas for Staged Rehearsal* [transcript]. Worcester: MRA/IofC archives, file UK 26.2–26.3

De Jongh, N., 1990. Havel, the Hot-Blooded [article]. *The Guardian*, 8 June. Surrey: Hugh Steadman Williams archive

Deak, Istvan, 2013. Could Stalin have Been Stopped? *The New York Review of Books*, 21 March, 2013. Available at: <http://www.nybooks.com/articles/archives/2013/mar/21/could-stalin-have-been-stopped/?page=1> [accessed 16 October, 2013]

Defty, A., 2013. *Britain, America and Anti-Communist Propaganda: 1945–1953* (2004). Oxford: Routledge

Dickson, K., 2008. *World War II Almanac*. New York: Infobase Publishing

Dilly, R., 1995. *Discovering Moral Re-Armament*. London: Freeway Publications

Driberg, T., 1964. *The Mystery of Moral Re-Armament: A Study of Frank Buchman and his Movement*. London: Secker and Warburg

Eagleton, T., 1983. *Literary Theory*. Oxford: Basil Blackwell

East London Advertiser, 1964. Review of *The Diplomats*. *The East London Advertiser*, January. Worcester: MRA/IofC archives, file 12.054

Economist, 2013. Margaret Thatcher: Freedom Fighter. *The Economist* [online]. Available at: <http://www.economist.com/news/leaders/21576094-now-especially-world-needs-hold-fast-margaret-thatchers-principles-freedom-fighter> [accessed 03 February, 2015]

Esslin, M., 1967. Introduction. In *Absurd Drama* (1965). London: Penguin
————1980. *Brecht: A Choice of Evils* (1959). London: Eyre Methuen

European, 1990. More Fun than Kissing Babies: Havel Courts Votes at Home but his Play Hits Trouble in London [article]. *The European*, 8 June. Surrey: Hugh Steadman Williams archive

Evans, A., 2012. Conversation between Pamela Jenner and Anne Evans, archivist for MRA/IofC archives. *Memories of Westminster Theatre* (personal communication). 29 October

Evans, C., J. Hore-Ruthven, J. Lester, N. Morshead, 1990. *Letter Regarding Closure of The Westminster Theatre*, [letter] 11 October. Worcester: MRA/IofC archives, file UK 26.6

Evans, H., 1972. Letter Regarding Reviews of Plays at the Westminster Theatre. *The Sunday Times*, [letter] (personal communication to Michael Henderson). 01 February. Devon: Michael Henderson archives

Evans, V. 1955. The MRA Plays. In *Report on Moral Re-Armament*. Ed Mowat, R.C. London: Blandford Press

Evening Gazette, 1963. Play With a Message or a Sermon? *The Evening Gazette*. 10 December. Worcester: MRA/IofC archives, file UK.26.0

Evening News, 1963. Apology by MP to Peter Howard, *The Evening News*. 11 July. Worcester: MRA/IofC archives, file UK 26.1

Feedback Reports, 1988. *Feedback Reports by Teachers Regarding Day of London Theatre* [reports]. Surrey: David Locke Archives.

Fleming, L., 1966a. *Letter of Acceptance* [letter] (personal communication). 10 October. Cambridgeshire: Fleming archives
————1966b. Revolution through the Arts [article]. *MRA Information Service*. Vol. 15, No.11. Cambridgeshire: Louis Fleming archives
————1967. What I Think for the New Arts Centre [article]. *Westminster Theatre News*, No. 16. January. Worcester: MRA/IofC archives, file UK 26.5

Frame, C., 1964. Fun and then the Moral [review]. *The Evening News*, 01 January. Worcester: MRA/IofC archives, file 12.054

Freshwater, H., 2009. *Theatre and Audience*. Hampshire: Palgrave Macmillan

Friends News, 1992. Friends Conclude Successful Spring Programme [report]. *Friends News*, June. Worcester: MRA/IofC archives, file UK 26.4

Friends News, 1999. Farewell to the Westminster. *Friends News*, March. Worcester: MRA/IofC archives, file UK 26.4

Friends of the Westminster Theatre, 1998. *The Future of the Friends* [report]. Worcester: MRA/IofC archives, file UK 26.4

Fuegi, J., 1987. *Bertolt Brecht: Chaos, According to Plan*. Cambridge: Cambridge University Press

Gandhi, R., 1986. Message to the Conference. *New World News* Vol. 34, No. 24, December. Worcester: MRA/IofC archives, files UK 26.6 - 26.8

Gazette de Lausanne, 1953. Report on *The Boss* [article]. *The Gazette de Lausanne*, December. Worcester: MRA/IofC archives, file UK 26.0

Gee, G., 1946. *Letter announcing the purchase of the Westminster Theatre* [letter]. April. Worcester: MRA/IofC archives, file UK 26.1

Gellert, R., 1964. No Hand Signals [review]. *The New Statesman*, 10 January. Worcester: MRA/IofC archives, file 12.054

Germanou, M., 1982. Brecht and the English Theatre. In *Brecht in Perspective*. Eds. G. Bartram and A. Waine. London: Longman

Gillard, D., 2011. Education in England: A Brief History. [online]. *Education England*. Available at <www.educationengland.org.uk/history>. [Accessed 03 March, 2015]

Gray, B. and N. Ruthven, 1983. *Clashpoint*. London: Westminster Productions

Guardian, 1968. The Year that Changed History. *The Guardian*, 17 January. Available at: <http://www.theguardian.com/observer/gallery/2008/jan/17/1> [accessed 11 January, 15]

Gunn, T., 1946. Readers Support Midlothian Miners [article]. *The Weekly Scotsman*. Worcester, MRA/IofC archives, file UK 26.1.1

Harker, B., 2009. Mediating the 1930s: Documentary and Politics in Theatre Union's 'Last Edition'. In *Get Real: Documentary Theatre Past and Present*. Eds. A Forsyth and C. Megson. London: Palgrave Macmillan

Hassell, G., c.1954. *The Westminster Theatre* [report]. London: David and Kay Hassell archive

Havel, V., 1989. *Temptation*. New York: Grove Press

Henderson, M., 1972. *Memo Regarding Press Coverage of Plays at the Westminster Theatre* Devon: Michael Henderson archives

Henderson, M., 1990. *Letter to David Channer Regarding Controversy over Performance at the Westminster Theatre* [letter]. Devon: Michael Henderson archives

Hennessy, P. 2007. *Having it So Good: Britain in the Fifties* (2006). London: Penguin Books.

Hobson, H., 1964 Standards of Daring [article]. *The Sunday Times*. Worcester: MRA/IofC archives, file UK.26.0

Hobson, H., 1973. Taking the Offensive [article]. *The Sunday Times*. 18 March. Devon: Michael Henderson archives.

Hodgson, J., 1980. *Is it True what They Say about MRA? – A Trade Unionist's Look at MRA*. London: Waterfront and Industrial Pioneer

Holdsworth, N., 2006. *Joan Littlewood*. London and New York: Routledge

————2011. *Joan Littlewood's Theatre*. Cambridge: Cambridge University Press

Holmes, C. 1991. Immigration. In *Britain since 1945*. Eds: T. Gourvish, and A. O'Day. London: Macmillan

Howard, A., 1964. Review of *The Diplomats*. *The New Statesman*, 10 April. Worcester: MRA/IofC archives, file 12.054

Howard, P., 1940. Four Things to Kick Up a Row About [article]. *The Daily Express*, 14 February. London: British Library newspaper archives

——————1941. *Innocent Men*. London and Toronto: William Heinemann

——————1945a. *Ideas have Legs*. London: Frederick Muller

——————1945b. *Men on Trial*. London: Blandford Press

——————1954a. *The Boss*. London: Blandford Press

——————1954b. *The Man with the Key*. London: Blandford Press

——————1956. *The Dictator's Slippers* (1954). London: Blandford Press

——————1961. *Frank Buchman's Secret*. London: Heinemann

——————1963. *Britain and the Beast*. London: Heinemann

——————1964a. *Mr Brown Comes Down the Hill*. London: Blandford Press

——————1964b. *The Diplomats*. London: Blandford Press.

——————1964c. The Modern Man [article]. *Westminster Theatre News*, No.3, November. Worcester: MRA/IofC archives, file UK 26.5

Howe, S., 2012. Decolonisation and Imperial Aftershocks: The Thatcher Years. In *Making Thatcher's Britain*. Eds. B. Jackson and R. Saunders. Cambridge: Cambridge University Press

Hugh, 1954. *Letter from Hugh to Frank* [letter] (personal communication) April. Worcester: MRA/IofC archives, file UK 26.0

Hurley, D., G. Hern, B. Hegarty, T. Keep, C. Stebbing, T. Jones, F. Briden, S. Young, J. Manning, F. Willets, 1951. *Correspondence from the National Amalgamated Stevedores' and Dockers' Union*, [report]. 23 November. Worcester: MRA/IofC archives, file UK 26.0

Hurley, D., 1952. A Stir in East London [article]. *New World News*. Vol. 8, No.1. pp. 4-5. London: MRA/IofC archives

Jackson, T., 1980. *Learning through Theatre: Essays and Casebooks on Theatre in Education*. Manchester: Manchester University Press

Kennedy, A., 1991. *Samuel Beckett* (1989). Cambridge: Cambridge University Press

Kentish Times, 1964. Diplomats' Conscience [review]. *Kentish Times*, January 10. Worcester: MRA/IofC archives, file 12.054

Kershaw, B., ed., 2004. *The Cambridge History of British Theatre*. Vol. 3. Cambridge: Cambridge University Press

Kiaer, S., 1990. The Facts [article]. *Westminster Theatre News*, August. Worcester: MRA/IofC archives, file UK 26.6

Kiaer, S., 1991. The Next Phase [article]. *Westminster Theatre News*, December. Worcester: MRA/IofC archives, file UK 26.4

——————1996. Future of the Westminster Theatre – An update [article]. *Friends News*, March. Worcester: MRA/IofC archives, file UK 26.4

——————1998. Westminster Theatre Sold [article]. *Friends News*, March. Worcester: MRA/IofC archives, file UK 26.4

————————2015. Conversation between Pamela Jenner and Stanley Kiaer *Conversation on MRA attitude to Margaret Thatcher* (personal communication) 20 March.

Kingston, J., 1989. Unusual Irish Views [article]. *The Times*, 11 November. Worcester: MRA/IofC archives, files UK 2.6., 26.7, 26.8

Krieger, J., 1999. *British Politics in the Global Age: Can Social Democracy Survive?* New York: Oxford University Press

Leaflet, 1997. *Give a Dog a Bone* [leaflet]. December 1997. London: Friends of Westminster Theatre. Worcester: MRA/IofC archives, file UK 26.4

Lean, G., 1985. *Frank Buchman: A Life*. London: Constable

Lean, M., 1998. Bringing Down the Curtain [article]. *For a Change*, Vol. 11, No. 3. Worcester: MRA/IofC archives, file UK 26.4

Lean, M., 2015. *Message regarding MRA and Christianity* [email] (personal communication to Pamela Jenner). June 18.

Lear, C. J., 1972. Letter Regarding Press Coverage. *News of the World*. [letter] (personal communication to Michael Henderson). 05 December. Devon: Michael Henderson archives

Lear, M., 1965. Why I gave £10,000 [article].*Westminster Theatre News*, No 7. Worcester: MRA/IofC archives, file UK 26.1.1

Leese, J., 1972. Evening News Theatre Review Policy. *The Evening News*. [letter] (personal communication to Michael Henderson). 27 November. Devon: Michael Henderson archives

Lee-Potter, L., 1990. Naked Truth About Rula [article]. *Daily Mail*, 15 June. Surrey: Hugh Steadman Williams archives

Leland, A., and M. Oboroceanu, 2010. American War and Military Operations: Casualty Lists and Statistics. *Congressional Research Service*. Available at <fpc.state.gov/documents/organization/139347.pdf> [accessed 18 October, 2013]

Leonard, G., 1990. The Vision Lives On [article]. *Westminster Theatre News*, August. Worcester: MRA/IofC archives, file UK 26.6 - 26.8

Lloyd-Evans, G., 1982. *To Whom it may Concern* [letter]. 2 February. Worcester: MRA/IofC archive, file UK 26.–26.3

Locke, J., 1990. First Floor Theatre — A Personal Note from Manager John Locke [article]. *Westminster Theatre News*. August. Worcester: MRA/IofC archives, file UK 26.4

Louis, Wm. Roger, 2006. *Ends of British Imperialism*. London: I. B. Tauris

Luttwak, E., 1994. Franco-German Reconciliation: The Overlooked Role of the Moral Re-Armament Movement. In *Religion: The Missing Dimension of Statecraft*. Eds. D. Johnston and C. Sampson. New York: Oxford University Press.

Lyon, J. and Hans-Peter Breuer, 1995. *Brecht Unbound*. Ontario: Associated University Presses

McGrath, J., 1984. *A Good Night Out* (1981). London and New York: Methuen

McKay, D., 1978. Maximov Speaks [article]. *Westminster Theatre News*, No. 81. February. Worcester: MRA/IofC archives, file UK 26.4

Manchester Guardian, 1946. Committee Buy a London Theatre [article]. *The Manchester Guardian*, 27 April. Worcester: MRA/IofC archives, file UK 26.1.1

Mann, R., 1989. *Memo on financing First Floor Theatre*, 6 April. [memo]. Worcester: MRA/IofC archives UK 26.2-26.3

Marr, A., 2008. *A History of Modern Britain*, 2007. London: Pan Books.

Meakins, J. B. , 1955. The Finances of MRA. In *Report on Moral Re-Armament*. Ed. R. C. Mowat. London: Blandford Press

Memo, 1998. *Programme Notes* [memo]. Worcester: MRA/IofC archives, file UK 26.4

Merrick, R., 1985. The Russian Committee of the British Foreign Office and the Cold War, 1946-47. *Journal of Contemporary History*, Vol. 20, No. 3. pp. 453-468

Mestrovic, M., 1989. Theater; from Prison, a Playwright yearns for a Stage. *New York Times*, 9 April, 1989. Available at: <http://go.gale-group.com/ps/i.do?&id=GALE|A175674942&v=2.1&u=anglia_itw&it=r&p=AONE&sw=w&authCount=1> [accessed 03 December, 2013]

Miller, A., 1994. Author's Foreword to the Second Edition (1992). In *The Theatre Essays of Arthur Miller* (1978). London: Methuen

Morrissey, M., 1963. They Laid it on Too Thick [article]. *The Northern Echo*, 10 December. Worcester: MRA/IofC archives, file UK.26.0

Morshead, N., 1968. *How We Raised the Building Fund and What We Need Now* [booklet]. London: Friends of Westminster Theatre

Motor Trader, 1946. *Forgotten Factor*: Motor Trade at the Theatre [article]. *The Motor Trader*. Worcester, MRA/IofC archives, file UK. 26.1.1

Mowat, R.C., 2000. *Peter Howard: A Re-Evaluation*. Oxford: New Cherwell Press

MRA, 1947a. *A Report of an Industrial Conference at the Westminster Theatre*, 27 March, 1947. Worcester: MRA/IofC archives, files UK 26.0 and 26.1.1

MRA, 1947b. *A Report on Contributions to the Westminster Memorial Trust Fund*, February 1946 to July 1947 [report]. Worcester: MRA/IofC archives, file UK. 26.1.1

MRA Information Service, 1971. 25th Anniversary at Westminster Theatre [report]. *MRA Information Service*, 20 November. Vol. 20, No. 8. Worcester: MRA/IofC archives, file UK. 26.0

Mueller, R., 2006. Learning for a New Society: The Lehrstücke. In *The Cambridge Companion to Brecht* (1994). Eds. P. Thomson and G. Sacks. Second Edition. Cambridge: Cambridge University Press

New World News, 1948. Stoke-on-Trent [article]. *New World News*, Vol. 4. No.1, 9 January. London: MRA/IofC archives

——————1955. An Answer that Works [article]. *New World News*. London: MRA/IofC archives

—————1956a. If You Fail the World Fails [article]. *New World News*, No.14. Autumn. Worcester: Robin Evans archives

—————1956b. Nations that will not think [article]. *New World News*, No.14. Autumn. Worcester: Robin Evans archives

—————1965. The Stage is Set [article]. *New World News*. No.27. October-December. London: MRA/IofC archive

—————1978. I was Sharply Moved [article]. *New World News*. Vol. 26 No. 28. Worcester: MRA/IofC archives, file 12.046

—————1986. Rajmohan Gandhi Message to Conference [report]. *New World News*. Vol. 34 No. 24. 6 December.

Nicholson, S., 2012. *Modern British Playwriting: The 1960s*. London: Methuen

—————2015. *The Censorship of British Drama 1900-1968. Vol. 4 The Sixties*. Exeter: University of Exeter Press

Nightingale, B., 1990. Tempted to Extravagance [article]. *The Times*, 7 June. Surrey: Hugh Steadman Williams archive

Northern Echo, 1963. Propaganda Play May Cause Row [article]. *The Northern Echo*, 22 November. Worcester: MRA/IofC archives, file UK.26.0

Oakley, A., 2003. *Marx's Critique of Political Economy*. Vol. II (1985). Oxford: Routledge

Osborne, C., 1990. Faust among the Bureaucrats [review]. *The Daily Telegraph*, 7 June. Surrey: Hugh Steadman Williams archives

Oxford Group Council of Management, 1995. *The Future of the Westminster Theatre* [Letter] (personal communication to the Friends of the Westminster Theatre). 11 December, 1995. Worcester: MRA/IofC archives, file UK 1.3

Page, C., 1963. Trippers saw Drama with a Difference [feature]. *Yorkshire Post*. Worcester: MRA/IofC archives, file UK. 26.0

Palmer, R., 1979. Moral Re-Armament Drama: Right Wing Theatre in America [article]. *Theatre Journal*. Vol.31, No 2, pp. 172-185

Passerini, L., 1999. *Europe in Love, Love in Europe*. London and New York: I.B. Tauris

Paton, M., 1990. Alluring Rula Runs Risk of being a Pain in the Neck [review]. *Daily Express*, 7 June. Surrey: Hugh Steadman Williams archives

Pelling, H., 1992. *A History of British Trade Unionism*. London: Palgrave Macmillan

Peters, E., undated. *A moral and spiritual awakening*. [online]. Available at: <http://uk.iofc.org./print/31225> [Accessed 04, March, 2015]

Petronius, 1990. Czech those Facts [article]. *The European*. 11-13 May. Surrey: Hugh Steadman Williams archives

Pincher, C., 1981. *Their Trade is Treachery*. London: Sidgwick and Jackson

Pinter, H., 1991. Writing for the Theatre (1962). In *Plays one*. London: Faber and Faber

Plastow J., and S. Tsehaye, 1998. Making Theatre for a Change: Two Plays of the Eritrean Liberation Struggle. In *Theatre Matters: Performance and culture on the world stage*. Eds. R. Boon and J. Plastow. Cambridge: Cambridge University Press.

Postlewait, T., 2002. The Idea of the 'Political' in Our Histories of Theatre: Texts, Contexts, Periods and Problems [article]. *Contemporary Theatre Review*, 2002, Vol.12, Part 3, pp. 9-33.

Proctor, M., 1968. *Give a Dog a Bone: The story of the Film and Play by Peter Howard*. London: Westminster Productions

Programme, 1966. *Programme for the Opening of the Westminster Theatre Arts Centre.* Westminster Productions.

Programme, 1975. *Programme notes: Return Trip*, 1975. Worcester: MRA/IofC archives, File UK 26.4, Worcester.

Promotional Leaflet, 1973. *Promotional Leaflet for GB*. London: Kathleen Dodson archive

Pryce-Jones, D., 1964. Bogeymen [article]. *The Spectator*, January 10. Worcester: MRA/IofC archives, File UK 26.6.-26.8

Ramchandani, G., 1988. *To Whom it may Concern* [letter]. 17 February. Worcester: MRA/IofC archives, file UK 26.3

Rawson, A., 2012. Introduction. In *Showcasing the Third Reich: The Nuremberg Rallies.* [e-book] Stroud: History Press. Available at Google Books http://books-google.com [accessed 17 July, 2015]

Reeves, T., 2000. *Twentieth Century America: A Brief History*. Oxford University Press: New York

Reid, J. and S., 1966. The Architects' View [article]. *Westminster Theatre Arts Centre programme*. Cambridgeshire: Louis Fleming archives

Report, 1946. *A Report on The Forgotten Factor*. Worcester: MRA/IofC archives, file UK 26.1.1

————1953. *A Report on The Boss*. December. Worcester: MRA/IofC archives, file UK 26.0

————c.1965. *What Goes on at the Westminster*. [report]. Worcester: MRA/IofC archives, file UK 26.5

————c.1971. *The Westminster Theatre*. [report]. Surrey: David Locke archives

————1974. *World Assembly for Moral Re-Armament – Caux 1974*. [report]. Worcester: MRA/IofC archives, file 12.044

————1988. *Westminster Theatre 'Theatre in Education' Tour of Indian Public Schools* January 12 – March 18. [Report]. Worcester: MRA/IofC archives, file UK 26.3

————c.1989. *Westminster Productions proposal to tour Soviet Union*. Worcester: MRA/IofC archives, file UK 26.5

Riley, D., 1995. Bertolt Brecht: The Man who Never Was [online]. *Green Left Weekly*. 1 March. Available at: https://www.greenleft.org.au/node/9798 [accessed 09 June, 2014]

Roberts, B. R. 1972. Letter Regarding Theatre Review Policy. *Sunday Telegraph* [letter] (personal communication to Michael Henderson). 29 November. Devon: Michael Henderson archives

Roberts, D., 1999. *The Royal Court and the Modern Stage*. Cambridge: Cambridge University Press

Roberts, P., 1986. *The Royal Court Theatre 1965–1972*. London and New York: Routledge

————1999. *The Royal Court Theatre and the Modern Stage*. Cambridge: Cambridge University Press

Roland, P., 2012. A Cathedral of Light. In *The Illustrated History of the Nazis*, 2009. [e-book] London: Arcturus. Available at Google Books http://books-google.com [accessed 09 October, 2015]

Roose-Evans, J., 1990. The Director's Temptation [article]. *Westminster Theatre News*, May. Worcester: MRA/IofC archives, file UK 26.4

Rorrison, H., 1983. Commentary and Notes. In B. Brecht, *Mother Courage and Her Children*. Trans. J. Willet. London: Methuen

Row, R., 1984. Sir Oswald Mosley: Briton, Fascist, European [article]. *The Journal of Historical Review*, Winter, 1984. Vol. 5

Ruthven, N., 1980. A Day of London Theatre [article]. *Westminster Theatre News*, June. Worcester: MRA/IofC archives, file UK 26.4

————1989. The Why: Small is Beautiful [article]. *Westminster Theatre News*, May. Worcester: MRA/IofC archives, file UK 26.4

Sack, D., 2009. *Moral Re-Armament: The Reinventions of an American Religious Movement*. New York: Palgrave Macmillan

Sale, J., 1972. *Punch Theatre Review Policy*. [letter] (personal communication to Michael Henderson) 20 December. Devon: Michael Henderson archives

Sandbrook, D., 2007. *White Heat: A History of Britain in the Swinging Sixties*. 2006. London: Abacus

————2011. *Never Had it So Good*, 2005. London: Abacus

Sanderson, S., 1946. *Statement to the Oxford Group* [report]. Worcester: MRA/IofC archives, file UK 26.0

Saviour, N., 2009. Christian Theatre: Art or Propaganda? [article]. *International Journal of Communication*. Vol.19.2. Bahri Publications

Schechner, R., 2006. *Performance Studies: An Introduction*. New York and London: Routledge

Shellard, D., 2000. *British Theatre since the War*. 1999. New Haven and London: Yale University Press

Shulman, M., 1967. At the Royal Court — Applause for a Barking Dog [review]. *Evening Standard*, July. Essex: Pamela Jenner personal archives

————1990. Satanic Curses [review]. *Evening Standard*, 7 June. Surrey: High Steadman Williams archive

Sinfield, A., 1983. *Society and Literature 1945–1970*. New York: Holmes and Meier

————1993. *Literature, Politics and Culture in Post War Britain*. 1989. Oxford: Basil Blackwell

————2004. *Literature, Politics and Culture in Post-war Britain*. 1997. London: Continuum

Smith, H., 1986. Ed. *War and Social Change*. Manchester: Manchester University Press

Smurthwaite, N., 1990. *Temptation to Shock at the Westminster* [article]. Worcester: MRA/IofC Archives, file UK 26.6

Spoerri, T., 1966. Peter Howard Festival at Caux. *Westminster Theatre News*, No.14. September. Worcester: MRA/IofC archives, file UK 26.4

Steadman Williams, H., 1969a. The Theatre: Where We Are and Where We Are Going [article]. *Westminster Theatre News*, No.32. October. Worcester: MRA/IofC archives, file UK 26.5

————1969b. *The Theatre of Change* [pamphlet]. London: MRA/IofC archives

————1974. Out into Battle [article]. *Westminster Theatre News*, April, No.58. Worcester: MRA/IofC archives, file UK 26.5

————1975. A Theatre of Change [article]. *Westminster Theatre News* No.64, April. Worcester: MRA/IofC archives, file UK 26.4

————1986. The Next Forty Years [article]. *Westminster Theatre News*, November. Worcester: MRA/IofC archives, file UK.26.0

————1990. Hugh's Column [article]. *Westminster Theatre News*, August. Worcester: MRA/IofC archives, file UK 26.6, 26.7, 26.8

————1994. A New Vision for the Westminster Theatre? [article]. *Friends News*, November. Worcester: MRA/IofC archives, file UK 26.4

Steadman Williams, H. and A. Thornhill, 1974. *Return Trip*. London: Westminster Productions

Sursham, T., 1990. *Temptation* Reviewed [review]. *Westminster Theatre News*, June. Worcester, MRA/IofC archives, file UK 26.4

Swinburne, N., 1962. The Stage is Set [article]. *New World News*, No. 27. October-December

T.F., 1964. *The Diplomats* is Delighting Audiences [review]. *Bromley and Kentish Times*. January 10. Worcester: MRA/IofC archives, file 12.054

Tardrew, W., 1964. Letter to Editor [letter]. *The Croydon Advertiser*. 24 January. Worcester: MRA/IofC archives, file 12.054

Taylor, P., 1990. Transformation Scene [review]. *The Independent*, 8 June. Surrey: Hugh Steadman Williams archive

Thames Valley Times, 1964. Review of *The Diplomats* [article]. *The Thames Valley Times*. 8 January. Worcester: MRA/IofC archives, file 12.054

Thatcher, M., 1987. Speech to Conservative Party Conference. *Margaret Thatcher Foundation*. Available at: <http://www.margaretthatcher.org/document/106941> [accessed 17 March, 2015]

————1990. Speech at Dinner for Czech President [Václav Havel]. 21 March. *Margaret Thatcher Foundation*. Available at <http://www.margaret-tatcher.org/document/108044≥ [accessed 18 March, 2015]

Theatre World, 1964. *The Diplomats* [article]. *Theatre World*, February. Worcester: MRA/IofC archives, file 12.054

Thirkell, A., 1973. Theatre [article]. *Daily Mirror*. Devon: Michael Henderson archives

Thomson, P. and Sacks, G., eds., 2006. *The Cambridge Companion to Brecht* (1994). Second Edition. Cambridge: Cambridge University Press

Thompson, N. 1963. Letters: *The Diplomats* [letter]. *The Northern Despatch*, 25 November. Worcester: MRA-IofC archives, file UK 26.0

Thornhill, A., 1954. *The Forgotten Factor*. London: Blandford Press

————1970. *The Forgotten Factor* [article]. *Westminster Theatre News*, No.37, August. Worcester: MRA/IofC archives, files UK 26.2 - 26.3

————1973. GB [report] *Westminster Theatre News*, No.51. London: Kathleen Johnson archives

Times, 1990. Times Diary: Play for Today [article]. *The Times*, 3 May. Worcester: MRA/IofC archives, file UK 26.6

Times Educational Supplement, 1967. On Stage at Westminster [article]. *Times Educational Supplement*, 22 September. Worcester: MRA/IofC archives, file UK 26.0

Tinker, J. 1978. Death Came as a Merciful Release for Us All [review]. *Daily Mail*. May. Worcester: MRA/IofC archives, file UK 26.4

————1990. Magical Trickery ... and Devilishly Sexy [review]. *Daily Mail*, 7 June. Surrey: Hugh Steadman Williams, archive

Tod, B., 1987. A Theatrical Dip into Cold Tea [article]. *ILEA News*. July. Worcester: MRA/IofC archives, file UK 26.2 and 26.3

Tomlinson, S., 2008. *Race and Education: Policy and Politics in Britain*. Berkshire: Open University Press

Tooms, E., 2015. *Reasons for the ending of The Day of London Theatre* [email] (personal communication to Pamela Jenner). 24 February

Trail, T.C., 1971. *Report on The Westminster Theatre*. Surrey: David Locke archives

Trewin, J.C., 1964. Matter of Principle [article]. *Birmingham Post*, January. Worcester: MRA/IofC archives, file UK. 12.054 and file UK 26.6.

————1967. Theatre [article]. *Illustrated News*, 18 February. Worcester: MRA/IofC archives, file UK 26.066

V.C., 1963. How Low Can Theatre Go? [article]. *West London Observer*. Worcester: MRA/IofC archives, file UK 26.5

War Cry, 1990. *Temptation*. No Deals with the Devil [article]. *The War Cry*, 9 June. Surrey: Hugh Steadman Williams archive

Weeks, J., 1989. A Day of London Theatre [article]. *Westminster Theatre News*. September. Worcester: MRA/IofC archives, file UK 26.4

Welch, D., 2013. *Propaganda: Power and Persuasion*. London: The British Library

West London Press, 1964. Subtle and Satisfying [article]. *The West London Press*, 10 January. Worcester: MRA/IofC archives, file 12.054

Westminster and Pimlico News, 1963. Filth Pouring from the Theatre [article]. *The Westminster and Pimlico News*, 30 August. Worcester: MRA/IofC archives, file UK 26.5

————1968. A Moral Dunkirk [article]. *The Westminster and Pimlico News* 6 September. Worcester: MRA/IofC archives, file UK 26.0

————1977a. Children Go Behind the Footlights [article]. *The Westminster and Pimlico News*, 18 February. Worcester: MRA/IofC archives, file UK 26.0

—————1977b. The Conscience of a Playwright [review]. *The Westminster and Pimlico News*, 18 April. Worcester: MRA/IofC archives, file UK 26.0

Westminster Theatre, 1963. Westminster Theatre brochure. *The Westminster Theatre*. London: MRA/IofC archive

Westminster Theatre News, 1964. *Give a Dog a Bone* [article]. *Westminster Theatre News*, No.3, November. Worcester: MRA/IofC archives, file UK. 26.4

—————1970a. *Give a Dog a Bone* [article]. *Westminster Theatre News*, No 39. December. Worcester: MRA/IofC archives, file UK 26.4

—————1970b. *Blindsight* [report] *Westminster Theatre News* No. 36. June. Worcester: MRA/IofC archives, file UK. 26.5

—————1971. World Tour [article]. *Westminster Theatre News*, No.42, June. Worcester: MRA/IofC archives, files UK26.2 and 26.3

—————1972. *Give a Dog a Bone* [article]. *Westminster Theatre News* No. 50, December. Worcester: MRA/IofC archives, file UK 26.4

—————1973a. GB – Taking the Offensive [article]. *Westminster Theatre News*, No. 52, April. Worcester: MRA/IofC archives, file UK 26.5

—————1973b. *Give a Dog a Bone* [article]. *Westminster Theatre News*, No.56. December. Worcester: MRA/IofC archives, file UK 26.4

—————1977. Egon Karter on Theatre [article]. *Westminster Theatre News*, No. 77, June. Worcester: MRA/IofC archives, file UK. 26.4

—————1979. 10,000 Children [article]. *Westminster Theatre News*, 1979. April. Worcester: MRA/IofC archives, file UK 26.4

—————1980. The Phyllis Konstam Memorial Fund [article]. *Westminster Theatre News*, June. Worcester: MRA/IofC archives, file UK 26.4

—————1981a. Day of London Theatre [report]. *Westminster Theatre News*, No 94. February. Worcester: MRA/IofC archives, files UK 26.6, 26.7, 26.8

—————1981b. Response to Jonas [article]. *Westminster Theatre News*, No.98. December. Worcester: MRA/IofC archives, file UK 26.4

—————1986. Turning Point. *Westminster Theatre News*, November. Worcester: MRA/IofC archives, file UK 26.0

—————1988. Back on Our Feet [article]. *Westminster Theatre News*, November. Worcester: MRA/IofC archives, file UK 26.4

—————1989a. Westminster Productions Declares it's Aims. *Westminster Theatre News*, February. Worcester: MRA/IofC archives, file UK. 26.4

—————1989b. The Dining-Room at the Westminster Will Soon Have a Dual Function. *Westminster Theatre News*, May. Worcester: MRA/IofC archives, file UK 26.4

—————1990a. *The Widening Gyre* [review]. *Westminster Theatre News*, January. Worcester: MRA/IofC archives, file UK 26.4

—————1990b. Gala Opening of FFT [article]. *Westminster Theatre News*, August. Worcester: MRA/IofC archives, files UK 26.6, 26.7, 26.8

—————1991. Westminster Productions Carries On [article]. *Westminster Theatre News*, February. Worcester: MRA/IofC archives, file UK 26.4

White, C., 1977. *The Women's Periodical Press in Britain 1946-1976*. London: HMSO

Whitley, J., 1963. Civic Theatre not for Propaganda [report]. *The Northern Echo*, 10 December, 1963. Worcester: MRA/IofC archives. File UK 26.0

Williams, R., 2005. *Culture and Materialism* (1980). London: Verso

Wolrige Gordon, A., 1970. *Peter Howard: Life and Letters*. 1969. London: Hodder and Stoughton.

Woolf, M., 1997. In Minor Key: Theatre 1930-55. In *Literature and Culture in Modern Britain*. Vol. 2: 1930-1955. Ed G. Day. London: Longman

Working Class Movement Library. n.d.[online]. Nationalisation of the Mines [article]. *Working Class Movement Library*. Available at: <http://www.wcml.org.uk/about-us/timeline/nationalisation-of-the-mines> [accessed 21 March, 2016]

Wrigley, C., 1997. *British Trade Unions, 1945-1995*. Manchester: Manchester University Press

Young, B., 1978. *Sentenced to Life* [review]. *Financial Times*, 18 May. Worcester: MRA/IofC archives, file 12.046

Appendices

APPENDIX ONE

Edited transcript of an Interview with Hilary Belden, daughter of Kenneth Belden, on 29 April, 2013, at IofC headquarters, Greencoat Place, London.

Mum and Dad met the Oxford Group separately in the 1930s. During the war Dad was in the fire service and Mum was cooking at Tirley [Tirley Garth MRA Centre, Cheshire]. At the end of the war both wondered what they would do. Dad went into book work and publications for MRA and Mum, who had been trained as a social worker, felt a calling to continue working with MRA. She went to London and discovered she would be working with my Dad. They spent a year working with each other getting out about a million books They were passionate about publications, about good typography and good design. They got married in July 1946. Mum's father had made quite a fortune so she had a little finance and they bought a big old Victorian house in Putney, visualising that they would share with other families. Ten months after they were married I was born. Caux was starting up and dad went over there. He sent a message back asking Mum to come for three weeks and bring the baby. We stayed for five years. They were right in on the starting up of Caux. We either lived in Caux or in Berne where my brother was born. They always thought they would return to the house in Putney but just as they were thinking about packing up and going back they were invited to take over the hosting and running of a big old house in Charles Street near the Westminster Theatre. At that time a number of leases were for sale on houses in the area and MRA bought them up.

I remember coming back to this beautiful house in Charles Street. It was completely empty and my parents furnished it gradually. We spent seventeen years there from 1953 to 1969. I went to school from there. Mum and Dad were warm inclusive people and it was a warm and inclusive house. Some of the MRA houses in the area had grand staircases to the first floor and then smaller staircases up to the servants' quarters. Our house had a main staircase that went all the way up the house and made it a very open welcoming home.

My brother went to boarding school at about the age of thirteen but I was there and when I was about twelve or thirteen my father had a real crisis. He began to think 'Am I in the right place, Am I wasting my life?' He talked to Frank Buchman about this who told him to go on a holiday. So we had three to four weeks in Cornwall. Dad lay under a tree with a rug over him. We had lots of family outings together. He was a fabulous Dad and it was there that he got his breath back.

We came back to London and he took over as chairman of the Westminster Theatre trustees. Dad always said it was a toss-up between him and someone else and he had the thought that the next ten years would be his creative decade. It was almost a casual decision that he made to take on chairing the Trust. It coincided with the collective decision to do something big with the theatre. He loved the theatre, he thrived on it and I got passionately interested in it.

I was fourteen or fifteen when the Westminster Theatre was re-launched. The arts centre would never have been built without Dad. He was a hands-on practical man. He could see the detail as well as the bigger picture. He was also an amazing fundraiser and a great manager. He was very interested in improving conditions for the actors and making it a much bigger centre of operations. All through my mid to late teens the centre was going up. He said it was really something to put your signature to a contract for a quarter of a million pounds.

Every Friday evening our house had a reception with all sorts of people coming to the theatre. People would have a meal and I would be in my school uniform standing in the doorway handing out drinks. My parents were very interested in good food and would hunt for the best ingredients at the lowest prices in the markets. Guest would then go upstairs for coffee and talks about the house and the Westminster and would then go off to a show at the theatre. All these extraordinary people came to the house — everyone from trade union leaders to African politicians.

That all went on throughout my teens. When I was doing my A levels Dad had a big study with a cosy sofa and I used to go there when I had done my homework and sit companionably with him. He would say things to me like 'I've had a letter from Peter Howard saying he's just written a play about a black man, a bishop, a harlot and God. Well, what do you think of that?' Dad was like a teddy bear with mental machinery. He was a very warm and loving man.

I was interested in the theatre. It was the days of Gielgud, Olivier and Ralph Richardson. I was interested in the classics. From some quite early stage I was aware of having a critical view and not accepting, as my father had, that the entire agenda was a Theatre of Darkness. I knew there were some very interesting things going on.

I did go to see the plays at the Westminster and I loved some of them. *Give a Dog a Bone* was enormous fun and it launched the career of Elaine Page. My grandfather was dying in the first or second run of *Give a Dog a Bone* and my father was able to go and see him and not worry because the theatre had full houses. Getting audiences took a huge amount of work, partly because we were a bit out of the way and also because we had a strong sense we had a gospel to proclaim.

I grew up on the MRA stories like *The Forgotten Factor*. I understood what the Westminster was trying to do – it was trying to reach people and their lives and give them a chance to find a way forward.

I read English at St Anne's Oxford and I had thought about doing a PhD on the plays of Peter Howard. They reminded me of the medieval Mystery Plays – the idea of putting on the stage what you want to say. Thornhill, Howard and Belden were an interesting trio who had the ability to go well beyond propaganda. They were more interested in what goes on in people's lives, telling stories and saying where we are in the story. I would put Peter Howard's work into the area of Theatre of Debate and Theatre of Discussion. What made him a good playwright was his instinct for where the fault lines were and where the controversy was. He had had a redemptive experience. He absolutely believed in a redemptive experience but never believed there was an easy way to do it

Father had a vision and the vision changed. When the decision was made to sell the theatre it was very difficult for them. When my parents retired they moved to Knebworth where they both threw themselves into

Knebworth life and became involved with the local community. When he was about eighty he published his memories *The Hour of the Helicopter* and a collection of his poems.

One Christmas, either 1998/1999, Stanley [Kaier] showed him around Greencoat Place and I think Dad felt happy about the fact that this was what it was, whatever the past traumas had been. It had everything of what he thought important. I think that this brought a kind of closure.

[On why MRA was criticised.] There was a very strong tide of public opinion that rubbished MRA. We grew up in an environment that was very hostile and embattled. We were challenging people's morals and people didn't like it. I went to a grammar school in Putney and my parents wondered whether MRA had adversely affected me. I met my old head years later at a school reunion and she said 'I never agreed with your parents but I did like them'. My parents worried that it would have a bad effect on my Oxford career but one of my tutors had been involved with MRA.

APPENDIX TWO

Edited email from Peggy Buckman to Pamela Jenner on 8 January, 2012.

My introduction to MRA was an invitation to a play or rather a musical. At that time in the mid-fifties I was training as a midwife in East London. A colleague invited two of us students to the musical, *The Vanishing Island* which was touring the world. The show enlarged my world-view as nothing else had ever done. The word ideology had not been in my vocabulary. On stage the conflict of ideas that governed nations and people was acted out before me. It was a life changing experience as I began to understand how the selfish living of the West provoked the hatred of the East and the part that each one of us, including me, ought to be playing to change things. For me it meant that my faith as a Christian needed to be lived not just talked about. I had to put right certain things that had been wrong in my life. I began to understand how a very ordinary young woman could play a part in the wider world. I can still remember much of that play.

For most of the 1960s I was living and working in London and was able to see all the series of plays and saw each play several times sometimes accompanied by friends and colleagues. I became more and more involved in the work of MRA and went to the Sunday morning meetings in the Westminster Theatre when coach loads of people came from all over the country to meet to share their experiences, having seen the current play on Saturday evening. I also spent many a day off from midwifery in the basement kitchen of 12A Charles Street helping to cook meals for a large number of people. So I learned quite a lot about cooking too. Once I began to teach midwifery I would invite some of my students to the theatre. On one occasion I remember my whole class of students came with me on a coach and the hospital matron came too. When I told her of my invitation to the students she had responded, 'I want my students to go to the Westminster Theatre.'

Later, living and working in South London, just ten minutes by train from Victoria Station the possibilities increased. Here with local Friends of the Westminster Theatre we were able to arrange theatre parties, invite friends and neighbours and give hospitality to the folk who came into London at each weekend to the plays. Also I was involved with a mixed team of people who worked in the Health Service in a series of 'Medical Receptions', which ended with an evening in the theatre seeing the current play.

The Christmas pantomime *Give a Dog a Bone* was especially memorable. And it played year after year. It had the marks of true pantomime, humour, audience participation, the battle between good and bad, right and wrong and the three magic words which helped to deal with every situation, Please, Thank you and Sorry. Adults enjoyed it as much as children. One memorable visit for me was when the Sunday School from the church I attended in Tulse Hill all came and loved it.

Peter Howard's last play *Happy Deathday* for me raised many issues that needed to be addressed in Britain at the time, among them faith versus scientific research and atheism. It was also made more meaningful because Peter had died before he had completed the play but his words went on resounding in the nation. The play became a film, shown widely.

I will attempt to summarise what Peter Howard's plays have meant to me through the years. The plays presented me with a challenge to change the way I thought and acted and to give God the chance to work through me to change myself and to bring change to others, in my job, in social relationships, in the local church. I have tested and found to be true that God guides and provides. This is just as true in retirement as at any other time in my life. Peter Howard's plays of the 1960s transformed my life.

APPENDIX THREE

Edited transcript of interview with Christine Channer on 1 December, 2011, at IofC headquarters, 24 Greencoat Place, London.

[Channer's parents met Frank Buchman at a house party in 1937. Her father was an industrialist and mother a magistrate.]

They were very struck by the meeting — it re-made their marriage. We saw this. We had difficulties at home. I danced all the way through school and when I was sixteen started training seriously. My parents were always trying to get me to see the plays at the Westminster. I heard they were giving free sandwiches at the theatre and I was a struggling actress so I went along and saw *The Forgotten Factor*. I met the actors afterwards and I was very struck by the people — it was an American company that had come over. They were so straightforward and accepted you warts and all. I was with a dance theatre at the time and they kept in touch.

My parents suggested I went to Caux. I was at the time one of four dancers going with the Glyndebourne Opera to the Edinburgh Festival and it was just two weeks before rehearsals started so I went to Caux. I was quite blown away. I never read a newspaper. I wasn't into the world. This was just after the war. There were Germans and French there. There was incredible reconciliation going on, I saw it all happen in front of me. I met a young German from the Hitler Youth. He had been imprisoned by the British. He had a fundamental change in his life whilst at Caux.

Phyllis Konstam the English film actress who worked with Olivier on Broadway and was married to British Number One tennis player Bunny Austin, was there with an American film actress. I was hugely impressed.

They invited me to lunch. Phyllis said they were creating a big international musical and invited me to go to America with it and help with the choreography. I sent a telegram to England to cancel the arrangement to go to Edinburgh and began working on the show which ended up going on Broadway. I was invited to America by MRA and also went to Hollywood Bowl.

The first half of the 1960s I was producing and directing plays and touring with students in India with MRA and with Rajmohan Gandhi (Gandhi's grandson) putting across MRA ideas. I returned to England in 1965 and performed at the Westminster. Every Sunday morning the theatre had a public meeting. There would be miners coming from various parts of the country. At the time there was the theatre of the kitchen sink, the theatre of cruelty, and this was a direct alternative to that. There was no Christian theatre at that point, no moral theatre. For some of the professional actors who came in to our company it was a new field for them and some of them didn't think much of the ideas but it was a job. Others were very interested. It was a melting pot. The theatre was throwing away all the drawing room theatre and establishing it in the kitchen.

We felt we were really flying the flag for some honour and dignity in the country. The Westminster was a bit off the beaten track. You had to work hard to get the audience. One of the plays we did was *The Ladder*. The actress playing the mother said: 'This play is just bare bones, there's nothing there'. But it is a wonderful challenge to give it flesh and blood. I think we got a good reception. It opened people's minds. I think they found it refreshing to have an alternative. It was very strange in the 1960s in the UK at the time. The *Marat de Sade* produced an absolute outrage. We rose to the challenge. We went out to meet people afterwards. We met people in the audience.

At the time we felt the theatrical establishment didn't want to know us. We felt we had to fight against them. They labelled Frank Buchman as being pro-Hitler. Tom Driberg was very against MRA. Tom Driberg was a number one enemy. He would turn up all over the place. The Westminster Theatre was revolutionary — we were fighting up-stream with a strong current floating down and we were pedalling our way up. Everyone knew what it stood for.

[Channer was also involved in the Day of London Theatre schools programme.] We could have three hundred children attending. This was something new before Theatre in Education was launched. It gave children an experience of the theatre. We would start with a slide show of history of the theatre, costume design, how a play is written, how you get it into production and then stage a play in the afternoon. The teachers were always very impressed.

[On taking part in *Clashpoint*] The cast was a good mix of Carib/Brits, Indian/Brits, Coloured South African/Brits and us white/Brits, and we were touring all the trouble spots as well as the Day of London Theatre. That is where one got the most public feedback ... How one can quantify the effect one just doesn't know, but all one can say is that the audience hung about for a long time after the curtain had come down just wanting to talk and discuss. The ideological thing about it was that it was created to answer a problem in the country. We were living in each other's pockets on tour, which is what usually happens, and hurt feelings, misunderstandings, etc, would get aired in the time we always had together before the show.

Things needed to be sorted out before we went on stage for the play to have the special power it did have. It wasn't a great masterpiece of writing, but it was a genuine piece written for the sake of people and the country so it had to have that integrity between us to hit home.

[On plans to close the theatre] I fought against the whole business of the theatre. I very often felt we were battling with knives in our backs from our best friends. It was very difficult as we were giving all of our art for 'nowt' and we felt that some of our team were not behind us. That was a truly horrible period of conflict and grief, especially for those of us who had sweated our guts out there.

APPENDIX FOUR

Edited email from Fiona Daukes to Pamela Jenner on 12 March, 2013.

When the Westminster Theatre was to be commissioned after it had been purchased, my mother was one of those there. She had given a large part of the gratuity she had received from the RAF towards its purchase. She and my father had been deeply involved in the Oxford Group, and it was surely because of the wider horizons he discovered through that involvement that he died as he did. He volunteered as a Chaplain with the RAF soon after war was declared. He was then, in 1941, posted overseas to what is now Ghana. He was on board a very crowded troop ship, which developed engine trouble, went back to Liverpool and later tried to catch up their convoy. Early next morning they were torpedoed. My father and his chaplain room-mate wore each other's tunics in the rush, and eventually we received my Dad's diary, the pages red where the colour had run, in the water. My Dad tried to comfort the wounded, and to get the men off the ship, saying to one man too afraid to jump, 'Go with God'. He survived. Then he found the stairs to the hold were destroyed and men were down there panicking and screaming in terror. He asked a marine to lower him down, but he replied, 'You will never get out', and Dad said, 'My love of God is greater than my fear of death, and I must be with my men'. The last he was seen was praying with the men as the water covered his shoulders. Six years later my mother finally heard what had happened, and he was awarded the George Cross. One survivor I met told me that he had seen him go down, but that he would never have forgotten him anyway as he had seen him on the day before making his way among the crowded decks talking and joking, and encouraging the men. When my mother was asked by a journalist if my father was a particularly brave man, she answered that he wasn't, but he had learnt to be obedient to that voice within, and for him it was surely just the next step.

This then was part of the heritage of the Westminster Theatre. Later, when funds were needed, I sold my mother's engagement ring, and my grandmother's engagement ring. Not huge sums, but special to me to give.

APPENDIX FIVE

Edited transcript of an interview with Kathleen Dodds, on 5 January, 2015, at IofC headquarters, Greencoat Place, London.

GB stood for Great Britain and was an attempt at satire, poking fun at some of the things that were going on and adapting to the culture of the time. We were about to go into Europe and this was a big deal about whether we were going to go into it. We never said it was called Great Britain. We were trying to find a view that had not been done to death. Each sketch had its own theme. It helped people to think for themselves and not just suck up to the trendy view — something in between. We were trying to show a more spiritual side. Arguments at that time were all about whether we could benefit financially or not from EU.

People's views about MRA were more negative than positive, they hadn't experienced it from the inside.

APPENDIX SIX

Edited transcript of an interview with Chris Evans, on 29 October, 2012, at Initiatives of Change archives centre, Worcester.

[Until June 2012 Evans was chairman of the Board of Trustees. He was treasurer of IofC from 1991–2003]

Throughout most of the 1980s and 1990s we were looking into IofC, to see where doors were opening, where the spirit was working and where it was having an effect. I thought I saw the spirit working more in other ways that working through the theatre. Initiatives such as Hope in the Cities were meeting a response that the theatre wasn't. The financial and human sustainability was an issue. The sheer effort of keeping it [the theatre] going. People were getting older, people's attention was moving elsewhere. The network around the country was unable to give it the energy they had done in the past. It was getting a steeper and steeper road to follow.

The debate went on throughout the 1980s. The theatre friends felt they were a beleaguered minority defending their path. I was concerned that there should be no spilt and I went around the country explaining the need to move. We deliberately invested to create a theatre space called The Barn in the new premises [Greencoat Place].

The buildings near the Westminster that we had leased were all coming to the end of their lease. The number of full-time workers had dropped hugely. We looked around London; where did we go? It was a cliff-hanger. Greencoat Place was the option around which people united quite easily. We converted a lot of car parking into useable office space and upgraded quite a lot.

APPENDIX SEVEN

Edited transcript of an interview with Robin Evans at 24, Greencoat Place, London, 30 January, 2013.

I was staying with various families in London. We used to meet as a team and decide which factory could usefully be approached to take people to the theatre. Each play had a different emphasis. I used to contact The Firestone Factory which made tyres near Ealing — I happened to have been in the army with the chief of personnel, he taught me desert warfare and then he became my platoon Sergeant. He was very helpful to us and sent a number of groups to see the plays. When we visited factories some were not interested but most were very open to the idea. We gave special terms for a good-sized group. After the play we would talk to individuals at the theatre and they were very responsive.

Ronald Mann was impresario for the theatre. David Fillimore was a specialist in travel organisation and used to get groups from America booked in for a tour of England including a play at the Westminster. We also had bus loads coming from the coalfields.

APPENDIX EIGHT

Edited transcript of an interview with Louis Fleming on 25 November, 2012 at Chestnut Way, Mepal, near Ely, Cambridgeshire.

The idea for the theatre came from Frank Buchman who wanted to the change the views of the actors in Hollywood. He believed if people like them could change then the world could change. He felt the way to get people to change was through the theatre and through film. The MRA plays began in America in 1938–39.

Buchman was the driving force behind it. He knew a lot of Hollywood producers and actors who supported MRA. It was decided to make a film of one of our plays, *The Good Road*, which we took to Germany in November 1945. We toured Germany when it had been flattened. The opera houses were still standing. We played Munich, Stuttgart, Frankfurt, Dusseldorf and other cities with the backing of the occupying British and American armies. We were based in a Munich art gallery which was the army centre in 1946. Buchman was looking at rebuilding of nations and he took the musical *The Good Road* into Germany and then to Holland. Prince Bernhard was one of the backers. They played the Haymarket theatre in 1948 in dense fog. We performed plays in many countries, in many languages and with many volunteers. By 1950 we had a team of around two hundred young people all under the age of 25.

[Fleming was originally born in Britain and went to Canada at the age of nine. After leaving school he joined the Royal Canadian Navy. When he left the navy in 1946 he went to a conference in Michigan at a hotel, Island House, on Mackinac Island, which the Governor of Michigan let Buchman have the use of.]

There was a theatre there that was in a barn. I'd had a lot of electrical and mechanical training. I saw these British, mostly from Oxford and Cambridge, who had been too old to enter the services and were handling the technical side of the plays. I helped them out. I liked the theatre but had no idea I would become involved as a result of soldering two wires together! The next thing I was building lighting boards and dimmer boards. In 1948 MRA put on the musical *Ideas Have Legs* and before I knew it we were staging it at the Hollywood Bowl and I was doing the lighting. We then went to the centre at Caux, Switzerland, and became involved in the theatre there, modernising and redesigning it. Buchman had a plan to move into Germany. He became a great friend of Chancellor Adenauer of West Germany. MRA had a lot of support in America at that time but not in Britain. This was partly because of the gay people who did not support us and we were also attacked by Tom Driberg. MRA built a film studio on Mackinac Island in 1959 and I was very involved with that. I was director of that film studio. Most of what we did initially was for television.

My father-in-law Lionel Exton was a very successful Bournemouth businessman. He was behind buying the Westminster Theatre and contributed towards it. He left Bournemouth and bought a house in Eaton Square in around 1946. I married his daughter Valerie on 21 June 1952. [She died in 2008 and Fleming was married again, to Anita, in 2010.] Valerie was an actress in some of the plays and her sister Leone became catering director at the Westminster. We had a very modern restaurant in the extension when it was built.

In 1961, when Buchman died, I went to Caux. Peter Howard asked my wife and I at the end of the Caux conference in the summer of 1961 to go to the Westminster. They wanted to put on the musical *The Hurricane* with Muriel Smith, an American opera star. I did the lights and stage management. I was stage manager of the Westminster in 1961 and when we expanded the theatre I became the director of the Westminster Theatre Arts Centre in 1965. When I was director of the Arts Centre I was never told what my tasks were. Part of what I did was to look at which plays were going to be put on. I always considered whether or not they would attract an audience. I was in charge of everything except the money side.

We realised people were not going to come to the theatre of their own accord. We had to fight to attract audiences. From 1941 to 1961 all of MRA plays were presented free and were internally produced, there were no paid professionals, but then Peter Howard had the guidance that we should use professional actors. We got Nora Swinburne and Peter Howard wrote *Music at Midnight* especially for her. The Westminster eventually became completely commercial and started to charge West End prices. I now believe it was the wrong move to make it professional. What happened was that all the creative people who had given freely of their knowledge and services felt, when it became professional, that there wasn't a part for them. Peter Howard was one of the most dynamic men I have ever met. He was totally for the theatre. He completely focused on it and came up with the material to put on. If Peter Howard had not died the Westminster would definitely have carried on putting on MRA plays.

In 1975 I decided to go back to Canada as the Westminster had fizzled out as far as MRA plays were concerned. I can remember taking morning walks and thinking 'What on earth are we going to do with the Westminster?' There were people in the British leadership who wanted to keep the message 'pure and simple' and the American MRA group which was very active and felt totally undermined by the leadership. Buchman would have sent those British academics out of Britain so they didn't have a chance to set up their own fiefdoms and I think that would have been right.

I moved away from MRA. I found MRA was dissolving. Today it's MRA that is needed not IofC. IofC is made up of three to four NGOs and doesn't appear to be projecting or demanding that people live a certain quality of life. I think MRA was not liked because it was something different and people were fearful of that. Today there are so many people preaching about ideologies that it would have been successful. After Buchman died there was a massive political clash and it was felt that MRA should be run by a group of people and not one person. Now thinking about it many years later it is obvious that many organisations die when they lose their leader. Buchman and his passion for projecting a message through drama and film would not agree at all with those people trying to close the Westminster down.

[Fleming's reaction to *Temptation*] I would have supported putting it on. I knew Hugh [Hugh Steadman Williams] got the blame for putting it on but if I had been there I would have supported it. I looked at it as portraying life. I was not against it. The people who criticised the play were the same ones who caused me to leave in 1975.

In 1990 at the age of 65 I came back to the UK. The Westminster people asked me if I would like to work with the Christian Arts Trust but I got disillusioned because a lot of people who said they would get involved didn't. It fell because it was not supported. My highlight at the Westminster was *Give a Dog a Bone* and seeing all those children flooding in. It got across a simple message of being able to say: please, thank you and sorry. *Mr Brown Came Down the Hill* was my favourite Peter Howard play. It was a very modern piece. The set was very modern. I hired a commercial set designer for that play instead of using our full-time MRA worker Bill Cameron Johnson.

APPENDIX NINE

Edited transcript of an interview with David Hassell, on 1 May, 2013, at IofC headquarters, Greencoat Place, London.

In the spring and summer of 1947 I was in the stage crew of *The Forgotten Factor* at the Westminster. In 1948 I took part in the French version at Caux and at Berne in Switzerland. Those were glorious days of youth. I wore gym shoes, they call them trainers today, and I had to move the stage set. I felt I was on the edge of a revolution of the world, which the theatre was a major part of. Theatre was the spearhead for getting to the public. Even television was a minimal thing. It was in the days before videos. People came in great numbers to the theatre and the cinema. Lots came to the Westminster. We had a large team driving up audiences and organising coach parties.

There was something in *The Forgotten Factor* that turned a key for a lot of people, particularly the miners. We had lots of miners coming in organised parties from South Wales and elsewhere, Ernest Bevin said at the time 'Give me coal and I'll give you a foreign policy'. It was so different from the time of Mrs Thatcher when the mines didn't pay. In those days the economy still depended on the mines but there were bad industrial relations within the mines.

The Forgotten Factor worked in America so we brought it across to Britain. The unions responded very well to it in the States and it had a bearing on the war effort. It also had an effect in factories. Bad industrial relationships had threatened production for the war effort. *The Forgotten Factor* was a major contribution of MRA to the allied war effort. This was publicly recognised by Truman. The same thing happened in Britain.

Industrial disputes were holding up the construction of Mulberry Harbour in Birkenhead. It was solved by Tim Rignall a trade union leader who worked with MRA. He was a really tough character. So the work went ahead and this was a very direct contribution to the war effort.

Times move on and you now get people sitting at home watching television, videos, DVDs. You can watch plays on your mobiles. The whole technical, information and entertainment industry has moved on and is using very different methods to those in the 1930s when people went to the cinema once a week in their thousands and radio was the television of the times.

[David Hassel's parents were involved in MRA and he has spent most of his life working for the movement. He studied French Philosophy at Oxford.]

APPENDIX TEN

Edited email from Kay Hassell to Pamela Jenner on 26 April, 2013.

At the end of the Second World War my parents, Gordon and Gladys Hassell, were one of the twenty couples who decided to underwrite the money that needed to be raised to buy the Westminster Theatre where plays such as *The Forgotten Factor* could be staged. The thought was to give people a purpose for the peace. We knew what we had been fighting for. How were we to carry that spirit of unity into the rebuilding of war-torn Britain when the devastation lay around us, most foods were still rationed and returning ex-servicemen and women had little to look forward to?

On Remembrance Sunday 1946 the theatre was dedicated in a moving ceremony. The stage was lined with Service men and women, some on their demob leave. My brother David was stage right standing to attention. He was 21. I was 18 and about to go to college. A large force of people who worked with Moral Re-Armament had come over from the USA earlier in the year, bringing with them the cast of *The Forgotten Factor*. This was a play that had been written by Alan Thornhill, an Oxford don and a clergyman. Not a natural playwright you would think! But he had travelled extensively with Frank Buchman during the war in America, and had seen the need for putting the truths of how to bring unity, especially in industry, in a light-hearted and compelling way that would speak to workers and management alike.

Night after night the play was shown to packed audiences, many staying on after the show to meet the cast and talk about how lives could be changed and entrenched positions between Labour and Management could be resolved. Entrance to the theatre was free. We relied on the collection and on gifts to cover the costs. Of course, all the cast and back stage people gave their services voluntarily. My parents put people up in our home, which fortunately seemed to have elastic walls. We had a long tradition of hospitality, and our neighbours were used to the sight of Hassell children walking down the road with armfuls of blankets we had borrowed.

My father, J. Gordon Hassell, became Secretary to the Trustees and only retired in 1969 on his eightieth birthday. He had helped to steer the Board through the building of the new Arts Centre, which came into being in 1966. The premises were considerably extended and the roof was raised. The whole exterior was covered in Welsh slate. There was a great campaign to raise money for this. You could pay for a slate or two or more. I was teaching in North Wales by that time and gave the money for two slates. Alas, that left me nearly penniless for the rest of the summer holidays. Dad had to lend me some money to tide me over!

The pantomime *Give a Dog a Bone* by Peter Howard with music by George Fraser showed for thirteen seasons. It was a superb musical and it set a new trend in theatre for children. No smutty jokes or sexual innuendoes but hilarious moments and, yes, an answer to the 'couldn't care less' attitudes of the day. A London teacher was given permission to write a simplified version that her class of ten-to-eleven-year-olds could perform, and I took her script and produced it twice in my school. As this was a junior boarding school, the children were constantly singing the songs. One would hear 'Please, Thank You and Sorry' as they cleaned their teeth at bedtime, or 'I Dream of Ice Cream, Sausages and Cake' as they washed their hands for dinner.

Peter Howard became a leading figure fairly early on in the war. He worked on the *Daily Express* and went to one of the London homes where a number of full-time MRA workers lived, in order to expose the movement and deride it publicly. But he found a new purpose for his life. One of the most difficult things he did was to resign his position as one of the most highly paid political columnists and give his life to 'remaking the world'. He had bought a run-down farm in Suffolk and turned his attention to raising it from a grade C3 to A1. Soon it was buzzing with people who beat a path to his door. Six young women who had joined the Land Army came to the farm, and Service people spent their leave there helping with all the work.

I first met Peter [Howard] at Tirley Garth in Cheshire. This was a very large beautiful home in a big estate which had been the home of the Prestwich family. It was inherited by one of the daughters, Irene, who offered it for the use of some of the MRA team from London, where they could bring the office work to the comparative safety of the countryside. A number of us teenagers had been invited to Tirley to a 'Battle School' in 1944. Doe Howard was there with the children and Peter was expected. One afternoon at teatime, Doe did not realise that he had actually arrived. 'He's here,' I said. 'Do you know him?' she queried rather sceptically. 'No,' I replied, 'but it must be him. He winked at me.'

We had tremendous fun playing games where we were taught to play to win, going on expeditions to the local newspaper works, to a tannery in Runcorn, and taking part in the village fête. Here we entered all the different races and rather to our embarrassment, won nearly every one. Peter Howard had given me half a crown to spend, but at the end of the afternoon I returned it together with my prize money from the race I had won. On the

310

way back to Tirley he asked some of us if we would like to go to Hill Farm the next summer, to which we all gave a mighty "Yes!" So in the summer of 1946 a number of us arrived at Hill Farm. The boys slept under canvas and the girls in one of the cottages. We had meals in the huge barn. We worked in the fields and I for one found myself in the kitchen. I learnt how to skin a rabbit. We had Bible study and we learnt more about the "war of ideas." Often in the evenings we had dancing the barn; Scottish Reels and Strip the Willow and The Dashing White Sergeant. We were at the Farm when we got the news that the Atom bomb had been dropped on Nagasaki. It was very sobering news.

Some people found Peter Howard intimidating, but to me he was like a favourite uncle. His tremendous energy and outpouring of writing in letters, speeches and plays was like lava from a volcano. He cared particularly for all the farm hands. He wrote a play especially for the Hill Farm folk to perform, called *Rumplesnitz*. It was acted in the sitting room. Then it was put on in one of the local village halls. Both Peter and Doe gave a home to their childhood nannies. 'Nursie' was Doe's, and 'Nanny George' was Peter's. Nursie was bedridden and several of the women in the household cared for her by night and day. She actually died while I was there in the fifties. Nanny George did not long survive her; she had cancer but had put off seeing the doctor until it was too late. She had just wanted to care for Nursie, then she was happy to die herself.

When the Howards' daughter, Anne, was married, hundreds of people were invited to the wedding. The reception was held in the grounds of the farm. There we were all dressed up in our finery, leaning on gate posts and avoiding muddy patches on the ground. It was wonderful. But when Peter died so unexpectedly in 1965 his funeral was also held in the village church. I believe that the organist played tunes from *Give a Dog a Bone* and other themes from the music of George Fraser, who had collaborated with Peter. I could not be present on that occasion, but I think that previously Peter had told his family to provide hot soup for everyone afterwards as it was February and they would all be cold.

Peter Howard was very canny. He could 'read' people and he understood their inner conflicts and need for honesty, forgiveness and restitution. This, because he had had enormous inner battles himself, and had given himself entirely to God, to listen to His leading and obey His commands. Peter fought for the souls of people and nations. You were always on your toes when he was around. No shirking, no second best, no hiding in corners. Alan Thornhill once told me that Peter, who was then the world leader of MRA, had asked him to be his mentor and confessor. Alan said it made him feel very humble taking on that role. I am honoured to have known the Howards.

APPENDIX ELEVEN

Edited transcript of an interview with Jill Hazell, on 6 December, 2014, at IofC headquarters, 24 Greencoat Place.

I used to come and sell books and records during *Give a Dog a Bone* and used to change in the usherettes' room in the basement, which used to be the crypt of a church. One day I walked into the wardrobe instead of the usherettes' room by mistake and saw an empty dog suit hanging there drying out. I had never given a thought to what went on behind the scenes. Judy Pearson was the wardrobe mistress in those days and she invited me to have a coffee. I ended up ironing a whole load of peasants' shirts! I used to come to the theatre twice a week to sell the books and it was very romantic seeing the actors. Suddenly a job came up. MRA was making a film on location of the play *Happy Deathday* and I was asked to be dresser and wardrobe assistant. I later became wardrobe mistress at the Westminster and loved it.

APPENDIX TWELVE

Edited transcript of an interview with Michael Henderson conducted by telephone 20 January, 2015, 8.30pm.

[Henderson spent time in America with MRA and was on the board of the Oxford Group. Henderson, Thornhill, Steadman Williams and Dodds teamed up to devise a revue, GB, and used newspapers as inspiration.]

Revue was quite new to us. Use of music and theatre was a recruiting tool and training ground – a specific attraction for young people and a way of getting them together. With GB we want to compete, to give something. After Howard died we didn't have very many people to write the plays we wanted, hence doing revue. I helped to write GB but I was very much a junior partner. It was great fun doing it. We were responding to change, to what was happening in society. The response from the audience was very satisfactory.

By the 1980s people in MRA were getting very tired and exhausted. Everyone worked for the theatre. There were parties coming every weekend and meetings every Sunday morning. We had a duty to fill the theatre with people. It became too much. I signed a pledge that I would get ten people into the theatre a week. A lot of people did that. There was a huge effort to do it.

The Westminster's greatest time was just after the war in 1946 and the role it played in British industry with *The Forgotten Factor* was very effective. We had a presence in public life. You could invite people to the theatre. You would open the paper and read about the Westminster.

I travelled so much. I was evacuated to America in the war and then my parents suggested going to Caux [in 1947]. I left school in 1950 and worked in Caux as a switchboard operator, actor, lighting crew, helped build sets, played a lead in a play and translated from German to English. In the 1960s I was MRA press officer.

APPENDIX THIRTEEN

Edited transcript of interview with Stanley Kiaer on 29 September, 2011, at IofC headquarters, 24 Greencoat Place, London.

[Kiaer spent five years working in the City of London for the shipping industry and five years working for the pharmaceutical industry. He went to work full time for MRA in 1964 and became secretary of the trustees that owned and ran the Westminster Theatre. He was responsible for the general administration of the theatre throughout the 1960s. He was a founder member of the Friends of Westminster Theatre and for some years was its chairman. In 1968 Kiaer founded the Institute of Business Ethics and was its director until 1999. He was secretary of the Oxford Group and is currently secretary of Westminster Productions.]

I came across the Oxford Group in the early 1950s through attending a conference at Caux when I was in my last year at Cambridge studying classics. I was very impressed with the atmosphere and sense of purpose, the idea that there is a plan for everyone's life and you could find it and if you wanted to see a difference in the world to place trust in yourself.

Those returning from the Second World War and those who had lost people in the war wanted to create a theatre for the world they had left behind. In 1946 there was a decline in the theatre and money was raised to buy the Westminster Theatre. At the end of the war twenty men in industry, the professions and the Armed Forces, with their wives set up a memorial fund to honour those who had lost their lives and to fulfil the aims for which they sacrificed everything. The Westminster Memorial Trust was formed. The aim of the theatre was to encourage growth in character. We initially used supporters of MRA as actors but then began using professional actors and actresses – this was a new departure for us.

The Friends of the Westminster Theatre, formed in April 1964, raised funds under the leadership of Harley Street dentist the late Dr James Dyce who did a lot of work on the front line in the battle fields of the Second World War. The aim of the Friends was: to make the Westminster Theatre and its purposes more widely known; to bring people or encourage them to come to the theatre and to strengthen financial support for the theatre. Every year the Friends raised money to buy tickets for children from children's homes to come and see the annual pantomime *Give a Dog a Bone* which ran for thirteen years with two thousand children a year coming to see it.

When Peter Howard was alive the theatre was very important in the work of MRA. His plays went around the world, as a means to change character, not as an event in themselves. The 1950s was a time when the whole morality of the country was called into question. It was a battle we fought and lost. In the Sixties there was a great shift in what was acceptable and not acceptable. There is an eternal struggle. People know more about kitchen sink drama than they do about Peter Howard. We have to continue that initial thinking of encouraging growth and character and to hold up the hope that things can change and people can change and give the very best of the arts in the process.

[Financing of the theatre] Friends raised money. There were lots of supporters around the country who tithed their income and were prepared to make sacrifices. You had this belief that if you did what God told you he would provide. [When Kiaer was made redundant, in the late 1950s, he gave his £500 compensation to MRA]. The Theatre was run as a commercial enterprise and many of the productions made a lot of money. However the Westminster spent a lot on advertising; buying full pages in the *Express* and elsewhere. Frank Buchman was very keen on the use of plays to promote the message and they were performed around the world — some with professional actors and others with supporters. The theatre can make an impact where a meeting can't. You can lose yourself in the theatre — it can depict something you have been going through.

The Westminster had the revolutionary message put forward by Buchman that human nature can be changed. That was the revolution. If people changed and if they accepted absolute moral change and if they listened to their inner voice they would be different. The revolution was to put those ideas into the plays.

Politicians were scared stiff of Howard. While at the *Daily Express*, he wrote a column always attacking some politician. Then to his horror Beaverbrook became a member of the cabinet and told Howard he couldn't write his column any more. A secretary at the *Express*, who had met the Oxford Group thought Howard should meet Garth Lean. That meeting led to Howard eventually working full time in MRA and his wish to contact people at the top of Governments who could affect global change. In the 1960s for instance Prime Minister Kishi of Japan saw one of Howard's plays and went around South East Asia as a result apologising for what Japan had done during the Second World War. Howard's plays were simplistic – about the eternal struggle between good and evil. I am not claiming Howard's plays were brilliant but they were about the battle of ideas. Double agent Tom Driberg absolutely loathed MRA and would follow us around the world damning every good thing we did. He worked for MI5 and the Communists.

Although the Westminster would be packed, there would often be no review of the plays because the theatre world didn't like us. The message we were giving was a challenge to their way of life. Howard had a theatre he had to supply and he had a message he had to get out. His plays were the weapon. People would be invited to the theatre and then to have supper in one of the MRA homes in central London. You would meet people after a play and talk about the experience at a reception. Then there would be meetings. Buchman saw the theatre as a fishing ground.

The Westminster staged a programme for schools entitled The Day of London Theatre. Pupils would come in the morning and have lectures on costume and how the play was set up; then see the play and meet the cast afterwards. In the 1960s the church was getting all wibbly-wobbly and panto was pretty vulgar, which was why we staged the *Give a Dog a Bone* panto and put on other children's plays like *The Gingerbread Man* and C.S. Lewis's *The Lion the Witch and the Wardrobe*. As far as the main stream theatre was concerned we didn't win the battle but we certainly affected national life.

APPENDIX FOURTEEN

Edited transcript of an interview with Stanley Kiaer on 12 November 2012 at Greencoat Place, London.

[Regarding the play *Temptation* which took place at the Westminster Theatre in May 1990, directed by James Roose-Evans and starring Rula Lenska.]

Havel was an interesting figure and Roose-Evans to my mind was a good director who had most thoughtfully directed an excellent play *The Best of Friends* about Shaw [George Bernard Shaw]. It was the kind of thing we were after. The one major mistake we made in commissioning Roose-Evans was that we had no rights on the final shape of the production. When it was produced some people found it too sexy. Rula Lenska was in it and there was a picture of her, in a review, of her legs, with her putting on stockings. This went all around the country. The Friends who supported us said what on earth is going on at the Westminster? People were divided over it. The play would have been fine in any other theatre but it did not represent what we stood for. This should have been a great success. We had outside backing for it. When Hugh [Steadman Williams] saw it in rehearsal he asked the director to tone it down but he refused. We had a similar situation with another play *Music at Midnight* where we didn't like the way it was being directed because it cut out the Quiet Time but we retained artistic rights and we spoke to the director who then changed it.

Temptation lost us our reputation and some our support. It also lost money because our supporters did not come and see it so it did not attract an audience. People were divided in their opinions. Friends of mine came and thought it was fine. I remember sitting through it, I was always hypersensitive about plays. I felt this play could go on at any other theatre and it would be terrific but not at the Westminster where we had to have a certain standard that we could not go beyond. As a result of *Temptation* the money at the Westminster ran out and the Oxford Group took back the running of it from Westminster Productions and closed the theatre. At the time I was secretary of Westminster Productions. We had a battle royal to stay solvent but we did. Running a theatre is very expensive, especially now. It was a thing of its time — it fulfilled a post-war need to rebuild.

The theatre tradition goes back to Buchman. He used the analogy of the fishing rod. He said you made contact with people and out of that came the transportation that began with seeing a play. When we first began putting on plays at the Westminster the cast was made up of MRA supporters. After the play, the cast would come down to talk to the audience and we also did this with Theatre for Schools. Everything depended on the play. Howard's death was a real blow to the theatre. We had to find new authors who could combine real life and teaching and create didactic theatre.

The theatre was also my home. My children were born and brought up there. From the mid-1960s onwards I was part of a team administering the theatre with Don Loughman as theatre manager, Louis Fleming as administrator of the Arts Centre and Hugh Williams as playwright and chairman of Westminster Productions.

I remember I was in the foyer once at a Theatre for Schools event. A lot of teenage girls came running across the theatre very excited. I shouted 'stop' and told them that they were now in a theatre and should imagine they were great ladies and sweep in to the auditorium. They all did just that.

The Day of London Theatre for Schools was a great success and very profitable until the government introduced legislation requiring every parent to give signed permission when a child went on a coach to the theatre.

[Reason for the demise of the Westminster.] Standing up for faith and the battle between good and evil in a secular age; massive increase in costs and the deaths of Peter Howard and Alan Thornhill as playwrights.

APPENDIX FIFTEEN

Edited transcript of interview with David Locke on 13 November 13, 2012, at Carshalton Beeches, Surrey.

[Locke first came into contact with MRA when he was 19 years of age. It was January 1954 and he was doing his National Service in the RAF. He was feeling quite lonely after being posted to a station 'in the wilds of Norfolk'. He went into a chapel and met the chaplain.]

I started to go in the evening to the service. At that time my Christian faith was a bit shaky but I felt this man had something. I liked the way he talked and what he said. He was a supporter of MRA and I told him I felt I should do something about moral leadership. He started to talk about the four standards of MRA and that resonated with me and I changed in my whole motivation in life. Instead of trying to please everyone I began to get some moral discipline in my life. In June of that year I went to Caux where I got a wider vision and I started to have Quiet Times in the chapel; it was all quite exciting.

[Locke worked full time with IofC from 1964 onwards. Before that he had a job and shared a flat in Mill Hill, working for IofC part time and organising coach parties to the theatre every two to three weeks.]

We would go up and down the street knocking on doors and inviting people to the theatre. Lots of people did this. By 1964 things were getting more organised and Ronald Mann took charge of the promotion. He invited me to talk with him about the theatre and I thought he would ask me to be the representative for North London. I thought: 'There is no way I am going to agree to do this – I am happy with what I am doing but I don't want to do more'. In fact he asked me to give up my job and work full time with his team which was a much bigger thing but funnily enough quite a bit of me really wanted to do that. I thought about it and agreed to work for him initially for six months.

[Locke became part of a team promoting the Westminster Theatre and his job involved attracting audiences. There were about six or seven in the team led by Ronald Mann and they worked from a small office in Mayfair. They would get reports from the box office every day on the number of vacant seats for the next three to four weeks. There were a variety of price ranges with the top price ticket £1.]

We would monitor the situation both in the long and short term. We would visit social clubs at factories. I was born in Enfield, North London and I remember visiting the factories there on the Great Cambridge Road and making friends with the social club secretaries. We would organise events at the Westminster and invite the social secretaries of these clubs to come along and also have a meal at one of the MRA houses. We had lots of houses in Charles Street, Mayfair. We would invite them to see the play and then encourage them to bring along coach parties. We would also get a list of all the voluntary organisations in an area. We would contact the secretaries of these organisations. Very often this would be a personal door-step visit after a phone call. Sometimes it would be through a letter. We would use different techniques at different times. We would tell them all about the theatre and offer them a special group rate.

I worked on this from 1964 to 1968. In 1967 we had a change of management structure. The professional theatre manager retired and Donald Loughman, manager of our theatre company Westminster Productions, took over with the dual role of manager of Westminster Productions and also manager of Westminster Theatre. We combined these two roles and I became his assistant in both roles. I learnt the job from him between 1967 and 1973. In that role I was dealing with house management, responsible for greeting people, the usherettes, theatre catering, organising cups of tea on trays in the interval, dealing with back stage staff and stage hands. We had permanent technical staff in addition to those who came in when needed. One of my principle jobs was to deal with all the wages. Donald Loughman and the board of Westminster Productions did the negotiations for the contracts with the actors — usually through their agents.

Most people coming to the theatre enjoyed it and quite a lot of people became regulars because they liked the integrity of the plays. There was a quote in one of the newspapers 'You know where you are at the Westminster' and a lot of people felt that. MRA in those days had a resident force of people up and down the country who were enthusiastic about MRA. The theatre was the main weapon — the main tool to get across our ideas to people all over the country and we would organise coaches to bring people from places like Wales and the North of England to London particularly at a weekend.

Each of the London houses took a different night to host receptions. For instance people involved with MRA and concerned about Middle East issues would invite people from the Middle East on a particular evening for a meal and then a visit to the theatre. We held special events. We noted that all the Mayors coming to the Buckingham Palace garden parties in the afternoon from around the country had nothing to do in the evening so we would invite some of them to one of the houses and then on to the theatre. We probably gave them free tickets. A lot of free tickets were given out. Getting audiences was like a military operation. We would meet every morning to look at the vacant seats. If we were low in numbers we would contact nurses and hospitals nearby and discuss other places we could contact. It was quite a struggle at times.'

[In the 1980s Locke joined the board of Westminster Productions with Hugh Steadman Williams, Stanley Kiaer and others. He was on the board at the time of the *Temptation* production.] It [*Temptation*] was a very difficult time. Ronald Mann got this guy James Roose-Evans to direct the play. He seemed to be a good guy. Like so many directors he wanted artistic freedom and we trusted he would do what we wanted. I remember sitting there in the dress rehearsal and I felt very divided. It was very suggestive. This wasn't quite MRA but at the same time it was artistic. I didn't personally make a great deal of fuss but others felt vehemently that it was absolutely atrocious. Without MRA support it was doomed. By that time we were struggling along and I had come to the conclusion the days of the theatre were over. I love theatre and I loved the way of doing things through the theatre but we just didn't have the plays any more. Peter Howard was an amazing guy and he turned out all these plays but no-one else was doing that and the theatre needed money invested in it.

[Regarding First Floor Theatre.] We wanted to get into experimental cutting-edge theatre. We were probably influenced by the Royal Court and its Theatre Upstairs. We were very conscious of the Royal Court and what they were doing.

[Regarding the closure of the theatre.] In the 1960s it [the Westminster] provided a focus for the MRA team. Something we could all do together to take the message to the country and it was an enjoyable way of doing it. After all, churchgoing was declining rapidly — many people hesitated to go into a church, but a theatre was a neutral space. As a result thousands came to the theatre over many years. Some came and enjoyed the entertainment. Others came and were influenced. However, some people came and their lives were changed.

Because Peter Howard had died we did not have the plays to put on. His plays continued to be performed for some years but there were no new ones from him. Alan Thornhill, Nancy Ruthven and Hugh Steadman Williams provided some material but this was not enough. We then moved to putting on Christian-type plays but, as Leone Exton [who ran the catering services at the Westminster] said, they did not have the last act, by which she meant that of real change in people which was the essence of the MRA message.

APPENDIX SIXTEEN

Edited transcript of an interview with John Locke conducted at IofC conference centre, Caux, Switzerland, 11 August, 2013.

[Locke began working at the Westminster Theatre in 1977 and left in 1990. He is on the board of Westminster Productions and in the past has been a member of the board of Aldersgate Productions.]

The Westminster was the only Christian theatre that was a member of the Society of West End Theatres. Membership of this society recognised the Westminster Theatre as a full 'West End Theatre'. This was a very exclusive group limited solely to those theatres within a certain geographical area. It meant important access to first night Fleet Street papers, critics and to other publicity. It also carried important responsibilities with regard to the issuing of contracts. Actors had to be paid at Equity, West End rates, rather than the lower outer London or provincial rates. The Westminster had to make a living from the box office, there was no subsidy, and there were two fundamental issues with this: (1) The Westminster Theatre itself wasn't a large theatre; with about six hundred seats it was small for a London West End Theatre and therefore its ability to make a profit was also relatively limited. Any West End Theatre will be required to take sufficient at the box office to cover weekly running costs and to amortise the original production costs over a specific number of weeks. Production costs can be high so the risks in failing to take sufficient at the box office to cover both production and running costs are relatively high. Relatively few West End shows manage to do this, because there is no subsidy, and financial risks are therefore considerable for anyone considering being an 'Angel' and investing in commercial theatre in London. Running a West End theatre is, therefore, a very challenging business. (2) The Westminster was limited with the type of show it could put on as a consequence of the size of the theatre and the conditions of the owner of the building. The freeholder, the Oxford Group, appeared to only want plays with an explicit Christian or a positive theme attached to Christian values. The problem was mainly that making a Christian theatre commercially viable was becoming very difficult. Throughout the sixties, and after that, much of the successful commercial theatre had been of an, apparently, more negative kind; Theatre of the Angry Young Man variety. While much of this was brilliant in its theatrical presentation and its writing it certainly could not be referred to as 'Positive'. It has been said that 'The devil has all the best tunes'. The struggle to find powerful writing that made good theatre that would be popular with audiences was a constant theme of our meetings. But there was a further issue as much of what was put on also appeared to be attracting an older audience. We needed to reach out to the many young Christian groups both in London and elsewhere to broaden the appeal of the Theatre. Westminster Productions, therefore, had a vested interest in promoting Christian theatre with young adults.

At the Theatre there was a largish room that was being used mainly as a staff restaurant that was underused. We also knew a substantial number of Christian-based theatre companies that were touring, such as Riding Lights, but did not have a base in London. We felt we could use the room upstairs as a showcase and invite these groups to London and the Westminster Theatre could become the home of Christian positive theatre in the country. The Board of Westminster Productions conceived it with the approval of the freeholders — the Oxford Group. From what I recall I believe that it was Ronald Mann who actually had the idea in the first place.

We thought about either using First Floor Theatre for other groups or running seasons ourselves – inviting groups in and paying them to promote Christian drama or running it as a facility house or a commercial paying house. There were a number of options but a key feature, initially, was that the venue had to pay for itself. The last thing we wanted was a further drain on Westminster Productions. Carol Henderson was appointed as artistic director and I was the manager. I had been assistant manager at the Westminster for nearly a year before that. I was appointed by Hugh Williams to be assistant manager to Don Loughman. It was in 1988. It was a chance of a lifetime. However, there was a difference of perspective between Carol and myself as to how to achieve the objectives the Board of Westminster Productions had set. An appeal had been launched and £100,000 was raised to start First Floor Theatre. I did not think this was a substantial enough sum to enter into contractual agreements with paying artists and companies and that this money should be used entirely for the capital outlay and to support First Floor Theatre through the initial, no doubt, difficult years. As I saw it companies needed to take the responsibility for filling the place as much as the Westminster. I wanted to operate First Floor Theatre on a box office split from the very beginning as this would establish the nature of the venue and its relationship to incoming companies. Carol wanted an initial impact, to hit the ground running. She felt it would take too long to promote the theatre as a venue space; that our position would not necessarily be trusted because of historical reticence about the Westminster Theatre and we needed to approach existing groups and build a programme that would be attractive to Christian audiences. She wanted two seasons of ten weeks twice a year in which we paid incoming companies a straight fee, rather than part fee/part box office or all box office. She also thought we should spend a larger sum of money promoting the seasons in the Christian press. The Board supported these initial proposals and we put together the two seasons. The cost of equipping the theatre was about £20,000 — we did it very economically but all facilities and equipment remained of high quality. We built a stage, got lights and a sound system. But even if we filled it every night we would not cover the costs of the season. The cost was £30,000 for each season. By the end of the second season we had spent £80,000 of the £100,000. Carol's seasons were of outstandingly high quality but managing them on a theatre basis, whilst operating the Westminster Theatre, also presented a number of logistical problems in terms of audience management, timing of intervals, getting audiences in and out with different show times. There were also certain frictions with those in the building who were not happy at the loss of the space as a staff restaurant. However we got through and overcame those, relatively unimportant, problems. What was difficult was persuading incoming companies to participate in the promotion of their show as there was no pressure that would arise from a box office split, for audiences attending, all the pressure was on us!

During the second season after a lot of lobbying and promoting I got Westminster City Council to give the first grant they ever gave to a West End theatre company and certainly the first ever grant The Westminster Theatre had received from Westminster City Council on the basis that we were providing a studio theatre for local young people. They gave £1,000. This was a phenomenal break-through but I was concerned that at the end of the second season there was insufficient money for the next season. As it turned out the issue was sterile as there was insufficient money to continue running the main house.

[Regarding *Temptation*.] *Temptation* made front page of *The War Cry* [the newspaper of The Salvation Army] in a positive way. And although mixed reviews greeted the play's opening night, much of the discerning press had a positive outlook. The interpretation of Havel's play was very powerful. Unfortunately, many of the full-time staff working in the building and elsewhere were highly critical of the style of production. My experience of what then happened was fairly disgraceful as a number of devoted full-time workers, who had given their lives to MRA, were pilloried and subjected to the most unjustified and in some cases completely false accusations. I found myself speaking to intelligent, discerning Christians, in the building, telling me utter falsehoods about the production, which, it turned out, they had not seen themselves. It was tragic because, although controversial, the production had offered the Westminster a way out of the rut associated with the internal MRA playwriting which, although good in its time, now lacked the popular appeal. This friction was unhelpful even to MRA's core aims as the show had proved popular with fellow traveling groups, as witnessed by *The War Cry* front page, picking up on the 'Don't deal with Sin' theme. It was a great pity because the Day of London Theatre and the Narnia plays were being very positively received at the Westminster. The controversy with *Temptation* therefore brought to a head the general feeling within MRA that the theatre was an expensive luxury they could ill afford and its day was past.

Temptation had a big outlay, it folded having lost money and *Temptation* pulled FFT [First Floor Theatre] down with it but FFT was in some difficulties because it did not have enough money for a third season. It had two absolutely scintillating, glorious, exciting seasons that were spectacularly successful. It cost £30k to £40k to mount two seasons, not a large amount and the seasons were very popular. The first season had seventy to seventy-eight per cent capacity and the second over eighty per cent capacity. We took full page ads in Christian newspapers and magazines. It was a wonderful conception – theatre with a positive approach that attracted audiences of all persuasions and not only Christian audiences. The Westminster Theatre was a gift – a marvellous place in which to work. What it did over the years was of incalculable benefit to Christian theatre and to using theatre generally as a means of communicating a positive message to the world.

After the theatre closed, the Oxford Group said we could buy it for use as a Christian Arts Centre and we made a desperate effort to raise the money. We needed many donors and time ran out. I was so distressed at the closure and the way I had seen my good friends Hugh [Steadman Williams] and Stanley [Kiaer] treated that I felt I did not want to stay in the theatre. I left it in 1990. I thought I wanted to do something utterly ordinary. I got the local paper on the day I was told it was all over and saw an advertisement by Brighton and Hove City Council for a housing services support worker. I applied and got the job and retired twenty-one years later as part of the management team of housing services. I took retirement and then got involved with Renewal Arts [the artistic arm of IofC] and performed the one man show *Legend of the Fourth King*.

I believe passionately in using drama as a means for spreading uplifting, inspirational messages. I am very proud to have been part of the Westminster Theatre and the inspirational work of Hugh Williams, Stanley Kiaer, Ron Mann, Nancy Ruthven and others. It was truly marvellous and an honour to work with such gifted, generous, devoted people. Working at The Westminster Theatre was, for me, a pinnacle of my professional life.

APPENDIX SEVENTEEN

Edited transcript of an interview with John Locke, on 27 May, 2015, at IofC headquarters, Greencoat Place, London.

The day of the gala opening of First Floor Theatre (FFT) [19 April, 1990] was the very day when we recognised that the company was challenged to the point where its very survival was in jeopardy. The irony of this was that First Floor Theatre represented a genuine new future for Christian Theatre and Theatre of the Positive. However, without the main stage theatre, First Floor Theatre had no future. What followed was a period of about twelve weeks during which time we tried, by every means at our disposal, to raise the several million pounds needed to secure the future and allow our work to continue. However, despite the very best efforts we did not prevail. I received my letter of notice on 5 July, 1990.

There needs to be some clarification on the original intended purpose of First Floor Theatre. The original intention of FFT was that it would be a facility for other Christian groups to use. On appointment Carol [Carol Henderson, artistic director] wanted an immediate profile. She argued at the time that Christian companies might not be persuaded to use the facility, or share the costs, without First Floor Theatre being already known. Carol, therefore, wanted to pay companies the full cost of their appearance; effectively employing them. This was against the alternative of actually charging companies to appear and use this central London venue or accepting appearances on a box-office split basis. Or, of course, a combination of the two which could be managed at a lower cost to the company than many other commercial venues would charge. Following a launch appeal, we had a capital of £100,000. With this financial structure, even had the theatre survived, there would have been some difficulty in ensuring a viable long-term future. After two brilliant seasons, FFT was proving to be very expensive. And it was supposed to be a boost to Westminster Productions, not a drain on its facilities.

To my mind the best play staged at FFT was *Adult Child/Dead Child* with Jaqueline Macdonald. Her performance was electrifying and this was a highly original production. For me, of everything we did at FFT, that has to be the pinnacle. It looked at complex and difficult issues involving child abuse and did it with gripping theatre and a superlative performance from Jacqueline Macdonald.

There were five issues going on simultaneously in the theatre from April 1989 until the closure.

1. The whole issue of survival was being debated even before *Temptation* opened. The difficulty was finding a production that people wanted to see but that met both the objectives of the company and, at the same time, could be financially viable at The Westminster Theatre. The Theatre was smaller than many West End theatres in terms of seating capacity, therefore production costs had to be kept lower in order to ensure we covered running costs of the theatre and met a weekly contribution towards the original production expense "amortisation" as it is generally known.

2. Westminster Productions came up with *Temptation* as a means of putting the theatre on the front line of public recognition with a producer who would make the headlines.

3. The difficult issues that arose around *Temptation* were founded in the fact that James Roose-Evans had directed the play in a way which was

original and challenging. Consequently, there emerged substantial conflict between MRA and Westminster Productions as to the nature of the production, how the issues were being portrayed and the actual staging. Even had the play been a huge financial success there were those who would still have objected to it on political and moral principles.

4. *Temptation* was an expensive production and, throughout the West End, audiences were falling following the stock market crash of that year and the security issues that seemed to be disproportionately affected by Iraq's invasion of Kuwait. A further irony here was that while audiences for the main theatre were challenged, First Floor Theatre audiences were doing well, with successful seasons, audiencewise. However we were running through its money and the box office take was not covering costs. There were concerns and discussions about the viability of FFT and the amount it was costing. There was, really, insufficient money for a third season. If we had survived until the spring of 1991 we might had been able to raise further resources with a let to the Soho Polytechnic, which needed premises at that time as they were temporally homeless.

For me there were a number of regrets and disappointment at the conduct of certain others. Regarding *Temptation*: I had people coming up to me in the Westminster being highly critical when they hadn't seen it and were relying on what had been told them by others. I challenged them to go and see it. The newspapers exaggerated what went on and those who read these reports relied on them rather than seeing the production for themselves. For instance one report that I heard spoken about was that Rula Lenska was very scantily dressed on stage. In fact, the actress was dressed from head to toe all the time — she, simply, just had a slit in the side of her dress which otherwise went from neck to ankle. It is always a pity when you see great men and great ideas brought down by lies. This was an opportunity for MRA to have owned the message of *Temptation* and promoted the theatre into the modern era, addressing Christian values in a challenging way. The production was challenging and it was a message that needed to be said. However, the show lost £10,000 in a week so was not covering costs or getting back the large production costs.

Buchman was interested in getting to the people in power as motivators of Change but the theatre draws in the ordinary people and they will then bring their influence to bear on those in power. Just as the Day of London Theatre got to the hearts and minds of the masses, the power to change will come from the ordinary people and that is the value of the Westminster Theatre, First Floor Theatre and its legacy.

The greatest achievement of the Westminster Theatre was, quite simply, that it survived for so long and flourished in a hostile atmosphere that became deeply suspicious of its purpose and intentions. The historical remarks made by Frank Buchman and the personal history of Peter Howard, and his association with certain East End political elements, had often been quoted by those who knew neither the context nor the accuracy of either. Because of this the Westminster Theatre had suffered, to some degree, during the time that MRA both owned and ran it. However, the Theatre had increasingly been viewed as old-fashioned and many of the plays that had been mounted had failed to attract a wider appeal beyond MRA supporters and fellow travellers. There were significant exceptions as in *Give the Dog a Bone* the theatre's successful Christmas show, the Day of London Theatre, the hugely successful educational programme run by the theatre and the successful run of the Narnia plays. During the period of MRA's production and, subsequently, Westminster Productions management of the Theatre, it was both the variety and the complexity of the undertakings that were so impressive. As the only Theatre in the country to base its ethic on Christian values and themes, without necessarily proselytising the Christian faith, it set a unique and courageous path in the face of bigotry, opposition and professional dissent.

[Reasons for closure of the theatre.] MRA decided, collectively, that there were too many other areas of interest in which they were becoming involved and that Theatre should no longer hold the supremacy it once did as part of their mission. From this perspective the Westminster Theatre simply did not give value for money. The achievements of the Theatre, far greater than its eventual fate, will, in the course of time, hopefully be recognised.

APPENDIX EIGHTEEN

Edited transcript of an interview with Mahala Menzies conducted on 20 March, 2015 at IofC headquarters, 24 Greencoat Place, London.

My mother was Elsie Griffin, international opera singer [1895-1989]. I was the understudy to Polly Rankine, but never actually got on the stage. I toured around the UK with the company and did backstage work. In the Midlands in the coal fields, where the battle for communism was taking place, we put on the play and it did change the atmosphere in the mines. The play was a focal point. There is something about a group of people sitting in a darkened room watching a story unfold in front of you that makes you want to see it through to the end. There is just you and what is going on on the stage. In the end you are left with making your own decision. Everyone was engaged with the play, it was very popular.

APPENDIX NINETEEN

Edited transcript of an interview with Geoffrey Pugh on 30 January, 2013, at IofC headquarters, 24 Greencoat Place, London.

[Pugh is brother of Fiona Daukes. Their father was Cecil Pugh, a padre in the air force. He got involved in MRA in 1929 after graduating from Oxford in theology in 1925. He was a congregational minister who lost his life in the war and was awarded the George Cross posthumously. His wife used his gratuity to help towards buying the Westminster Theatre.]

I was invited to go and live in Manchester around 1966/67. *Annie* the musical was on at the Westminster in London about the work of Annie Jaeger who came from Stockport. Bill Jaeger, her son, who had introduced me to the Mayor of Stockport whilst I was in London, asked me to go to Stockport and get as many people as possible to travel to the Westminster to see *Annie*. I contacted a headmistress who was fascinated to hear about there being a musical in London about a Stockport character and she said she would help us.

A friend of mine who was a lecturer at an FE college decided to hire a special train from Stockport to London at a cost of £2,000 and we then set about filling it. The headmistress we had started off with got pupils to take part. I was having tea with my friend in the Co-op and a little old lady came to our table. She asked what we were doing and I told her about the train. She said she couldn't come on that one but she would go on the next one so we thought we would have to have another one. We ended up organising three trains from Stockport and taking around 1,000 people to the Westminster.

People would come down to the Westminster in large numbers particularly at the weekends — including people from Welsh Mining villages, male voice choirs. They would stay over in the homes of MRA activists all around London and then on Sundays the choirs would help to entertain and we would give news of MRA. Wendy, my wife, invited her boss, a chartered accountant, to the theatre. He heard there was trouble in a shipyard. He was so interested he offered to pay for a coach to come from Scotland where the shipyard was. They did come and as a result of the visit the trouble was resolved and the future of the shipyard was assured.

APPENDIX TWENTY

Edited email from Ray Purdy to Pamela Jenner on 4 April, 2012.

I was thirteen when I arrived in Southampton aboard the *Queen Mary* on 30 April, 1946 with my parents and a large number of MRA workers, led by Frank Buchman, the founder. We came by train to London and then drove through the streets in buses to the MRA headquarters at 4 Hays Mews. The evidence of the wartime blitz was all around us and it made a deep impression on me. In the street was a large crowd of British MRA workers, and the laughing and crying and joyous reunion of these long-time friends from both sides of the water, who hadn't seen each other during the long years of war, was something to see. I was a member of the cast of the stage play *The Forgotten Factor* by Alan Thornhill, which had been mounted and shown across America, and which Frank Buchman brought to Britain as a vehicle to help revitalise and arm the country for the coming ideological struggle for post-war Europe, which he foresaw. In July I went for the first time to Caux, Switzerland, where Mountain House was opened as a world training centre for MRA. *The Forgotten Factor* came too! When we came back to Britain, the tour with the play continued through the Midlands and Scotland. All through that winter of 1946-7 the play was performed. Night after night, busloads would come, from collieries, factories, schools, farms and towns all over the country. It was an amazing winter. I experienced pea soup fogs and bitter cold, but I count myself so lucky to have been part of this initiative.

I remember the dedication service [of the Westminster Theatre], with the ranks of servicemen on stage, all in uniform, who had given quite sacrificially from their pay to purchase the theatre. They felt it could be used as a training centre where people from all over the country could come to learn how to bring about the world for which they had fought and so many had died – a world which could be changed the way they had been changed, by starting with themselves.

I first met Peter Howard when my parents and I were invited to his farm in Lavenham, Suffolk. We had heard a lot about him in America, and read his books, but this was a chance to get to know him and his family. It was to be a life-long friendship. He gave the address at our wedding in 1964 at Mackinac Island, Michigan, and my wife and I were in South America with him and others at the time of his death in 1965. Of course, in later years, a whole galaxy of other plays were performed at the Westminster Theatre, most of them written by Peter Howard. It is just possible that the existence of the theatre, with its technical competence, experienced crew and stable of dedicated directors and actors provided a ready-made platform for the creative genius of Peter Howard to flourish and grow and speak to the country, and later to many other countries, through this alternative medium to his books. Having performed there, as well as other venues, myself, I realise I have received a priceless gift, a love of theatre and an awareness of how it can be used to move men and women and affect the way they live their lives. This 'inspiration factor' is what I now look for in films and plays, presented, of course, in a thumping good story!

As you can see, these memories are very strong, even if a long time ago. I feel very privileged to have known Peter [Howard], and to have known the Westminster Theatre. Oddly enough, some of the stage equipment from the Westminster Theatre has found its way up to the wee theatre of the

Church Hall here in Kirkcudbright, Scotland, where I still occasionally 'tread the boards'. It feels just like home!

APPENDIX TWENTY-ONE

Edited email from Peter Rundell to Pamela Jenner on 20 March, 2015

My father, Robert John Kenneth Rundell (known as Ken), became involved with the Oxford Group, as it then was, when he was at Oxford in 1938. He was a 'County Scholar' from a Cornish grammar school, the son of a builder, and the first generation of his family to go to University. He was an active Methodist before University (he remained a lay preacher on the Cornwall circuit from the age of sixteen until his death at the age of 90) and at Oxford marched with the International Brigades down the High Street. However, he found the Oxford Group's ideas convincing, and when he was called up in 1940 (after a struggle over his earlier conscientious objection) he remained in close touch with his MRA friends (as the Oxford Group became). When he was demobilised in 1946 or 1947 he was one of the servicemen who gave their demob gratuities to buy the Westminster Theatre, and he remained actively involved with the theatre from time to time thereafter.

When he came down from Oxford again – like many whose studies were interrupted by the war – he returned to complete his degree, in his case reading theology after the war (classical mods before). When he graduated he went into full-time work with MRA, which he continued for many years. For the first few years he worked in the MRA press team, as he had been editor of *Isis* (the Oxford University magazine) and was a member of the Institute of Journalists (one of the two Trades Unions for journalists).

My father was away from the UK quite often in the 1950s and 1960s (we were in Nigeria 1956–58 and in Caux, the MRA conference centre in

Switzerland, 1960-64) with MRA. When we returned to London as a family, he took on a role in the Westminster Theatre – MRA's main public outreach forum – and soon identified the need to bring in more children and young people. Partly recalling the Jesuit remark about 'give me a boy until he is nine and I will give you the man' (the saying was in the male form, as much Jesuit and evangelical thought was in those days), he wanted to reach an audience that might not yet be formed in the cynicism and self-indulgence he perceived in contemporary culture. However, he recognised that only organised groups would bring the scale of outreach he sought, so he hit on the idea of integrating lessons about theatre into a programme which would include the afternoon performance (which was rarely heavily booked on weekdays).

Of course this only made sense when the age group targeted by the educational element was suited to the play. So primary schools were a natural audience for the Christmas pantomime *Give a Dog a Bone*, while secondary schools might be attracted to more mature shows like *Blindsight* or *Happy Deathday* (the latter subsequently filmed, the former I think sunk without trace). The programme included elements on costume (modifying the outline of a female costume by changing details like sleeve shape, trimmings, neck decoration *etc.* with Velcro used to attach elements that could be pulled off and stuck on, much to the relief of the wardrobe mistress, who commented that this made it so much simpler than when they had needed to sew each item on), diction, theatrical movement, lighting and scenery. There was also a section on the history of theatre, including classical and medieval plays, which Bill Cameron-Johnson illustrated (illustrations now in 24 Greencoat Place I think); this tended to bring out the social role of theatre in particular. I think a section on the history of the Westminster

Theatre itself, notably the role of the founder of the Westminster Chapel which was the original building on the site (he was the last man to be hanged at Tyburn for forgery), was also part of the programme for the older children.

I think the end of ADOLT [A Day of London Theatre] came partly because of the changes in the way schools operated; it became more and more difficult to fill the theatre with school parties as funding dried up. My mother fell ill (with motor neurone disease) in 1975–76, and my father made caring for her his priority, so his role would have ended then; I cannot recall whether the programme was still alive at that point or not.

Educationally I think, looking back, that the programme was the first in what has become relatively routine today; outreach by theatres to potential future audiences. While elements of the day were perhaps amateur by today's standards (the sections on diction and movement would hardly pass muster with a media-savvy class accustomed to *Strictly Come Dancing* and reality TV), I still recall other elements like the lighting and costume sections as admirably suited to an audience whose next experience of theatre might be in a school play or community drama group. It retained throughout a didactic thrust which might no longer work, together with a set of strong messages from MRA which were delivered in a more direct form than would be effective today.

APPENDIX TWENTY-TWO

Edited transcript of interview with Hugh Steadman Williams on 3 October, 2011, at IofC headquarters, 24 Greencoat Place, London.

[Hugh Steadman Williams became involved in MRA in 1961 as a trustee of the Westminster Memorial Trust, developed to run a series of plays under their own management.]

I was asked to come and be assistant stage manager and understudy the smallest part in the play *Music at Midnight*. In 1963 we took *Music at Midnight* touring across the US and I was deputy stage manager. From then until 1969 I did that work, except for 1966 which I spent in East Africa on a production of an MRA show. In 1969 at the AGM I was appointed deputy stage manager.

The motive of MRA then was to counter the culture in the 1950s and 1960s of deliberately debunking and going against moral and spiritual values. John Osborne deliberately did that, as did Shelagh Delaney and *A Taste of Honey*. It got even more extreme with Edward Bond's *Saved*. Even the National Theatre had a season of Theatre of Cruelty. *The Romans in Britain* had one particularly violent scene of homosexual rape. [Williams said he was highly embarrassed by what he regarded as the overt sexuality in Joe Orton's play *Entertaining Mr Sloane*.]

Peter Howard wanted to create plays of a very high standard in terms of production. He had professional designers, actors etc. and competed on an artistic level with the West End but all his plays had to have a message. Most of his plays were allegories. *Through the Garden Wall* was about the division between East and West Europe. *Mr Brown Comes Down the Hill* really talked about what would happen if Christ came down to earth again. The critics had a different set of views. They seemed to think our Christian plays were propaganda and other plays were not; but this double thinking we found very annoying. A character in a Howard play said: 'Every positive is propaganda and every negative is news.' Lots of Howard's concepts were brilliant and parts of the plays were brilliant but he was living a busy life. He got up at 4AM to write plays before breakfast but you cannot write great works of art like that. Shaw [George Bernard Shaw] spent months on his plays. Howard did not have this leisure. They had an unfinished look about them. They were rushed. I think if he had been able to concentrate on playwriting he would have been a very good playwright.

Harold Hobson said at the time in *The Times* that in most theatre you get sex, sadism, Shakespeare and sometimes all three. He added that plays at the Westminster were 'pure and simple and it certainly makes a change'. Some critics treated us very fairly but others refused to review the plays, saying they were just Christian propaganda.

The Royal Court was a revolution in theatre. Up until the 1950s plays had been about middle-class families in drawing rooms having extra marital affairs. Suddenly there were working class playwrights — Pinter, Osborne, Shelagh Delaney, Orton and there was a revolution going on. Unfortunately, the Westminster was seen as trying to perpetuate the old drawing room theatre. We were regarded as too conservative. Our revolution was for people to live the values and standards of MRA. Peter Howard said people would not survive without a change in character. Many people were aware of this alternative theatre. The Westminster was trying to give a balancing factor. Everyone was pushing the boundaries. It's difficult to say what effect we have had. Using theatre in a revolutionary way was part of the whole event for MRA. Towards the end of 1960s and in 1970s we had the Day of London Theatre. Children would come to lectures, demonstrations, a matinée and a discussion afterwards. We put on plays like *Mr Wilberforce MP* by Alan Thornhill. I could see a deficiency in the plays we were staging. I wanted to do better. We had Henry Cass, former Old Vic, as director. Production values were very high. It was in the writing. This is not a criticism of Peter Howard but this was only a small part of his working day and I don't know if you can produce great drama like that. Even Howard was subject to the censors — *Mr Brown Comes Down the Hill* was censored and the Lord Chamberlain took out some lines about Jesus Christ. Howard and Brecht were didactic playwrights. For them the message was all important. They wanted to spread a message.

APPENDIX TWENTY-THREE

Edited transcript of interview with Hugh Steadman on 30 July, 2013 at IofC headquarters, 24, Greencoat Place, London.

The eighties were a very difficult time for the Westminster as there was a constant battle about whether we should keep the theatre or not. In the mid-1980s the management introduced The Pause, when we would do nothing at all. However, during The Pause a number of video productions were made. In 1988 Westminster Productions, which had literally been the production company, took over the running of the theatre. We revamped the restaurant, introduced the First Floor Theatre and The Pause ended.

I was the chairman of Westminster Productions and we had a twofold policy: (1) to bring in decent plays that had originated elsewhere, on to the main stage; co-producing with outside companies; (2) to express the spiritual side of MRA in the First Floor Theatre. In 1990 we took a big step — to put on a main stage production under our own management. The First Floor Theatre was opened by Cliff Richard but it could not stand on its own. It was only financially viable if it could be supported by the main theatre box office.

There were a series of disasters in 1990. We decided to bring from America a musical *Cotton Patch Gospel*. It was a southern folk-style musical. We had put up some money for it and then found someone else who would also back it financially. While it was in rehearsal in New York this backer pulled out. Finance was needed at that time for Tim Rice's *Chess* and this person decided to back that instead. We had to pay the cast for three weeks rehearsal and then we had an empty theatre for a month. We had to pay off the cast. We were already in a weak position by the time we staged *Temptation*. It was just after Czechoslovakia became democratic and Václav Havel, the outspoken dissident, became president. We looked at what he had written. We read several of his other plays but we like this one which was based on a Faust legend. I raised sponsorship from APV, a big food processing company with a large interest in Czechoslovakia. They put up £25,000. We also had £25,000 from a Japanese electronics company plus private investment. Altogether we raised £200,000 to the total cost of £250,000 so we borrowed £50,000 from the bank. When the play closed after six weeks instead of the expected six months we were faced with repaying the bank loan.

Westminster Memorial Trust, which was part of the Oxford Group, offered to bail us out but the trustees — who were not theatre people at all — made it a condition that we would stop altogether and close the theatre. They had been angling for this throughout the 1980s and we had to do it. I had to give notice to twenty-five people. It was terrible. The only way we avoided bankruptcy was by selling equipment. We had equipped the First Floor Theatre very well with modern lighting equipment. The Caux Foundation bought it from us for the Caux Theatre for £25,000. That saved us from bankruptcy but left us with nothing. We tried to persuade the Trust to let us do Christmas shows with Vanessa Ford Productions but they wouldn't even allow that. We had to close the theatre down and then they tried to sell it, but it took seven years.

We had hoped the Christian Arts Trust might buy it and create a Christian Arts Centre. We did two feasibility studies with Ronald Mann, who was the secretary of it at the time. I took over as secretary in 1991. We formed a special committee from all sorts of groups and churches. Transforming it into an arts centre would have cost eight and a half million. We applied to the Arts Council. They would have given us five and a half but we still needed to raise £3million and we found we just could not do it. Even top Christian businesses were not prepared to put money into it. One man in America promised us half a million but he turned out to be a crook; a pyramid seller who ended up in jail. We failed to come up with the money but it did a lot of good because it brought a lot of Christian organisations together and we formed great friendships as a result. Eventually it was agreed that if we could get two and three quarter million we would sell the Westminster.

[Regarding choosing James Roose-Evans to direct *Temptation*.] Roose-Evans produced *84 Charing Cross Road* and *The Best of Friends* about George Bernard Shaw. We felt he was the right man. I was so busy raising the money and doing the publicity that I never actually got to rehearsals. I was the producer and didn't get there until the dress rehearsal and by that time things were irreversible. We had spent a lot of money and could not consider putting a halt to it, but it wasn't the production we hoped it would be. I know Roose-Evans had experience of MRA in the 1940s and it was not a happy experience. I feel he had it in for us and used the production to undermine our values. We kept standards of absolute purity and there were scenes simulating the sex act, a scene of copulation, and very sexy scenes with Rula Lenska. Roose-Evans was a homosexual and in those days a lot of MRA people were homophobic. Maybe he felt he had to put the knife in.

Bernard Mann was helping me on the board at Westminster Productions. We had a meeting with James [Roose-Evans] and tackled him head on about the explicit sex scene. He said: 'I'm a non-stipendiary clergyman in the Church of England – the only director who is. I wouldn't do anything to undermine Christian values' – but he did. After I had seen the dress rehearsal I spoke to James. I told him I would lose the audience and he said 'yes, but I will get you a whole new audience'. But it was not a success. We did not get good reviews. We didn't get the audiences. I got him to modify some things by use of lighting but it still upset the MRA family terribly. There was a huge outcry. My name was mud. Monsignor George Leonard, head of public affairs for the Catholic Diocese of Westminster, saw the dress rehearsal and said he didn't think there was much to worry about. A URC clergyman saw it and said it just fell short of redemption but highlighted an important part of the Bible message and underlined a neglected doctrine, about hell. The whole set ended in flames.

A lot of young people in MRA were very supportive but the old guard sat in the foyer night after night trying to persuade people not to go in. I very much regret I didn't get to rehearsals sooner. We could have modified it and changed direction. There had been an earlier production of it by the Royal Shakespeare Company in their studio theatre which was not as explicit. I don't think James [Roose-Evans] pulled it off artistically. I think he got carried away by his own agenda. The wife of the translator saw it and walked out saying 'It is a travesty'. Someone came from the Czech Embassy and I asked what Havel would have made of it. They said they did not think he would have approved. He may have been warned off it by the cultural attaché of the Czech Embassy in London who had seen the play and said he did not think it would be to Havel's taste. He explained that although in his private life Havel was quite a ladies' man, he did not like overt sexuality on the stage.

[Regarding the tension between the Americans and British in MRA and Steadman Williams' views on Peter Howard's plays.] The tension was between the message and the art. In America MRA created *Sing Out* touring shows, mainly consisting of songs. One musical was *Up with People* which was very upbeat, showing the bright-eyed American youth. But on this side of the Atlantic we felt to get sponsorship you had to get people like Coca Cola and they toned down the message. The Americans sold off a lot of our assets such as the Mackinac Island conference centre and all the money went into the shows.

Even in Peter Howard's time there were those for whom the message was everything and they didn't care much about the art. I always maintain the better the art the more powerful the message. I often felt Peter Howard had too many roles. He was the leader of MRA; he was very dynamic, his writing was often done between meetings; he did not give it the time it needed. The plots were brilliant, the characters amusing, but they could have done with a lot more work. He felt this himself. The tension was always there. If the plays had been better there would not have been the tensions. When Peter Howard died some people felt the cutting edge of the theatre had been lost and it no longer had the sharpness of the message. There was more interest in the message than the theatre so we didn't have the support.

When we closed First Floor Theatre the next play we were going to do was my play *Skeletons*, which people say was my best. It was performed at Caux several years running.

In the 1960s there was definitely a counter culture. The more liberal culture won the day but at least we gave people the choice, we showed another side. Most industry now is controlled by large corporates. Plays like *The Forgotten Factor* are not representative of the work place today. Capitalism has changed so much. There are not the family firms anymore. Today it is big business even in the theatre — you cannot for instance have experimental theatre in the West End.

In the 1960s *The Diplomats* had a lovely set. It had a £5,000 capital investment; *Temptation* cost £250,000. Things have changed.

We were going against the tide, swimming upstream and it was all too powerful. It's disappointing but I understand the reason for it. The plays were probably not good enough and with MRA, after Peter Howard died, people felt the plays did not have the cutting edge of the message.

APPENDIX TWENTY-FOUR

Edited transcript of interview with Hugh Steadman Williams on 15 January, 2015, at IofC headquarters, 24 Greencoat Place, London.

Alan Thornhill was a clergyman. In 1967 he wrote the books and lyrics for *Annie*. In the middle of rehearsals he had a heart attack and was confined to bed. He asked to see me, handed me the script and said I had to see it through. We then decided we would work together and write *High Diplomacy* – which starred Muriel Smith and Donald Scott. I went on with *Anything to Declare* – a young people's revue which was taken round the world. I was away eighteen months on that.

Thornhill told me about Frank Wilson an ordained minister who had thought to open a centre for drug addicts – God spoke to him. It had more than sixty per cent success rate because he gave them a living faith in Jesus Christ. He introduced us to one young man who had come back for the second time. He said he found the faith to come off drugs, went home, and his parents, who were both academics and atheists, argued him out of it so he went back to drugs. [Thornhill and Steadman then wrote *Return Trip*, based on this incident, in four weeks at MRA's India headquarters in Panchgani.]

[Regarding cancellation of a tour of the Soviet Union with the schools programme.] She [Nancy Ruthven] had already taken a similar tour to India. But sadly she was killed in a car crash and it was never pursued any further.

[Regarding the musical *GB*.] The 1970s was the age of satire with *That Was the Week that Was*. We felt they were satirising virtue and we thought, why not satirise vice. It was new for MRA to go into satire, we satirised the fashion industry, politicians, banks and got some good reviews.

[Regarding The Pause at the theatre in the mid-1980s.] There were big disagreements and a lot of people felt the Westminster was taking up too much of our resources and too many people. They felt it wasn't worth it but there were others like me who were passionate about it. In the end it was suggested a Pause for a couple of years when we would have no productions. In that time we made a video of a play by Keir Hardy *The Man they could not Buy,* a video of *Clashpoint* and a video of *Poor Man Rich Man* [by Steadman Williams.]

The main achievement of the Westminster was that it provided a useful counterbalance to what was going on in the theatre at that time. What it did not achieve was artistic excellence.

[At Louis Fleming's funeral on 19 January, 2015, Steadman Williams describes Fleming's time at the Arts Centre as becoming 'increasingly unhappy'. The following is an extract from the tribute:] An unfortunate split had occurred between the work of MRA in Britain and that in America. The deeper the divide became the more an atmosphere of fear and control came to dominate the British work. Lou, because of his many associations with friends in America, was regarded with suspicion. He was increasingly side-lined and found that decisions were being taken elsewhere and that he had become largely a figurehead. To Lou, a big man with big vision and big ideas and immense capabilities, this eventually became intolerable. In 1975 he resigned and returned to Canada.

[Regarding plans to establish a Christian Arts Centre following the closure of the Westminster.] The Christian Arts Trust made a grant of £50,000 for a feasibility study which was carried out by Theatre Projects Consultants. They came up with a brilliant design. To realise that together with the purchase price and some endowment would require £8.5 million.

We approached the National Lottery Arts Fund who were very encouraging and indicated that if we could find twenty per-cent of the total they would fund the remainder. This is where we hit the buffers. We approached several wealthy Christian business people but they just did not rate the arts as highly as we did and we got nowhere. So we just had to give up our scheme.

APPENDIX TWENTY-FIVE

Edited comments from feedback forms following performance of *The Diplomats,* on 8 June, 2013, at IofC headquarters, Greencoat Place, London.

Male, non IofC: I think the play is interesting from a social and cultural history point of view, in the same way that other cultural artefacts are interesting and worth studying because of their social or political context and not because of any great artistic spirit. I do find the play's message rather contrived and obvious and was surprised that a modern audience was, on the whole, so positive about it

Male, non IofC: It would be a success [in 2013] with a liberal audience, who would find the ending enlightening.

Female, non IofC, journalist: The political messages are fascinating and as true today as they ever were. But I think today's politicians would hate to admit that. I believe this play transcends the decades and is as relevant now as it ever was. Everyone was scared of the 'Reds under the Beds', but only because they never bothered to actually listen to what their beliefs were. The threat is more subtle today, but nonetheless significant. The staged reading was very professional — much more so that I had expected and entertaining.

Male, non IofC: This is a wonderful example of everything that at that period in the twentieth-century was regarded by the establishment as the pinnacle of what this country should be in the future. I suspect you could put this play on and an appropriate audience would love it because they want the world to be like that.

Male, non IofC: It could be a success today as long as it is treated in the proper sense of being humorous, but based on facts pertaining to 2013, and makes people laugh. It could ensure people see both sides of an argument, then laugh and might agree to a good solution.

Male, IofC supporter: The characters are too generalised but the very stereotypical nature still applies, or at least in the eyes of the newspapers. It could not be a success today without even more trimming or perhaps, more to the point, some lines need to be changed, but the basic concept and structure is good.

Female, IofC supporter: The actors developed some convincing characterisation and the effect was to make it seem that the play would work with elements of farce — the lighter the 'touch' the more convincing the play would be. But it is clear that the characters are to be presented as stereotypes and as I grew up in the Cold War these stereotypes made sense to me — I don't know how it would work for people who grew up after the Cold War.

Male, IofC supporter: It would be slammed in 2013 as far too simplistic. It could however be re-written with the message more subtly presented. The interaction between the characters is very convincing. It is clearly a message play and re-written it could work today.

Female, IofC supporter: The play is way too didactic ... it puts my back up.

Female, IofC supporter, who attended opening of the Westminster Theatre in 1946: Points in the play such as the importance of listening to each other, actually hearing what the other person is saying, comes across. People are still embarrassed by the mention of God as a powerful spiritual being.

Probably why some reviews were so negative. We are becoming more tolerant of other faiths now but children especially are not given clear instructions in the Christian faith, nor given a purpose in life.

Male, IofC supporter, who attended opening of the Westminster Theatre in 1946: It might succeed (in 2013) if understood as a period piece, as *Downton Abbey* is. All drama is 'unrealistic' in a sense because it is a condensed human experience but it is possible for it to ring true both psychologically and spiritually. The original production had possibly a bit more 'gravitas' but nevertheless I felt the reading was remarkably effective.

APPENDIX TWENTY-SIX

Edited email from Anthony Thomas to Pamela Jenner on 13 April, 2013.

Stanley Kiaer invited me to be a representative of the Theatre [Westminster] in the London Borough of Bexley, and I publicised the Westminster extensively to clubs, institutes and factories, arranging for them to take parties. I also attended the plays in a personal capacity, as did many of those in MRA in order to fill the Theatre. To this day, a day never goes by without my writing in my Quiet Time book, 'Fill the Theatre' and this includes The Barn [a dual use theatre/conference space at the IofC headquarters in Greencoat Place]. Every time there is an event I publicise it to twenty or so of my friends, even if most of them do not come. I live in hope that sometime they may. If nothing else it shows it is alive and kicking!

Since being connected with the Theatre I realise the power of theatre to change lives. Witness the faces of children watching *Give a Dog a Bone*, and the effect of The *Forgotten Factor* on the miners who saw it and returned to increase production of coal in their pits.

As Shaw [playwright George Bernard Shaw] said 'It is a factory of thought, a prompter of conscience and a temple for the ascent of Man'; wise words. Peter Howard once said, 'I write my plays to bring about a change in man' — that is why his, and Alan Thornhill's plays, are so important. They have, and still can, change society. I firmly believe in theatre to bring about a change in society for the better. We need plays that not only depict the human condition — many do that — but point the way to changing it. Howard's and Thornhill's plays do that. They are full of hope that things can and will be different.

Peter's [Howard] was a committed life, given to changing the world, whether it was youth or the elderly. He was funny, yet deadly serious, not afraid of rebuking when necessary, but always concerned with the lives of those he touched, and he touched the lives of many, not only in life (as you know he worked with Beaverbrook), but through his books and especially his plays. As a young man I worked as a switchboard operator in Clive House, Berkeley Square (Frank Buchman's London home), a shy auditor, and often had breakfast with him [Howard]. He was full of fun, and sometimes asked me to 'share' my morning quiet time with those sitting around the table! On one such occasion I shared the thought that it was wrong to criticise others' leadership, and I needed to take more responsibility myself! He made me 'share' the thought again! 'Say it again', he said! On another occasion he said, 'You think too much about yourself.' I remember him 'taking the mickey' out of one poor lady who was taking life too seriously! He was a great family man, and loved his children. I think he missed them very much when he was on his world travels. As he did, Doe, his wife.

APPENDIX TWENTY-SEVEN

Edited transcript of interview with Anne Wolrige Gordon, daughter of Peter Howard, on 10 June, 2013 at IofC headquarters, 24 Greencoat Place, London.

My father discussed his plays a lot around the table. *The Dictator's Slippers* is based on a meeting he had at Caux. He met Brecht and *The Dictator's Slippers* is based on what Brecht said to him. He met him in Switzerland in the early 1950s. Brecht was very avant-garde in those days. The establishment in Britain didn't like Brecht's plays but they were accepted by the left wing radical element. My father was not interested in Brecht's politics but in his playwriting and the way he introduced ideas on stage. Father was also interested in change in the theatre. When musicals became popular staging changed — for instance stages were moveable; sets could be changed in motion. All these things my father really was inspired by.

I remember my father discussing the role of women with my mother. His portrayal of women was showing how they should *not* be treated. He believed women were equal to men.

I have seen every one of his plays. He put people he knew into his plays; he always used people from real life and we would often try and guess who they were. My favourite plays are *Mr Brown Comes Down the Hill*, *The Ladder* and *Through the Garden Wall* (and of course *Give a Dog a Bone*). His plays were very progressive for the time. Lots of standard MRA plays were good but his plays always progressed, they were always different, you could be quite surprised by them and a lot of people were surprised. My father was a brave man and a brave playwright.

I was in *The Vanishing Island* and we were trained in Hollywood. I was eighteen and the youngest member of the cast. We had had tremendous success with it in New York and Detroit and arrived in Hollywood having had great reviews. My father wanted top Hollywood actors, choreographers and directors to look at it as he wanted it improved. They tore it to strips. We were all told to improve one hundred per cent and my father said 'Hooray, well done'! We all worked hard. These top choreographers and musicians gave their services free. It was phenomenal. We had most rigorous training and what a transformation. We then went around the world including Japan, the Philippines and Manila.

My father read a lot of plays, particularly Shaw and Brecht, and their structure will have influenced him. He never got the idea he was good. He always felt he could improve. He did not write to amuse himself. He wrote because the plays were required for a reason, for a specific purpose. I think *The Diplomats* was written for a Canadian ambassador. He often said he would go to Hill Farm and spend his time writing but he was much too involved in the world for that to happen. I have an image of him deciding to write a play and then there would be a telephone call and the play would be ditched.

I don't think my father felt theatre censorship was realistic. We went to the Royal Court; he said you have to know what you are up against in order to answer it. We went to see *Oh, What a Lovely War!* – we went with Phyllis Austin. If you don't know what is going on you don't have the tools to answer it. You need to know what is going on in other people's lives.

My father didn't think much of kitchen sink [theatre] but he thought there was an answer to it. He felt that theatre could get the message across.

He felt the theatre could give people a picture. They had drama unfolding before them. In a theatre, regardless of what play it is, there is a direct engagement with the audience and you have to win them. That really interested him. Theatre is no longer the top means of communication in our age and my father would have moved on, probably to television. In the theatre cost is a huge problem in putting on a production today.

We used to have Sunday morning meetings at the Westminster and some of them were incredibly stodgy — all gloom and doom with people with notebooks taking things down. When my father was there he would gallop down the aisle and on to the stage and you could feel the windows open. He would say: 'Put away your notebooks, don't listen to me, think for yourselves' — it was like an electric shock. He lifted it all. That's what I loved about him. It was like fresh air, vigour; he wanted people to think for themselves. I have taken from this that, in any situation in which I find myself, there will always be someone in that situation who is key to altering it and something I can do to help that. I always felt very close to my father. I knew quite often what he was thinking from across a room. I didn't need to ask.

He felt the theatre had limitless opportunities. He could see how it was progressing, He foresaw the technical skills of the future where scenery would be redundant and it would be all about lights and special effects.

About the Author

Pamela Jenner was awarded a PhD in 2016 for her thesis on Moral Re-Armament at the Westminster Theatre. Dr Jenner was a journalist for more than thirty years, working on both newspapers and magazines, but in 2009 decided to enter the world of academia. She achieved a First Class BA degree in Drama from Anglia Ruskin University in 2012 and then progressed to a PhD. The thesis has enabled her to combine her love of theatre with her interest in archival research and investigative journalism. She is now an Associate Lecturer with the Department of Music and Performing Arts at Anglia Ruskin University, Cambridge and Senior Tutor in Journalism at Harlow FE College, Essex.

11326666R00224

Printed in Great Britain
by Amazon